11/2

CREDIBLE

CREDIBLE

WHY WE DOUBT ACCUSERS
AND PROTECT ABUSERS

DEBORAH TUERKHEIMER

HARPER WAVE

An Imprint of HarperCollins*Publishers*

HarperCollins books may be purchased for educational, business, or sales promotional use. For information, please email the Special Markets Department at SPsales@harpercollins.com.

FIRST EDITION

Designed by Nancy Singer

Library of Congress Cataloging-in-Publication Data has been applied for.

ISBN 978-0-06-300274-6

21 22 23 24 25 LSC 10 9 8 7 6 5 4 3 2 1

For Survivors

CONTENTS

AUTHOR'S NOTE

The stories that I share in *Credible* represent a range of experiences associated with the aftermath of sexual assault and harassment. Without a doubt, countless stories of how courageous people experience this aftermath could have appeared in the pages that follow. I have elected to highlight cases that portray patterns in our treatment of sexual misconduct accusers and amplify voices seldom heard. The chosen stories reflect both commonalities and particularities in the experience of coming forward with allegations of abuse. On occasion, names and identifying characteristics have been changed to protect privacy.

I use the words "victim" and "survivor" interchangeably unless one is suggested by context or the preference of the person described. Both words are intended to convey the harm of sexual misconduct; the nonlinear, often incomplete process of healing; and the strength it takes to persevere in the wake of abuse. As the author Donna Freitas writes, "I am both a survivor *and* still a victim, and somehow I will always and forever be both."

While boys and men are also victims and survivors of sexual misconduct, it is no coincidence that the vast majority of abuse victims are girls and women. Nor is it surprising that most abusers are men. My use of gendered pronouns to reference perpetrators and victims depicts abuse that is typical in that it involves a male perpetrator and a female victim. For perpetrators, the same power that can be leveraged to prey on vulnerability confers protection from consequences. Most sexual misconduct—still today—goes unaddressed, leaving intact the hierarchies that enable it. Gender is inseparable from sexual violence and its aftermath. This reality shapes the stories that follow.

INTRODUCTION

One morning in late February 2020, I approached the Criminal Courts Building in lower Manhattan, where I worked as a prosecutor in the early years of my career. Back then, I specialized in gender violence cases, many of which I remember well. Those cases—and especially the victims—were on my mind as I made my way into the courthouse. What brought me back that day was the case against Harvey Weinstein. I'd been following the monthlong trial closely from my perch at Northwestern University. Now I could finally observe the proceedings in person.

I was in the courtroom when, after five days of deliberations, the jury announced it had reached a verdict. This fact alone was extraordinary. The vast majority of sexual assault complaints never result in an arrest, much less charges, a prosecution, or a conviction. Around the country, only an estimated 20 percent of sexual assault cases reported to the police lead to an arrest. In some jurisdictions, the arrest rate is even lower. Those allegations that do somehow make it to trial tend to be more vexing for jurors when the accuser and accused are acquainted, as we know. And when the accused is a powerful man, accountability is the rarest of exceptions to the general rule of impunity.

Weinstein's path to the courtroom catalyzed what felt like a new era. Almost two and a half years earlier, groundbreaking reporting on the Hollywood mogul's predations turned whispers into a loud chorus of public accusations. The hashtag #MeToo went viral. People from all walks of life came forward to share their stories, exposing abuse in publishing, fashion, music, sports, advertising, comedy, philanthropy, hospitality, retail, law, factories, academia, technology, places of worship, politics, and more. This was over a decade after Tarana Burke began the "Me Too" movement, which was in fact designed to empower survivors of sexual violence, particularly women and girls of color. By the time Weinstein stood trial, the movement had pushed sexual abuse to the forefront of our collective conversations and consciousness.*

After #MeToo went viral, activists and advocates capitalized on the momentum to demand systemic change. They achieved several notable successes. The use of nondisclosure agreements—a key issue that gained major attention when Weinstein's decades-long use of NDAs to keep women silent came to light—was restricted in more than a dozen states. A few states expanded their definition of sexual harassment to encompass a broader range of behaviors, including less severe harassment, and to protect more victims, like independent contractors and interns. And several states extended the statute of limitations for filing a sexual harassment claim.

Despite these initial successes, efforts to reform our institutions and the culture surrounding them have all but stalled. Hard-fought legal gains fall well short of where we need to be. Still today, across the states and in federal court, in both civil and criminal cases, even the most evolved jurisdictions preserve laws that downgrade the credibility of accusers.

The problem is worse outside the legal system. Here, our daily

---

* The way I'm using these terms, sexual assault and sexual harassment (both physical and nonphysical) fall into the category of sexual misconduct or sexual abuse.

lives require urgent judgments about credibility. When a coworker tells you about an incident of harassment. When you hear quiet warnings about your boss. When a friend discloses a sexual assault, perhaps from long ago and perhaps from the recent past. When you learn on social media that one acquaintance has accused another of misconduct. When you read about the latest allegation against a politician, actor, or athlete you admire.

Judging credibility is a mighty power—because credibility is itself a form of power. Whenever we judge credibility, we are in a position to value, or to devalue, the speaker. Yet as a society and as individuals, we wield this power in troubling ways. This is true of even the best intentioned among us, including those fully open to the lessons of #MeToo.

Unbeknownst to us, we are shaped by a cluster of forces that I call the *credibility complex*. These forces corrupt our judgments, making us too prone to both discount the credibility of accusers and inflate the credibility of the accused. The most vulnerable women experience credibility discounting at its most extreme, while men who are protected by greater status or position are the beneficiaries of massive credibility boosts.

There are two major drivers of the credibility complex. The first is culture. The credibility complex penetrates the deepest layers of our culture, which we can think of as our communal system of meaning, however contested. The social anthropologist Adam Kuper defines culture as a "matter of ideas and values, a collective cast of mind." Fractured though our shared system of meaning is, it exists. What's key here is that this culture cannot be isolated from a social context defined by stark power imbalances. In the stories that follow, hierarchies, inequalities, vulnerabilities, and privileges all play a pivotal role.

A main way our culture is refracted is through the behaviors and attitudes of individuals. You'll see in the chapters that follow that the credibility complex is powered by people. Some of these people work within systems that routinely mete out credibility discounts and credibility boosts. Police officers, school officials, and workplace personnel figure prominently in the accounts to come. So do friends, roommates, parents, and coworkers. None of us can transcend cultural norms or avoid their imprint on our inner workings. As cultural psychologists recognize, the human psyche is both a product of culture and a producer of it. When it comes to the credibility complex, individual psychology mirrors *and* fuels collective responses to allegations of abuse.

Like it or not, we are all marinated in many of the same cultural juices. Some of us are more attuned to the influence of these cultural forces than others, and some of us manage to adjust for commonplace errors and biases of which we become aware. Some are informed by distinct experiences with sexual misconduct, which also shape decision-making around credibility. And most of us have gleaned something about abuse from the many #MeToo stories. But no one is immune from cultural influences—not even survivors.

Law is the other major driver of the credibility complex. The function of law in molding our communal values and attitudes often goes unnoticed. "Law operates even when it appears not to," writes the legal scholar Naomi Mezey. In all our relationships, including the most intimate, Mezey explains, legal rules set "the very baseline from which we negotiate our lives and form our identities."

These rules are sprawling, for law is a labyrinth. It is criminal statutes that penalize certain conduct, statutes that outlaw certain forms of discrimination, judicial opinions that interpret these laws, rules that dictate what evidence is allowed in court, and procedures that govern the litigation of cases, both civil and criminal. These sources of law are all vital to the credibility complex.

Because law bakes in cultural understandings, it reveals blind spots that might otherwise be concealed. But "law does more than reflect or encode what is otherwise normatively constructed," as the sociologist Susan Silbey has observed. Law also forges culture—as Silbey puts it: "law is a part of the cultural processes that actively contribute in the composition of social relations." Law lays bare the credibility complex while fortifying it.

———

Back in 2017, Weinstein had become the poster child for #MeToo villainy in the court of public opinion. The court of law was different. There, he—like all criminal defendants—was presumed innocent unless his guilt was proven beyond a reasonable doubt. The prosecution's case rested on the word of the accusers, whose credibility was central, and it was attacked at every turn.

Cross-examination by Weinstein's defense team was tough and painful, tapping into enduring suspicions about women who report sexual abuse. The accusers were portrayed as liars who were out for fortune or fame. They were blamed for putting themselves in vulnerable positions. They were presented as vengeful and regretful about what the defense argued was consensual sex. They were pressed about why they had waited years to come forward, remaining friendly with Weinstein after their alleged assault.

These are age-old tactics used to discredit women. They surface not only inside the courtroom, but outside of it, where accusations of sexual misconduct are first brought forward, most often to those within a trusted inner circle. The traps set for the Weinstein jurors are traps into which any of us can fall.

As the jurors shuffled back into the courtroom, I watched the court officers surround Weinstein in preparation for the verdict to come. This moment, I knew, was not just for Weinstein's brave victims, but for survivors of sexual abuse everywhere, and for all those watching to see if justice could be delivered against the odds. *Guilty.* The accusers were believed: what they described happened; what happened was wrong; their suffering mattered. The women had been found credible.

The verdict against Weinstein represented a tremendous victory. But I worried about what this moment required. It took so many women—the six who testified at trial, but also the dozens who came forward publicly against Weinstein, mounting pressure on police and prosecutors to build a case. If credibility only comes in numbers, what becomes of the more typical lone accuser? And if credibility is only bestowed on certain accusers—most of Weinstein's victims were white women—what happens when women of color and other marginalized women speak up about abuse? These were urgent questions—a reminder that the work of #MeToo was woefully incomplete.

Throughout my career, first as a special victims prosecutor and then a legal scholar, I have seen how the credibility complex provides impunity for perpetrators of sexual abuse. And I've come to believe that, in order for this to end, we must shift our approach to credibility. This belief is informed not only by my work but by my experiences and observations as a woman in this world. Many powerful people are deeply invested in maintaining the patriarchal status quo. This status quo will endure until we reckon with credibility and its essence: power.

The credibility complex distributes this power unevenly, and unfairly. We'll see that marginalized survivors suffer most from our widespread tendencies to discount the credibility of accusers. Women of color, poor women, women with disabilities, LGBTQ individuals, immigrant women—these are the accusers least likely to be believed, whether by formal officials or by their family and friends. Their word is treated differently because of where they are situated in a society of rampant hierarchies. Survivors often anticipate this unequal treatment and, to avoid it, stay silent about their abuse.

When women do come forward, the credibility complex leads us to too readily dismiss them. To disbelieve their version of events. To fault them for their violation. To disregard their suffering. All the while, the credibility complex causes us to elevate the interests of men accused. To embrace their denials. To absolve them of blame. To prioritize their desire to avoid accountability. Most of us fall prey to these tendencies—not because we're bad people or because we want to stack the deck against survivors, but because we remain steeped in this culture that has always discredited victims of sexual assault and harassment.

There is an alternative: by confronting the influences that distort our decision-making, we can better wield our power to decide who's credible.

The stories that follow illuminate, in the most intimate of ways, the workings of the credibility complex. We will see how women who were harmed by misconduct are harmed once again—this time, by the aftermath of abuse. Some of the figures in these stories will be familiar to you—Harvey Weinstein, Jeffrey Epstein, R. Kelly, Larry Nassar, Bill Cosby, Brett Kavanaugh, Donald Trump. But we will view familiar facts through a new lens—the lens of the credibility complex.

Most of the stories in this book belong to women whose abusers aren't famous and whose accounts never made headlines. These women too suffered—not only from the abuse, but from its fallout. They too were failed—not only by the abuser, but by those around them who were unable or unwilling to offer a helpful response. Some victims turned first to friends, coworkers, or family members. Others reported to a workplace supervisor, to a college disciplinary official, or to police and prosecutors. These are the people whose judgments unwittingly fell short, hurting the women who trusted them.

We can do better. Each of us is part of the solution, as we are all part of the problem. If we rewire ourselves to respond more fairly to the accusations that come our way, law reform and culture change will follow. Over time, we can dismantle the credibility complex. It starts with understanding how this complex operates.

1

ALONG AXES OF POWER

WORKINGS OF THE CREDIBILITY COMPLEX

Whether we realize it or not, we're prone to credibility judgments that work to the detriment of people who lack social power. We doubt their authority to assert facts—even facts about their own lives. An assertion that threatens the status quo sets the credibility complex in motion, and the complex kicks into high gear when that statement comes from someone who is marginalized or vulnerable. Dismissal is our default.

The rule is simple: credibility is meted out too sparingly to women, whether cis or trans, whatever their race or socioeconomic status, their sexual orientation or immigration status. At the same time, the intersections are critical—just as there is no female prototype, there is no singular experience of what I call the *credibility discount*.

Once you have a name for it, you see credibility discounting everywhere. It's not isolated or idiosyncratic—it's patterned and predictable. It happens in the workplace, when your contributions are treated with disrespect. In medical settings, when your description of symptoms is cast aside as untrue or unimportant. In the course of salary negotiations, when your requests are dismissed as unseemly

posturing. In the classroom, when the value of your insights is minimized. In intimate relationships, when you're somehow held responsible for the conduct of others. And on and on. Even when you sense
these moments might be gendered, you may not see them as linked
to judgments about your credibility. By understanding the workings
of the credibility discount, you'll know why these moments leave
you feeling diminished.

When a woman comes forward with an allegation of abuse, the
widespread societal impulse to discount credibility is at its apex. Here,
gender, power, sexual entitlement, cultural mythology, and legal protections collide. It's where I conceived credibility discounting, and
what I consider to be its paradigm.

Even without giving name to the experience, most accusers know
it well. Many come forward only to be dismissed. Many more are
silenced by the prospect. Maybe they were dismissed the last time. In
all likelihood, they've seen other accusers dismissed. The credibility
discount can feel inescapable.

This discount can also feel far-reaching—and it is. Credibility
entails much more than belief in the truth of the allegation. For an
allegation to be deemed credible, we must also believe that the conduct it describes is blameworthy, and that it's worthy of our concern.

Consider that a person who comes forward with an allegation of
abuse makes a trio of claims: *This happened. It was wrong. It matters.*
Each claim is crucial. If any one of them is rejected, whether by a
loved one or by an official responder, the accuser will be dismissed.

The listener may decide that the alleged conduct didn't happen.

Or that it wasn't the fault of the accused, but the fault of the
accuser.

Or that it wasn't harmful enough to warrant concern.

Regardless, the outcome is the same. The listener isn't convinced,
and the status quo is preserved. Unless all parts of the allegation—*it*

happened, it's wrong, it matters—are accepted, the allegation will be dismissed as untrue, unworthy of blame, or unimportant. These three discounting mechanisms can overlap, and they often blur together—but each on its own is enough to sink an allegation.

Most women who come forward with an abuse allegation against a man will confront the credibility discount. When a woman comes forward against a *powerful* man, she will confront an even steeper discount. To be clear: men who are victims of sexual misconduct may also experience credibility discounting when they come forward. But my focus throughout the book remains on those who are most threatening to the patriarchy: female accusers. In a patriarchal society where male sexual prerogatives are at stake, discounting operates with special potency.

There is a flip side to credibility discounting—and it's what I call *credibility inflation*. Together, discounting and inflation define the credibility complex. Just as the credibility discount is three-dimensional, applied to the full trio of claims, so too is this credibility "boost." It ensures that abusers are rarely held to account and permits the systems that tolerate them to carry on as usual.

All this can seem natural and intractable. Credibility inflation is such an ingrained pattern of thought that it often disappears altogether from view. But it is every bit as integral to the workings of the credibility complex.

Our society confers a hidden benefit on powerful men. As the philosopher Lauren Leydon-Hardy remarked to me, we are taught to "assign an excess of credibility" to these men. They are granted the authority to speak definitively about past events, along with their meaning and significance. They receive what I think of as an extra generous credibility boost. Indeed, this boost is "socially normative," Leydon-Hardy says, meaning that the "roadmap" we collectively use to navigate our lives tells us "over and over again" to recognize male authority—authority not only to make decisions, but to understand the world.

When we evaluate an account along with a denial, our common response to the accusation is unduly skeptical *and* our response to the denial is unduly trusting. This response is easiest to spot in the context of an archetypical "he said, she said" contest. But not all allegations prompt a denial—at times, we never hear the accused man's version of events, or he admits what he did. Yet he can *still* receive a credibility boost—only now in the realm of blame (*it wasn't his fault*) and care (*he matters too much to suffer consequences for his actions*).

This upgrade is especially pronounced in relation to the blame we place on the accuser and our indifference to her suffering. You can think of this as an interlocking system: each of the mechanisms for downgrading the credibility of accusers has a corresponding mechanism for inflating the credibility of the accused. While accusers are routinely distrusted, faulted, and disregarded, the men they accuse are readily believed, absolved of blame, and granted outsized importance.

We may barely notice when the accused's implausible denials are trusted as a matter of course. Or when misconduct is justified as the fault of the victim. Or when misdeeds are excused as not harmful enough to warrant intervention. But these boosting mechanisms have the very same effect as their opposites on the accuser side.

This should come as no surprise, since discounting and inflation are rooted in the same source—a complex that assigns credibility along axes of power.

———

Rose McGowan is the woman who initiated a chain of events that would topple Harvey Weinstein. For decades, the producer's misconduct was an open secret in certain circles. But no woman had come forward against him publicly. This began to change in the fall of 2016, when the actress and activist McGowan tweeted that an unnamed "studio head" had raped her. Her Twitter thread made its way to top journalists already engaged in early stages of their reporting on Weinstein's alleged abuse of a stream of women. A year later, blockbuster exposés of Weinstein's predations would be published by Jodi Kantor and Megan Twohey at the *New York Times* and Ronan Farrow at the *New Yorker*.

In her memoir *Brave*, McGowan describes how she was summoned for a business meeting at the 1997 Sundance Film Festival, where her movie was premiering. Weinstein, who McGowan refers to as "the Monster," was working from his enormous hotel suite, where their meeting was held. When it finished, he said he would walk her out. Instead, McGowan says he pushed her into the jacuzzi, where he forced oral sex on her. She left the hotel in shock. As she wrote, "My life was never going to be the same."

McGowan would have had no reason to know it at the time, but at least a hundred women—two dozen of whom would become known as the Silence Breakers—would ultimately accuse Weinstein of sexual harassment or assault. It would take McGowan nearly two decades to come forward herself, propelling this cascade. Back in 1997, she believed she was alone, and chose not to report what happened. Like so many survivors—whether famous or not, whether accusing a power-broker or not—she absorbed the insidious messaging of the credibility complex and downgraded her own credibility.

"I kept thinking about how he'd been sitting behind me in the theater the night before it happened," she says. "Which made it—not my responsibility, exactly, but—like I had had a hand in tempting him. Which made it even sicker and made me feel dirtier. I know other victims feel this way too. We replay the tape of the event over and over, blaming ourselves. If only, if only, if only."

McGowan considered reporting to the police and thought better of it. "I knew if I came out publicly with this, nothing was going to happen to the Monster, but I—I would never work again," she reasoned. She assumed that those around Weinstein, his collection of powerful people in Hollywood, media, and politics, would continue to protect him. "Because it's okay," she writes. "It's the business. And it is just. a. girl."

Nearly two decades later, when Weinstein realized that McGowan would no longer stay silent, he began a smear campaign against her through his legal team and a collection of spies whom he enlisted in his efforts. As Kantor and Twohey would ultimately report, Lisa Bloom, a lawyer (successfully) pitching her services to Weinstein, offered to help battle "the Roses of the world," and especially McGowan herself. Bloom's memo to Weinstein proposed a "counterops online campaign to push back and call her out as a pathological liar." Bloom further suggested placing "an article re her becoming increasingly unglued, so that when someone Googles her this is what pops up and she is discredited."

The campaign was effective. As McGowan puts it, "They did a really, really good job. And people want to believe that stuff, you know? It makes them feel better about something horrible that's happened, you know? They can tuck themselves in at night, rest assured that it only happens to bad people, but that's not the case."

McGowan says that just after the assault, news of what happened somehow "spread like wildfire through Hollywood," and she was blacklisted. "It seemed like every creep in Hollywood knew about my most vulnerable and violated moment. And I was the one being punished for it. It's like being assaulted over and over.

"Everyone just wants it to go away so they can feel better," she observes. For sexual misconduct to seem to disappear, the "Roses of this world" must be discredited.

THE DISCOUNT BREAKS UNEVENLY

Specifics matter when we judge an accuser's credibility. When women belong to groups that are marginalized, subordinated, or otherwise vulnerable, their allegations are even less likely to be credited. Class matters. Line of work matters. Immigration status matters. Drug and alcohol use matters. Sexual history matters. Sexual orientation matters. Nowhere are the particulars more important than when it comes to race, which is "inextricable from gender," noted the legal scholar Trina Grillo.

The mistakes we make when judging credibility are not randomly distributed. Instead, they tend to run in one direction: against those with less power and in favor of those with more. This typically means that the alleged victim, who is already disadvantaged by comparison, loses, while the accused man, who already occupies a position of relative privilege, benefits.

Over time, there has been one notable exception. When white women allege sexual assault by a Black man, whites in power have a long and tragic history of too readily crediting the accusation. As the historian Estelle Freedman wrote, "Nothing better exemplified the dynamic of racial dominance than the response to rape." Myths about Black male sexual predators and the vulnerability of white women became entrenched during slavery, when accusations of rape against Black men, however specious, were routinely used to justify white violence, both within the legal system and outside of it. While rape allegations were strategically deployed against Black men, white men were permitted to rape their female slaves with impunity. Freedman recounted that by the late nineteenth century, two sets of racial beliefs defined rape around the nation: "first, that black women could not be raped, and second, that black men threatened white female virtue."

Even today this history shapes responses to sexual misconduct.

Many victims of color mention their race when describing the aftermath of abuse. The same is *not* true for many white women, who, as Grillo remarked, "often think of themselves as 'without a race' rather than as white." Whatever the accuser's race, it is entwined with how others perceive her credibility.*

Consider the story of Venkayla Haynes. Haynes is a recent college graduate who says she was raped at the beginning of her freshman year. When I asked her about the aftermath, she made clear that we needed to go back much further in time to understand her reluctance to report the incident to authorities. Haynes told me that she was twelve years old when she was sexually abused, repeatedly, by a member of her church who was heavily involved with the youth group. He "never really asked for anything" from the church, Haynes said, "but in return he would abuse the Black girls." She "knew what was going on was wrong," but as long as the abuse continued, she told no one. "I felt like someone just took my voice away . . . I went through the entire time of this abuse in silence."

Although Haynes stayed quiet about her abuse, another girl who was being molested by the same church member came forward. The girl's allegation was made public, and the church took no action. "He was back in church the next Sunday," Haynes remembers. "And he went right back to abusing me that same Sunday." Her abuse lasted for more than five years, until her family moved away. This was Haynes's first encounter with credibility discounting, and it would profoundly shape her view of the world and her place in it.

Years later, Haynes would resist the idea of coming forward with an allegation of campus sexual assault. She says she was raped by an

---

* In the accounts that follow, I provide a racial identification where accusers did so themselves, while finding other ways to avoid having whiteness disappear or tacitly become the norm.

athlete at a neighboring college. He was a close friend of hers, and also one of the first people Haynes had told about her childhood abuse. After the sexual assault, Haynes recalls that her initial response was not to involve the police. She explained to me, "Me being Black, me being a woman, I'm not someone who would quickly call 911 or trust law enforcement, because there are issues with sexual misconduct and police brutality and those are just very, very touchy subjects." She also remembered what happened years earlier, when nothing was done about the Black church member who was molesting her and other girls after one of his victims came forward.

As a newly minted college student, uncertain about whether to report her assault to campus authorities, Haynes had no doubt that she had been raped. But she wondered if she had "the strength" to speak up and whether, against the odds, she would be believed. She wondered if it was possible for her to be "protected this time around," or, as when she kept quiet about her childhood abuse, she would again have to "protect other people."

After much hesitation, well aware that her story might not matter to those around her, she decided to report her assault. The response of the college, Haynes describes, was to blame *her*. She recalls being told, "You shouldn't have gone to this apartment off campus. You shouldn't have worn this dress. You should not be hanging around these boys. You should be focused on your studies." She emphasizes, "All the blame was put on me."

Haynes ultimately dropped the case. "I feel like I was pushed to protect my abuser over my trauma and my feelings and my experiences," she explains. "And nobody wanted to protect me." She was left feeling that what happened to her was unimportant, which meant her "life wasn't valued." She later wrote, "Black women who are raped don't matter."

The credibility of Black women is discounted in ways that are distinct from how white women's credibility is discounted. Black women are not simply subordinated to a greater degree than white women; they are also differently subordinated. As the legal scholar Angela P. Harris has observed, Black women are not "white women only more so." When it comes to credibility, long-standing myths about Black women's sexuality inflect the disbelief, blame, and indifference that confront Black accusers.

Take the case of Anita Hill, the lawyer whose allegations of sexual harassment against Clarence Thomas led to hearings that, nearly three decades later, remain among the most pivotal moments in recent U.S. history. As the journalist Jane Mayer wrote, "The hearings devolved into a shocking showdown in which Thomas and his defenders did all they could to degrade Hill's character and destroy her credibility, accusing her, with no real evidence, of being a liar, a fantasist, and an erotomaniac." Skeptics of Hill's claims pointed to her failure to file a complaint against Thomas years earlier, when she left the Equal Employment Opportunity Commission (EEOC), where he was her boss. In fact, around that time, Hill did tell a mutual friend about two years of alleged harassment by Thomas.

"I don't believe it!" her friend responded. "What do you mean?" asked Hill. "Not that I don't believe you," the friend explained, "but [I] can't believe Clarence Thomas would do it." Hill began to cry. This conversation was reportedly "seminal in her thinking about whether to discuss the experience with anyone ever again." Hill later recalled feeling that "if my friend reacted this way, others on his side would react [the] same way." She did not raise the subject again for almost a decade.

When Hill came forward to publicly accuse Thomas, who by then had been nominated to the Supreme Court, she was again disregarded. Thomas was confirmed to the Court, while Hill's reputation was left in tatters. In conservative circles, she was widely portrayed as unhinged and loose, "a little bit nutty and a little bit slutty," as one political commentator wrote.

Reflecting on her experience, Hill notes that Black women "as a group" have long been "presumed to be unchaste and eagerly available." As slaves, "their sexual violation was not an offense," and victims "who might have the temerity to complain were accused of being delusional or imagining they had something to complain about." Centuries later, this same narrative was used to dismiss Hill's allegation. She writes, "Falsely casting me as an erotomaniac whose desire for an object prevented me from discerning reality from fantasy fit neatly within the myth of black women's sexuality."

When a Black woman comes forward with the trio of claims—*it happened, it's wrong, it matters*—the discount is at its steepest. Victims whose allegations are accepted as true are often treated with indifference, as Black women find their value diminished not only by society, but also within their own racial communities. Anita Hill identifies a compulsion to "deny our gender in order to maintain our racial identity," and says this pushes Black women to remain silent about their abuse. "Rules against protesting harassment, domestic violence, and even rape are reinforced by the stories about violence toward and lynching of black men," Hill adds. "The experience may hurt the individual, but disclosure, we are told, hurts everyone."

Each of the three discounting mechanisms—distrust, blame, disregard—is brought to bear with special vengeance on Black women. One study found that those victims who reported sexual assault to family members were met, in turn, with three common responses: denying the assault occurred, faulting the victim, or ignoring the allegation altogether. Those at greater risk for sexual violence are more likely to be met with distrust, blame, or disregard, diminishing the odds that they will pursue a formal complaint. Psychologists who study barriers to disclosure facing Black women have identified a "cultural mandate to protect African American male perpetrators from actual and perceived unfair treatment in the criminal justice system." (Other than sexual assaults against Native women, which the research suggests are overwhelmingly interracial, the vast majority of sexual assaults involve a victim and perpetrator who share the same race.)

For Black women, coming forward may be cast as an act of disloyalty. Salamishah Tillet, a feminist activist and scholar of African American studies, writes that "the stereotype of the black male rapist has . . . intimidated black women who were assaulted by African American men into silence out of fear of being labeled race traitors or, worse yet, of being seen as complicit with a criminal justice system that disproportionately incarcerated black men." The imposition of this code of silence on Black women results in "a form of self-denial that contributes further to the degradation," as Anita Hill once described it.

Tarana Burke, founder of the Me Too movement, continues to center her work on victims who are far less visible than celebrities. For the stories of these survivors to matter, Burke insists that their suffering must be regarded as important. Expecting otherwise, Black women are reluctant to speak up about their abuse, says dream hampton, the filmmaker who was an executive producer for the documentary series *Surviving R. Kelly*. "This is a way of shutting down black women," she observes, "that the victimhood of black men in the criminal justice system supersedes all other harm."

The journalist Jamil Smith writes, "Though the female members of our Black communities have constantly been asked to prioritize our collective racial struggle, sometimes at the price of their own dignity and safety, they are still labeled as unfaithful to our heritage and culture if they dare say a cross word about a Black rapist." In a world where concern for abusers trumps concern for victims, Black women are burdened with added reason to stay silent at their own expense.

Survivors of color, regardless of their race, are regularly perceived as less important than their abuser. "Women of color are differently situated in the economic, social, and political worlds," writes Kimberlé Williams Crenshaw, a law professor who coined the term "intersectionality" to illuminate the need to account for overlapping layers of identity and inequality. Whether an accuser is Black or Latinx, Asian American or Muslim—all this and more inform how her credibility is judged.

Native women encounter the credibility discount in ways that are similar to how other women of color encounter it—and aspects of the experience are also singular. Sarah Deer is a law professor, a MacArthur Fellow, and a citizen of the Muscogee (Creek) Nation of Oklahoma. Deer has devoted more than two decades to helping Native survivors of gender violence—survivors she describes as "not only the most victimized, but also the original victims, the first victims of political and politicized sexual violence." Native women suffer sexual violence at staggering rates: according to government estimates, more than half are victimized in their lifetime. In some communities, especially remote villages, the incidence of sexual assault is even higher. "It's more expected than unexpected," says one women's health advocate on the Yankton Sioux Reservation in South Dakota.

Officials discount the credibility of Native survivors so steeply that reporting can seem useless. When Native women are assaulted, they are well aware of the high probability that their allegation will be dismissed. "You may have seen your mother report, or your sister report, or your aunties report, or you heard of them reporting," Deer says. "And nobody did a damn thing. So why would you think your case would be any different?"

Tribal communities are often separated physically from the law enforcement officers responsible for protecting them and from the jurors who would in theory decide their cases. In the lower forty-eight states, the prosecution of sexual assault against Native women falls largely to the federal government—not the tribe, which lacks jurisdiction over non-Native offenders (who, again, are responsible for the vast majority of sexual assaults against Native victims). This creates a sense of remove, accentuating a disregard for Native women and their suffering on the part of the outsiders charged with pursuing and hearing their cases.

A lack of concern for Native women extends to local law enforcement officers as well. In Alaska, several police departments are notorious for failing to investigate sexual assault complaints from Native women. The observations of one former officer are telling. Gretchen Small served as a Nome police officer in the mid-2000s. Soon after she joined the force, she says, she realized the department was routinely dismissing Native women's allegations. In case after case, accusers were blamed and disregarded.

Small remembers a Native woman who reported that she was drinking at a bar and woke up in a hotel room with several men, one of whom described how five others had repeatedly raped her while she was unconscious. After hearing this victim's account, Small returned to the police station to pursue leads, only to be instructed by two fellow officers that the episode was "not rape" because the accuser was drunk. When Small reminded them that sex with an unconscious victim was indeed a crime, the officers "laughed and pointed to a stack of case files," explaining that "when a victim has a 'history of drinking or promiscuity,'" the case would "never be acted upon."

In Nome, as elsewhere, belief that the abuse occurred is not enough to prompt action. One local victim's advocate observed a lingering "mindset—not just within law enforcement but within community members—that when things like this happen . . . it's an individual's fault." Blame is not the only discounting mechanism deployed against Native victims. Disregard is a separate problem. Many police officers show an utter indifference to the plight of Native survivors. Small says she was once ordered to halt an investigation into a white man suspected of raping an Alaska Native fourteen-year-old. "He doesn't do girls," Small recollects the sergeant saying. "He only gets women at the bar drunk and takes them out in the tundra for sex . . . He's a good guy."

From this case and others, Small was forced to conclude, "Native women don't count." In fact: some advocates have stopped encouraging indigenous victims to report their assault. Although this feels bad to admit, Sarah Deer explains, it "compounds the trauma [of the assault] if you are willing to stand up and testify," and no one helps. For many survivors, Native and non-Native, this second harm is even worse than the original violation.

Marginalized survivors are well attuned to the prospect of being handily dismissed. As one trans woman who did not report her assault wrote, "I stayed silent because I knew that while many survivors are met with disbelief and doubt when they share their stories, trans survivors often also face a different kind of disbelief—one rooted in the perception that trans people are 'too disgusting' to be assaulted."

Steep credibility discounts provide survivors with added reason not to disclose abuse.

But the truth is universal: to come forward with an abuse allegation only to be dismissed without warrant is to be violated anew. Rather than run headlong into this collective dismissal, victims often stay silent. This silence results from what I call the *anticipated credibility discount*.

HOW THE CREDIBILITY COMPLEX SILENCES VICTIMS

Abby Honold is a lifelong Minnesotan. The oldest of six, she grew up in a middle-class family and attended the University of Minnesota, where she graduated in 2017. To get there, she says, was a "long, icky road."

A few years earlier, Honold had been raped when she was unconscious. "I definitely felt like it was my fault," she explains, adding that she was doing drugs with her rapist before he assaulted her. "I felt like that was 'on me.' If *I* thought that was 'on me,' what would the cops say?" Until we spoke, only a few friends and her doctor knew what happened.

The story of why Honold didn't report that rape to the police begins when another man, Daniel Drill-Mellum, sexually assaulted her about a year prior. Much about this first rape was different from the second. The first time, Honold was transported to a hospital in an ambulance soon after the assault. She *did* file a police report. She didn't blame herself—at least not initially.

Her complaint was terribly mishandled. She was treated as a liar—a young woman who engaged in consensual sex and then came to regret it. In the aftermath, Honold experienced nightmares in which she would call 911 and no one would answer.

This first rape was extremely violent. It happened just across the street from a party of hundreds of students enjoying festivities surrounding the Minnesota-Iowa football game. At the party, a mutual friend introduced Honold to Drill-Mellum, and she agreed to help him carry vodka from his apartment back to the tailgate. Shortly after they arrived in the apartment, Drill-Mellum pulled Honold into the bedroom and, over protest, roughly removed her clothes, leaving scratch marks on her legs.

Honold later explained, "I just froze." After throwing her down on the bed, he raped her—anally and vaginally—while biting her and suffocating her to brief unconsciousness. "I thought, *I'm going to die*, and I thought at least it was going to be over." But when he finished and she told him she was leaving, he raped her again. "This time,"

Honold said, "I didn't stop kicking or pulling or trying to stand up because I just knew how bad it was going to get."

When Honold finally managed to escape the apartment, she was panicked. It was noon, sunny and bright outside, and she found her way back across the street to the tailgate. "You could tell from looking at me that something had happened. My hair was messed up and my clothes were probably kind of messed up and my makeup was definitely messed up with tears all over. Students started to gather . . . and I could hear some of them saying things like, 'Oh my gosh, you think she got raped or something? Damn, that's so crazy.' Just hearing it was awful, and I got down in the fetal position . . . and I just started crying."

At the suggestion of another student in the crowd, Honold called 911. She recalled that first a police car, and then an ambulance arrived. She told me that the police officers advised her she could not have friends accompany her to the hospital because they could help change her story. She was not allowed to phone her mom. "You can call her later," instructed an officer. "This is pretty embarrassing for you."

"What did you say to this boy to make him know he was raping you?" another officer asked. "It doesn't sound like you said the word 'no,' honey, and boys really understand the word 'no.' You should try that next time." Honold remembers wondering whether there really was something she could have said that would have made her rapist stop.

On the way to the hospital, as she processed her interactions with the officers, she began to regret calling the police. She remembers thinking at the time, "You don't matter, what happened to you doesn't matter . . . it wasn't that bad and you're just whining, you're just being dramatic."

Shortly after she arrived at the hospital, Honold was visited by a detective. "Just so you know, this isn't going to go anywhere," he promptly informed her, noting that he had contacted the man Honold had identified as her attacker. "I talked to this kid, and he said this was consensual. What do you have to say about that?"

Honold was at a loss to respond to the detective's questions, which seemed aimed at trapping her into giving a wrong answer. In an effort to respond directly to what was being asked, she did the best she could do. As often happens in the wake of sexual assault, particularly when an interview is not informed by an understanding of trauma, many details were left out. Honold didn't mention the biting, the suffocation, or having been anally raped: "I was so fixated on what I thought he was asking me, and he was really set on getting me to go in chronological order. If I would start to blurt something out that I remembered, he would cut me off." The interview ended with the detective telling Honold in effect that her report "really isn't all that serious." As Honold recollects, the detective explained, "This is very 'he said, she said,' and we're not going to be able to do anything with this, but you should still get a rape kit."

She did, and she was interviewed again—this time, by a sexual assault nurse examiner whose approach was informed by the realities of trauma. The nurse posed a series of open-ended questions, many about Honold's sensory impressions of the attack. When asked what she tasted during the incident, Honold suddenly remembered Drill-Mellum's fingers down her throat and, afterward, something different about her mouth. When the nurse looked, she discovered that Honold's labial frenulum—a small fold of skin that connects the upper lip to the gums—was broken. The nurse also observed scratches and bite marks, some deep enough to scar, along with dozens of vaginal and anal lacerations. That night, on the phone with the case detective, she described Honold's injuries as among the most serious she had ever seen in more than seven hundred cases. "I can remember thinking this was kind of a 'perfect case,'" the nurse examiner later said. "You need to take this seriously," she insisted—and she recalls the detective replying, "You know, kids are into kinky shit these days."

Honold went home to begin a different kind of life on campus. The night she was raped, she received a voice mail from several of her male friends, who were clearly intoxicated, laughing and yelling, "Damn, we didn't know it was that easy." Quickly, word on campus spread that Honold had lied about her rape. "The story going around," she recalls, "was that I had walked up to Dan on the street and said, 'you want to go upstairs and have rough sex?' And then when it was over, I called 911 because he didn't want to be my boyfriend." Over the coming months, Honold heard herself referred to as "that crazy false accuser girl," "psycho," and "slut," while Drill-Mellum was depicted as "innocent," "someone who would never have done this," and "cleared by the cops."

Honold remembers this as a terrifying time. The police had dropped the charges against Drill-Mellum soon after his arrest, and Honold's trauma was intensified because "nobody believed anything." Because Drill-Mellum had apparently "gotten away with it," she worried that if he returned to rape her, again no one would care.

Today, Honold wonders if the rumor that she had falsely reported rape made her a target for people who thought no one would ever believe her if she complained. She felt this way herself—that any accusation she brought forward would surely be perceived as a lie. This helps explain why, nearly a year later, she chose not to involve the police when the second man assaulted her. "I can't do that again," Honold remembers thinking. "If I had reported again and faced a similar reaction, I don't know if I would have made it through that."

As it turns out, when two more women came forward with allegations against Drill-Mellum, he was charged with Honold's assault. "You should feel lucky that we're charging someone of his stature for raping someone of your stature," she recalls a prosecutor telling her, apparently alluding to the fact that her attacker came from a family that, compared to hers, was wealthier and more highly educated. Drill-Mellum later pleaded guilty and was sentenced to prison.

Although she hardly felt "lucky," her attacker's prosecution was meaningful to Honold. For a sex crime to reach the courtroom is exceptional. Typical was Honold's decision, the second time around, not to report. Like most survivors, she chose to keep quiet about her abuse.

THE CREDIBILITY COMPLEX WORKS IN advance to keep sexual abuse accusations from ever surfacing. We know that most sexual assault is not reported through official channels. Among the population most vulnerable to rape, young women ages eighteen to twenty-four, less than a third complain to police. Women in college report at lower rates—20 percent, according to one estimate, and less than 5 percent, according to another. Reporting rates for women of color, both on and off campus, are even lower. Government researchers estimate that for every Black woman who reports her rape, at least fifteen Black women do not report theirs.

Although college sexual assault survivors rarely turn to police, they are more likely to complain if the incident will seem "believable"— that is, if their assault involved the kind of physical evidence associated with violent rape by a stranger. But the vast majority of sexual assault does not conform to the template of a violent "stranger rape": more than three-quarters of victims know their perpetrator; nine of ten victims say that no weapon was used. Sexual assault usually lacks conventional hallmarks of believability, which leads many survivors to anticipate, rightly, that their allegations will be dismissed as untrue.

Many survivors also foresee blame and disregard if they come forward to formal authorities and even to loved ones, even if the *what happened* part of their claim is believed. Survivors understand better than anyone that however their credibility is discounted, it can lead to the dismissal of the accusation. Rather than disclose their abuse only to be disbelieved, blamed, or disregarded, most remain silent. The preemptive operation of the credibility complex helps explain why not reporting is the rule rather than the exception.

For some survivors, including Abby Honold, the expectation of unfair treatment—the anticipated credibility discount—is borne of past experience. Over the years, many survivors have mentioned to me, almost in passing, a prior incident of sexual misconduct that was badly handled. Sexual abuse during childhood and adolescence occurs with alarming frequency. Black girls are especially vulnerable, with estimates as high as 65 percent having experienced sexual abuse before age fourteen. Irrespective of race, sexual abuse during childhood or adolescence increases the likelihood of sexual victimization in adulthood. Most of these victims stay silent. For many who do disclose their abuse, a hard lesson is learned early on: reporting makes no difference.

There are other routes to silence. Survivors who are initially willing to disclose their abuse often change course after their credibility is discounted at an initial phase—typically by a loved one. Many women I've spoken with chose not to make a formal report because their first, informal disclosure was not well received. Psychologists have shown that "negative social reactions" from their confidants lead survivors to stop talking about the misconduct.

When a victim's initial account is discounted—whether by distrust, blame, or disregard—she often becomes silent. In many conversations with survivors of both sexual assault and workplace harassment, I've heard how responses to first disclosures dictated the path forward. When loved ones responded poorly, they reinforced the sense of futility that is also associated with more formal reporting. As survivors have said to me, *If my own friends didn't believe me, why would someone who doesn't even know me? If my mom blamed me, of course the police would too. If those closest to me didn't care about what happened, why would anyone else?*

The anticipated credibility discount can also silence survivors who have not personally experienced the discount but are steeped enough in our culture to predict that, if they come forward, they will be discredited. Many victims know how likely it is that their story will be met with disbelief, blame, or disregard. They know this from watching how other accusers have been treated by family members and friends, by police officers and other formal officials, and in the court of public opinion. This awareness is a huge impediment to coming forward about sexual assault when it departs from the stranger rape paradigm.

Disregard is an especially potent preemptive force. Sexual assault survivors often stay silent for fear their report will be treated as unimportant, or not important enough to warrant consequences for the man accused. To avoid this indifference, many victims choose to disclose their abuse only in a therapeutic setting. Nicole Johnson is a psychologist who researches gender-based violence intervention and prevention. In her clinical practice, Johnson has worked for years with survivors of trauma, particularly sexual assault. She told me that many of her clients believe that what they suffered will not be seen as serious enough to warrant reporting. In weighing whether to come forward, these women understand that concern for the abuser normally outranks concern for the accuser.

This understanding is a commonplace reason for silence on the part of victims whose violation is unlikely to matter to anyone in a position to hold the abuser to account. We see this across industries, where silence is a regular feature of sexual harassment in the workplace. Some 90 percent of employees who experience abuse decline to report through formal workplace channels. These workers share a widespread expectation of "inaction on their claim," according to a task force convened by the Equal Employment Opportunity Commission. Many workers also suspect that, if they do file a formal complaint, their claim will be disbelieved, or they will be blamed "for causing the offending actions."

With good reason, workers who have experienced nonphysical harassment may be especially skeptical that their complaint will prompt action. For most of our nation's history, the concept of sexual harassment did not exist. In 1975, Lin Farley, a journalist teaching a class on women and work at Cornell University, convened a session for students to talk about their experiences in the workplace. What emerged from this conversation among a racially and economically diverse group of women, Farley recalls, was a hidden yet "unmistakable pattern to our employment." "Each one of us had already quit or been fired from a job at least once because we had been made too uncomfortable by the behavior of men," Farley says.

Soon after, courts began to recognize the legal claim of workplace sexual harassment, which I'll explore in the chapters ahead. Until then, it was "something to just live through," as described by the legal scholar Catharine MacKinnon, who pioneered the claim. Only once sexual harassment was named could it be attacked as wrong, and illegal.

But even with this formal claim on the books, victims of workplace sexual harassment—particularly more marginalized workers—doubt that coming forward will do any good. Like countless victims of abuse, within the workplace and outside it, many suffer in silence.

ALEJANDRA BEGAN WORKING AS A janitor in Fresno, California, in 2003. Her regular shift lasted from five thirty p.m. until two a.m., Monday through Friday. Alejandra worked under a supervisor named

Mateo, who she says began harassing her within a year. According to Alejandra, Mateo would comment on her buttocks and tell her that he wanted to feel her wrapped around his penis. He would watch pornographic videos and masturbate in her presence. He repeatedly demanded that she perform oral sex on him or touch his exposed penis. And he once tried to rape her. As Alejandra recalls, Mateo frequently told her "nobody would believe her" if she came forward—a common silencing tactic of abusers. Alejandra says she endured the abuse for more than a decade before finally reporting it to the police and to her employer.

Victims of workplace sexual harassment must consider not only the prospect of disbelief, but also the danger of retaliation. Women are often seen as expendable employees—a view that reflects and perpetuates workplace hierarchies. Their abusers, meanwhile, are usually valued, as men and as more powerful employees. Unlike their seemingly dispensable victims, harassers will likely be protected by those with decision-making authority. This dynamic is a legitimate concern for workers at any level of income, but especially for those with little or nothing to fall back on. Robert Vance, a Philadelphia civil rights lawyer with decades of experience representing plaintiffs in sexual harassment cases, explains that because they need the paycheck, low-wage workers, if they report at all, tend to do so only when the job has become unbearable. Alejandra, the Fresno janitor, says her harasser repeatedly told her she would be fired if she reported him. "I spent many years suffering," she later remarked.

Maria de Jesus Ramos Hernandez came to the United States from Mexico, hoping to earn enough money to pay for her daughter's surgery. Soon after she took a job in a chiropractor's office, the sexual abuse began. Hernandez didn't immediately report the chiropractor. Like so many victims, she thought she would be dismissed if she came forward. Hernandez was also alone and without money or immigration papers, and didn't speak English. She had special cause for thinking the police would believe a man who was a respected member of society, and not her. And like many immigrant women who work in isolated settings—perhaps someone else's home or a small office—Hernandez had no witnesses to her abuse or its aftermath. Her word would be all she had.

Hernandez also worried that she would be blamed for tempting her employer or for encouraging his advances. Because of what he paid her, she felt she could not "deny him pleasure," so Hernandez was mostly passive throughout her abuse. As a woman of color without power in the workplace, as an accuser who would probably not be credited if she were to come forward, Hernandez was unlikely to complain. She was a perfect target for her harasser.

Notice how the credibility complex compounds vulnerabilities. Marginalized women receive the steepest credibility discount. As a result, they have special reason to stay silent. Abusers understand this, and often target victims who are least likely to disclose their abuse. In the end, those who are already subordinated are further violated.

ROWENA CHIU BEGAN WORKING FOR Harvey Weinstein in 1998, assisting in the London office with his European film productions. Later that year, at the Venice Film Festival, she found herself at a late-night meeting with the producer. There, she recalls, Weinstein told her "he'd never had a Chinese girl" before attempting to rape her. Decades later, with the benefit of hindsight, Chiu says she "fell into Harvey's trap" because of power imbalances that included race. "The idea of the Asian immigrant 'model minority' is a cliché," Chiu writes, "but at least in my British-Chinese family, we were afraid of standing out. . . . I learned the social benefits of being deferential, polite and well behaved. As with many Asian women, this meant that I was visible as a sex object, invisible as a person."

She describes "almost two decades of living with a secret trauma of such magnitude that I would attempt suicide twice," and "grappling with guilt that I took the job, that I hadn't left the room sooner, that it was somehow my fault." She kept her secret from her therapist, from her pastor, and from the man she would marry.

In the summer of 2017, Chiu was visited by Jodi Kantor, one of the *New York Times* reporters investigating Weinstein. Kantor had reason to believe Chiu had a story to tell—a story Chiu had told nearly two decades earlier to Zelda Perkins, a coworker who was herself the victim of Weinstein's abuse. Perkins had spoken with Kantor, but wouldn't provide the details of Chiu's account—Perkins said these were Chiu's to share or not.

When Kantor first approached Chiu, she was only months away from publishing, with Twohey, the bombshell Weinstein investigation—yet Chiu wouldn't speak about what happened. After the story broke, dozens of women came forward on the record with their allegations—and still Chiu kept her secret. There were many reasons why.

For one, back in the late 1990s, she had entered into a legal agreement with Weinstein that obligated her to stay silent in exchange for £125,000, or about $213,000. Chiu later explained that she and Perkins "had wanted to report Harvey to his superiors; instead, we were pressured into signing a nondisclosure agreement that prevented us from speaking to family and friends, and made it extremely difficult to work with a therapist or a lawyer, or to aid a criminal investigation."

Although it was not what either woman wanted, there seemed to be no alternative. They had tried to report Weinstein to his superiors, but the credibility complex had moved into high gear. As Chiu recalls, "multiple senior individuals acted to shut us down. Some outright laughed in our faces. The message was always the same: Who would ever believe us over the most powerful man in Hollywood?"

After signing the nondisclosure agreement, Chiu spent nearly two decades in what she describes as "constant fear"—"Fear of Harvey's abuse, control and power; that the story would come back to haunt me; that I would inadvertently slip up on my promise to never speak of this."

The nondisclosure agreement was terribly damaging. Yet Chiu says the "personal constraints" on speaking out were "a lot stronger" than the legal constraints. Like many women, especially women from "model minority" families, Chiu was raised not to "make a fuss" or behave in an "unpleasant" way. She became accustomed to not calling attention to herself or disrupting the status quo. She was taught to be "nice," even if that meant burying her own assault. "Remaining silent had become integral to my identity, both as a woman and as a person of color," she would later recount.

What ultimately prompted Chiu to share her story, first with Kantor and Twohey, and then in her own words in the pages of the *New York Times*? She said she was inspired by the powerful testimony of Christine Blasey Ford, whose decision to "speak up" about Brett Kavanaugh in September 2018 made a lasting impression. Several months later, Chiu had the opportunity to meet Ford at a gathering convened by Kantor and Twohey. Chiu shared her story with Ford, and she listened to the stories of the other women—twelve in total, along with several of their lawyers. The group met at the Los Angeles home of Gwyneth Paltrow, who had also come forward with abuse allegations against Weinstein. Each of the women gathered was a central accuser in the #MeToo era, except Chiu, the one woman in the room not yet to have broken her silence.

For Chiu, the group encounter was a momentous one. "Meeting

others who'd had similar experiences created a seismic shift within me," she explained. Not long after the gathering in Los Angeles, she went public with her allegation, which Weinstein denied. As difficult as it was to come forward, Chiu felt at peace with the decision. "I can briefly glory in the relief that I am no longer sitting on a sickening secret," she wrote.

Months earlier, just before that pivotal gathering came to a close, several of the women took a moment to reflect on the experience of speaking out. "We're still here," said Zelda Perkins, who added, "We walked through the fire, but we all came out the other side."

Most women who bring forward allegations of misconduct must walk through the fire: they will be distrusted, blamed, treated with indifference, or far worse. In all likelihood, they will be harmed again—this time, by the people they trusted to help them. We now turn to why.

2

OF PERFECT VICTIMS AND MONSTER ABUSERS

HOW MYTHS DISTORT OUR CREDIBILITY JUDGMENTS

A clump of misconceptions about victims and abusers is nestled deep in the credibility complex. These misconceptions saturate our culture and our law, imprinting themselves on us all and manipulating our response to misconduct. When an accuser's account departs from our understanding of victims, abusers, and abuse, however inaccurate this understanding, we are more likely to discredit the allegation.

This disconnect between myth and reality spans all three dimensions of credibility. You'll recall that *it happened* is one of a trio of claims nested in an accusation. The others, again, are *it's wrong* and *it matters*. Each of these claims must be believed in order for an accuser to be found credible. Across the board, faulty paradigms lead us astray.

STRANGER RAPE REMAINS THE COMPARATOR against which sexual assault allegations are judged. Most sexual assault is committed by friends, dates, partners, coworkers, bosses, mentors—by far, acquaintances and intimates are more likely than strangers to be the perpetrators of sexual violence. According to one estimate, more than half of female victims of rape reported that at least one perpetrator was a current or former intimate partner, while more than 40 percent were raped by an acquaintance. Yet we hew to the opposite archetype. The stranger rape paradigm continues to warp our credibility determinations.

Most of us are familiar with this paradigm, also known as "real rape," or "righteous rape." This is rape perpetrated, not by someone known to the victim, but by a stranger. It is committed by someone of low socioeconomic status. It entails a great deal of physical violence that leaves obvious signs of physical injury. It involves a weapon. It takes place at night, in a dark alley or a rough neighborhood. As experts on community responses to sexual assault have observed, these understandings of rape "impact not only law enforcement professionals, but also prosecutors, medical professionals, victim advocates, judges, jurors, and even the friends and family members of sexual assault victims." Although this paradigm defies reality, it has remarkable durability. It is embraced by wide swaths of society.

For almost fifty years, sociologists and psychologists have demonstrated the influence of rape myths, defined in an early study as "prejudicial, stereotyped, or false beliefs about rape, rape victims, and rapists." More recently, there's been an important shift in how experts think about rape myths. They look at false beliefs, but also our *attitudes* toward sexual violence. These beliefs and attitudes are widely and persistently held. And they serve a crucial function: as researchers put it, "to deny and justify male sexual aggression against women." In other words, rape myths are a pillar that supports sexual violence, which helps explain their longevity.

As the writer Rebecca Solnit writes in *Men Explain Things to Me*, ours is a culture saturated with "the idea that a man has the right to have sex with a woman regardless of her desires." Solnit adds, "this sense of being owed sex is everywhere." Sexual entitlement goes hand in hand with the stranger rape paradigm, which leads us to tacitly authorize most sexual violence. We recognize only a tiny sliver as real, as wrong, and as worthy of concern. The rest is cast aside as false, justified, or unimportant. This is how patriarchal structures are bolstered. "His rights trump hers," writes Solnit. When male sexual prerogatives are protected, especially within our everyday relationships, gendered hierarchies congeal and calcify.

Our everyday relationships include those with bosses and coworkers—another site of skewed credibility evaluations. Researchers have found that workplace sexual harassment, like sexual assault, is surrounded by a cluster of misconceptions. These misconceptions subtly influence how many of us respond to harassment accusers.

Rape and sexual harassment myths have staying power not only because they reinforce patriarchal structures, but because most of us would rather not confront an ugly reality. It turns out we are highly motivated to doubt the occurrence of sexual abuse. Kimberly Lonsway, a psychologist responsible for much of the research on community responses to sexual misconduct, observes that all of us have a vested interest in overlooking it. "We don't want it to happen as much as it does," Lonsway told me. "We don't want it to happen to our loved ones. We don't want to believe in it. It's a better world if it's not true."

Accepting the ubiquity of sexual abuse also disrupts understandings of ourselves and our relationships. As Lonsway explains, it can be profoundly unsettling to believe that abuse happens as often as it does, and that its perpetrators are mostly known to their victims and to us. These beliefs can force us to "rethink gender and sexuality," and even our own experiences. So we hold on to the faulty paradigms and avoid the uncomfortable truths.

NANCY HOGSHEAD-MAKAR IS A LAWYER who specializes in representing sexual abuse victims. She is also a former world-class swimmer who won four medals, three of them gold, at the 1984 summer Olympics. Several years before achieving this incredible feat, she was sexually assaulted while running on a tree-lined path at Duke University, where she was a sophomore. The attacker brutally raped and beat her for two hours.

Unlike the typical sexual assault by an acquaintance of the same race, what happened to Hogshead-Makar conformed to the conventional paradigm, which is maddeningly difficult to dislodge. "I sort of fit this narrative," she rues, and her assailant did too. "It was a stranger. He was African American. I'm Caucasian. I'm rich, he's poor. And I looked like I had been raped."

Duke provided the support she needed. Hogshead-Makar dropped two classes, and she was given a parking pass that allowed her to avoid a long walk through campus to get to her dorm. She was moved to a more centralized location. Everyone around her believed she'd been assaulted. They believed it had harmed her, so they worked to assist her in whatever ways they could. They understood that she was important, a valuable member of the community, and that she deserved their compassion. Her community rallied around her and restored, to the greatest extent possible, what she had lost. The response helped her move forward. Unlike most of her clients over the ensuing decades, she was found credible, and it made a world of difference.

As Hogshead-Makar fully recognizes, this outcome was exceptional and it cannot be separated from her privilege as a white, educated woman, and a star athlete. Nor can it be decoupled from her assailant's vulnerability as a Black man who—from what police were able to piece together—appeared to be an outsider to the university community. Hogshead-Makar laments how her identities, and those of her rapist, shaped the collective response to her assault. She insists that the care she received shouldn't be reserved for survivors who look like her, and that men who look like her abuser shouldn't be the only ones held to account. Her rapist was never apprehended, but this was not for want of effort, which she says felt more important than the absence of punishment.

Hogshead-Makar emphasizes that what she managed to achieve in the years following her rape shouldn't be used to minimize the trauma of sexual violation. Her story is far more complicated than the timeline alone would suggest, and she resists any neat packaging, however tempting—like, as she puts it, "Hey, Nancy was raped in 1981, and by 1984, she won three gold medals in the Olympics." She maintains that her accomplishments were only possible because she was given "extraordinary accommodations."

Most allegations fail to move us because they don't resemble Hogshead-Makar's—they don't resemble the stranger rape paradigm or the archetypes of the perfect victim and the monster abuser that flow from it.

MYTH VERSUS REALITY: VICTIMS

Our credibility judgments are hindered by a "perfect victim" standard. When an accuser falls short of this standard, all three claims embedded in her allegation are rejected: it didn't happen, it wasn't blameworthy, it doesn't matter.

The "perfect victim" is an amalgam of how we think women *do* respond to abuse and how we think women *should* respond to abuse. If an accuser fails to satisfy these benchmarks, she doesn't seem like a victim.

One expectation is that victims fight back. A woman must mount some kind of physical resistance that is then overcome by the abuser after a violent struggle: fight or flight. Only then does the violation register. In the fall of 2017, Amelia Wagoner, a sophomore at a college in Northern California, was sexually assaulted by a fellow student. At the time, Wagoner was a competitive athlete—she was a member of the school's rowing team—and this fact made her less credible.

"How much do you bench press? How much can you squat? How many hours do you work out a week?" Wagoner recalls the lawyer for the accused man asking her. "How did this happen? How could you let this happen if you're so strong?"

Wagoner described to me how "the lawyer just kept picking" at this idea that she was an unlikely, even undeserving, victim. She added that she didn't understand why her physical abilities were "so important." "If you freeze up," she explained, "nothing matters—how much you can bench or how strong you are. Your body's not working."

In 2019, former military linguist Ryan Leigh Dostie wrote an essay in the *New York Times* about women who were raped while serving in the army. Dostie describes how her own allegations were dismissed, along with those of other military survivors she knew, because the women didn't "act enough 'like a rape victim'"—a "mantra" that Dostie said was repeated by the investigators in her case.

In her first year in the military, Dostie says she and two other women she knew—a specialist and a staff sergeant—were sexually assaulted. The specialist came forward, only to be disbelieved because she "didn't uncurl her fists and shoot her rapists"—four of them. The sergeant was raped by a translator in a shed after a game of chess, but she kept silent about it until her military career ended years later. In Dostie's telling, the sergeant had good reason to believe that she would be blamed for being alone with a man. "Whatever had happened, that was on her. So the staff sergeant kept her head down," Dostie writes.

Dostie too deviated from the victim archetype. "Despite my own visible, documented injuries," she says, "I didn't cry hard enough, loud enough, in the military police station in the hours after my rape, in front of a group of men who had no intention of believing me anyway."

The problem of course extends well beyond Dostie and the survivors she happens to know. "Every rape in the Army is unreal, unbelievable," she writes. The idealized victim is in many ways the opposite of the ideal service member—what Dostie describes as "silent" and "obedient." And yet accusers are dismissed when they don't, according to the mantra, "act enough like a victim."

Outside the military, many girls and women are socialized to be acquiescent and physically docile. Even as traditional notions of femininity are challenged they retain their influence by dictating a gendered set of appropriate attributes and qualities—like sweetness and gentleness. This antiquated standard continues to constrain how many girls and women behave, and it is one of many reasons why, in the midst of sexual violence, victims may not satisfy our demand for a physical fight.

Another reason for apparent passivity is self-preservation. Fearing that resistance would increase their chance of death or more serious injury, some victims make a conscious decision not to fight.

Other victims have developed a coping mechanism, often originating from childhood sexual trauma, of remaining still during abuse. Psychologists have learned that this coping mechanism can be activated, almost automatically, when a threat looms.

Victims can also freeze as a reflexive response to trauma. As neurobiologists discover more about the brain, they've been able to identify the circuitry responsible for various states of immobility that can occur when we're under attack. A state of severe threat can trigger predictable responses, whether the traumatic event is a school shooting, a natural disaster, military combat, sexual assault, or severe harassment.

Mounting evidence is revolutionizing our understanding of how victims respond to trauma. Yet we continue to impose a tacit burden on them: a burden to resist. It's a unique burden—one entrenched not only in our culture but in our law.

——

The logic built into our criminal law is crystal clear: *Accusers who don't physically resist their abusers aren't victims.* And, related, men who force sex on women who surrender can't be held responsible.

The law's resistance requirement, as it's known, has evolved over the past century. A woman once needed to resist "to the utmost" to legally qualify as a victim of rape. Some states later softened the requirement to recognize victims who offered "earnest" or "reasonable" resistance. But these changes have preserved the requirement's underlying premise—unless they mount a fight, women are responsible for the conduct of their alleged rapist.

The older cases don't bother to disguise the harshness of the rule. In 1906, the Wisconsin Supreme Court reversed the rape conviction of a man whose teenaged victim, Edna Nethery, failed to satisfy the utmost resistance standard. Nethery was walking across a field to her grandmother's house when she came upon Grant Brown, the son of a neighboring farmer. Brown "at once seized her, tripped her to the ground, placed himself in front and over her, unbuttoned her underclothing, then his own clothing, and had intercourse with her." For her part, Nethery testified, "I tried as hard as I could to get away. I was trying all the time to get away just as hard as I could. I was trying to get up; I pulled at the grass; I screamed as hard as I could, and he told me to shut up, and I didn't, and then he held his hand on my mouth until I was almost strangled." Brown "allowed her to arise" after Nethery promised not to tell. When she finally got to her grandmother's house, bleeding, she "at once exclaimed, 'Grant Brown has [done something] to me. O! what shall I do?'"

Accepting the truth of these allegations, as was required since Brown had already been convicted at trial, the appeals court held that Nethery didn't do enough to resist—therefore, Brown was not guilty of rape. "There must be the most vehement exercise of every physical means or faculty within the woman's power to resist the penetration of her person, and this must be shown to persist until the offense is consummated," explained the court. By this standard, Nethery's conduct was said to fall short. "Except for one demand, when first seized, to 'let me go,' and inarticulate screams, she mentions no verbal protests." Even more damning, Nethery didn't physically fight her assailant—at least not to the court's satisfaction. A woman must deploy her strongest "means of protection," the court emphasized, as "she is equipped to interpose most effective obstacles by means of hands and limbs and pelvic muscles." Nethery failed to do what was expected of her, the blame was hers, and Brown walked free.

This most extreme version of the burden placed on victims persisted for many decades. By the 1980s, most states had somewhat relaxed the "utmost" resistance standard to require "reasonable" or "earnest" resistance. But victims still needed to prove themselves worthy of the law's protection by fighting their assailant. In 1983, after a jury found a man guilty of rape, an appellate court took the unusual step of reversing the conviction. In the court's view, the accuser, Cassandra Weeks, hadn't done enough to ward off her rape. Evidence showed that Weeks was waiting on the corner of a street for a ride from her cousin. An acquaintance drove up, and Weeks got into his car to talk. The man brought Weeks to a secluded area, where, as the court described, he "slapped her in the face three or four times while threatening to kill her," and "threatened to use a weapon which, he had indicated, was under the seat of the car." He forced Weeks to have intercourse.

The court concluded that, by not doing more to resist, Weeks acted unreasonably. "Certainly" she was afraid, conceded the court, while quickly adding this: "It is important to note that all of the witnesses who saw the victim immediately after the alleged rape testified that they did not see any cuts, bruises or evidence of any physical attack. Her own testimony indicates that she did not make any efforts to resist. The victim asserted at trial that the defendant threatened to kill her, yet, he did nothing to warrant a reasonable person in these circumstances to believe that resistance would not prevent the rape." Slaps in the face and a gun nearby were not enough.

The resistance requirement is no longer as rigid as it was in the 1980s, but it remains "a model standard of behavior" by which courts and juries judge rape accusers. The standard varies among the states. Some like Alabama retain a formal requirement, while others like Delaware define terms like "non-consent" and "force" in ways that condition legal protection on resistance. Still today, "a female's resistance—or lack thereof—has not lost its potential relevance in rape prosecutions," writes the legal scholar Joshua Dressler. "Proof of resistance may be helpful—or even critical—to the fact finder's determination that a rape has occurred."

With rare exception, states that have lifted their physical resistance requirement continue to apply what is, in effect, a verbal resistance requirement. Across the country, from Washington to New Hampshire and places in between, the victim must *demonstrate* her unwillingness to engage in sexual conduct in order to qualify as a victim of assault. The default is that she consents, simply by being.

Unlike the affirmative consent rules that are now commonplace on college campuses, criminal law consent definitions put the onus on the accuser to refuse sex. Otherwise, under prevailing legal definitions, a woman who does nothing—who has remained inert throughout a sexual encounter—is said to have consented to it.

For instance, in New York, the victim must "clearly express" her nonconsent. This requires that a "reasonable person" in the accused's position would understand her "words and acts" as an "expression of lack of consent." Consent definitions serve to modernize the traditional resistance requirement and expand the category of deserving victims. But let's be clear: rape law leaves intact an age-old focus on the accuser and whether she did enough to thwart her assault.

———

A victim's behavior following the assault can also disappoint our expectations and lessen her believability. When an accuser's emotional response is different from the response we envision, her story seems suspicious. Both "suppressed" and "intensified" emotions—or "underemotional" and "overemotional" responses—are familiar to psychologists who work with sexual assault survivors. Yet our preset ideas of how victims react to their abuse distort our credibility judgments.

For example, victims who don't display obvious signs of emotional distress are often discredited by law enforcement officers and civilians alike. In the acclaimed 2019 television miniseries *Unbelievable*, a young woman called Marie is charged with lying about her rape and later vindicated when police catch her attacker, who turns out to be a serial rapist. Skepticism of Marie's account began not with the police, but with those closest to her. Her foster mother, Peggy, suggested that something was strange about the way Marie recounted her rape. "She was detached. . . . Emotionally detached from what she was saying," Peggy told the investigating police officer.

Shannon, Marie's former foster mother, was suspicious for the same reason. "I remember exactly," she told journalists. "I was standing on my balcony and she called and said, 'I've been raped.' It was very flat, no emotion." When Shannon and Peggy spoke, each confirmed the other's doubts. And when those doubts were shared with the police, Marie became the suspect, derailing any meaningful investigation into her rapist.

These reactions aren't unusual. A meta-analysis finds that accusers "who present with controlled affect" are perceived as less credible than accusers who are visibly upset. This is a burden placed uniquely on rape accusers, who are expected to "experience negative emotions that are much stronger than those experienced by other victims of crime." The assumption that sexual assault victims will display extreme emotion warps our judgments. Because "emotional demeanor is not diagnostic of witness honesty," as the meta-analysis concluded, we downgrade the believability of certain victims for no good reason. Women who fail to display the appropriate level of emotion are dismissed.

Jim Markey, a retired Phoenix law enforcement officer with over thirty years on the job, fourteen of those supervising sexual assault cases, points out that many first responders disbelieve accusers who appear very calm. But the acceptable emotional range for survivors is exceedingly narrow, creating a troubling bind that evokes a twisted version of the tale of Goldilocks. Like their *too calm* counterparts, women who are *too agitated* are unbelievable. "Hysterical" accusers seem especially suspect when their allegations depart from the stranger rape template. As Markey explains, patrol officers often think, "This person wasn't injured, there weren't any weapons, I don't understand why they're acting like this." When the label of hysteria has been attached, it's likely the accusation has already been discarded.

"Hysterical" women are deemed unreliable reporters, just as they have been for centuries.*

Kevin Becker is a clinical psychologist who has specialized in trauma for nearly thirty years. When we spoke, Becker stressed that victims of trauma tend to defy conventional understandings. "The affect may not always match what you expect. And it may not even match what people are saying," he explained. A person who is recounting "a really gruesome situation, really graphically," may lack the emotions we think victims should display. Becker told me that certain unanticipated responses—including laughter—can be explained by the neurobiology of trauma and, in some cases, survivors' coping mechanisms. Yet without a sound framework for interpreting them, these responses only fuel our doubt.

WE ALSO ASSUME THAT A woman will immediately cut all ties with her abuser—another prime example of how the "perfect victim" script works against survivors. If a woman and her abuser maintain any kind of relationship, her story will fall short on all three dimensions. We see her as untrustworthy and reject her account as untrue. *The abuse didn't happen.* We assign responsibility to her for inviting or encouraging the behavior. *The abuse wasn't wrong.* And we perceive the misconduct as unworthy of our concern. *The abuse doesn't matter.* After all, we think, it couldn't have been *that* awful if she kept in touch with him.

Take the Weinstein case as an example. Among the many chal-

---

* It was once believed that the uterus was "a free-floating entity which could leave its moorings when a woman was dissatisfied, to travel around the body and disrupt everything in its passage," resulting in "hysterical" symptoms.

lenges facing the prosecution was the need to explain to the jury why Weinstein's victims kept in touch with him after the abuse, in some instances with friendly and even intimate exchanges. As one forensic psychiatrist testified at trial, victims of sexual assault and harassment often remain cordial or intimate with their abuser. "Most individuals think, 'I can put it behind me, I can move on with my life and forget about what happened to me. I don't want it to get worse. I don't want this person who sexually assaulted me to ruin my friendships or put my job in jeopardy," the expert told the jury. Apart from a fear of repercussions, preserving the relationship may feel to the survivor like a way to show—both herself and her abuser—that he didn't defeat her. By moving forward as if nothing ever happened, she tries to diminish his power.

MYTH VERSUS REALITY: ABUSERS

The credibility complex rests on a set of long-standing misconceptions about abusers as well. Just as we're skeptical when an accuser diverges from the perfect victim in our mind, we're skeptical when the accused man diverges from our imagined perpetrator. Misunderstandings about who offenders are and how they behave lead us to doubt accusations of abuse, to blame accusers, and to disregard abuse when it's inflicted by a "good man." Our doubt is linked to the persistent myth of the monster abuser, the corollary of the "perfect victim." In much the same way, the archetype leads us to deny, justify, and excuse abuse.

The caricatured bad man is relentless, violating all potential victims in his path. This vilification of the mythical abuser has real consequences. It leads us to believe that "ordinary" men don't engage in sexual misconduct. When only men marked as deviant resemble an allegorical offender, all others are presumptively innocent. Survivors themselves often adopt this framework—as always, no one is immune from cultural biases. Nicole Johnson, the clinical psychologist with a focus on sexual violence, notes that many of her clients struggle to integrate the "monster picture that we've painted of a rapist" with their own perceptions of their attacker: "If a rapist is a monster, and this person who I have some positive feelings towards, possibly even loved, did this thing to me," as many victims reason, says Johnson, "I have to figure out how to make sense of that." For survivors, the need to reconcile the good in their abuser with the terrible damage he inflicted can create enormous cognitive dissonance. This dissonance often gives way to denial, justification, and excuse, which then leads to silence.

A similar conundrum arises when an accuser chooses to come forward. If those evaluating her credibility compare the accused man to the archetypical villain, the allegation seems implausible. We're easily swayed by defenders who insist that the accused is a "good husband," a "good boss," or "from a good family." And if the accused is a well-known man who we collectively respect, we are even more prone to disbelieve his accuser.

Barbara Bowman presents a case in point. She is an artist in Scottsdale and one of dozens of women who accused Bill Cosby of sexual abuse. Bowman says she was seventeen years old and an aspiring actress when Cosby assaulted her on multiple occasions. She first disclosed the alleged abuse to her agent, who did nothing, and then to a lawyer, who accused her of "making the story up." Almost thirty years later, writing in the *Washington Post*, Bowman recalls that "their dismissive responses crushed any hope I had of getting help; I was convinced no one would listen to me." She was "a teenager from Denver acting in McDonald's commercials. He was Bill Cosby: consummate American dad Cliff Huxtable and the Jell-O spokesman."

Although she never went to the police, over the years, Bowman began telling her story publicly. "Still," she says, "my complaint didn't seem to take hold." Nor did the complaints of the other Cosby accusers whose allegations had long been reported in the press. As Bowman observed, public outcry began "in earnest" "only after a *man*, Hannibal Buress, called Bill Cosby a rapist in a comedy act" in the fall of 2014.

In the end, sixty women came forward against Cosby, who denied all the allegations. Four years later, he was convicted of assaulting Andrea Constand, who testified that her former mentor drugged her and sexually assaulted her while she was immobilized on his couch.

IN LATE 2019, A JURY deadlocked in the sexual assault trial of a prominent Bay Area ballet teacher. The man was charged with raping two young teenagers who were his students at the time; a third student also testified about an incident of abuse that prosecutors did not include in their formal charges. In his defense, the ballet teacher denied raping the girls. One, he claimed, had lied. The other girl, he said, was flirting with him, but when he tried to have sex with her, he couldn't get an erection.

After the mistrial, the jury foreperson explained why she was suspicious: there were too few victims for the girls who testified to be believed. "Three alleged victims over more than twenty years of teaching and hundreds of students?" she asked. This made no sense to her. The kind of man who would molest girls could only be a "hardcore pedophile."

A version of this defense that's less explicit but grounded in similar logic is that the accused is not "the type" to commit misconduct. Men who abuse women are thought to abuse women across the board. Based on this fallacy, the testimonials of those women who weren't victimized by an accused man are regarded as exculpatory evidence. When we decide that only a certain *type* of man could harass or assault a woman, we too readily reject the possibility that a man of otherwise good character might transgress. This can lead us to dismiss the accusation outright, obviating the need to complicate our opinion of the accused man.

Of course, our judgments about whose character is "good" may themselves be skewed. We tend to regard those who occupy a privileged social status as having positive character traits. When supporters of the accused attest to his character, they fortify this flawed presumption. The lure of "good man reasoning" is powerful. It predisposes us to discredit accusers who come forward against the men we can personally vouch for, and even those who accuse the men *other women* can vouch for.

In the wake of misconduct allegations, women who were not harassed by the alleged abuser typically follow to refute the accusations. A friend of Les Moonves, the former CBS chief who resigned in 2018 following numerous sexual assault and harassment allegations, says he is kind and decent. An executive at CBS says her "experience with him on a professional and personal basis has never had any hint of the behavior" alleged. A colleague of Jeff Fager, the former chairman of CBS News accused of harassment, says, in her experience, "Jeff is supportive of women and decent to women." Three dozen of former senator and comedian Al Franken's female colleagues from his time at *Saturday Night Live* write in an open letter, "Not one of us has ever experienced any inappropriate behavior." More than sixty women who worked with former NBC News anchor Tom Brokaw, accused of harassment, say he "has treated each of us with fairness and respect."

Cataloging the testimonials in support of these accused men, the journalist Megan Garber writes, "that kind of familiarity doesn't scale to a defense. There's saying *I know him*, and there's assuming that the knowing itself is an exoneration." It is not. As Garber observes,

"What *I know him* overlooks, of course, is the obvious: An abuser will not abuse everybody. Not just because of dull pragmatism, but also because people are complex and variable and, as a rule, containing of multitudes."

Until we see the ordinariness of abusers, we'll continue to dismiss the countless women who are abused by them. The "monster abuser" will garble our credibility judgments, immunizing a range of abuse. The same is true of the "perfect victim." In the next three chapters, I look at how these archetypes and other traps set by the credibility complex prime us to discount the credibility of accusers and inflate the credibility of men accused. As we identify these traps, we'll be better positioned to lessen their influence. First, I'll focus on the realm of trust—how we evaluate the claim *it happened*.

3

WHOSE TRUTH?

HOW VICTIMS ARE DISTRUSTED

Aja Newman calls herself a city girl. She's a Black woman who was raised in New York City as the youngest of seven, and she never left. Now in her thirties and the mother of school-age children, Newman is unguarded when she recounts her sexual assault.

In January 2016, she was working as a baggage handler at LaGuardia Airport. One evening, shoulder pain that had been bothering her throughout the day began to intensify. When the pain worsened and her hands started tingling, Newman decided it was time to check herself into the emergency room at a hospital in East Harlem—the same hospital where she and her six siblings were born.

After receiving anti-inflammatories for the pain, Newman was able to move her shoulder enough to change into a hospital gown. As the medical team switched shifts, Newman was introduced to the overnight attending doctor, who ordered a dose of morphine that put her to sleep. Soon after, the doctor came into her room and, over her objection, injected her again. Lab tests would later show that, on top of the morphine that had been prescribed, Newman was given an unauthorized dose of propofol, a powerful drug used for general anesthesia and sedation. She began to slip in and out of consciousness.

Later, Newman would remember how the doctor who had drugged her quickly moved her bed and squeezed himself between the bed and the wall. "One of the first things I felt was him groping my breast," she described to the journalist Lisa Miller. Newman couldn't see, perhaps because her eyes wouldn't open, but she could hear the doctor masturbating while he molested her. "I'm trying to move. I'm trying to fight. And it's like either he's really strong or I'm not doing anything at all," she explained. She says the doctor wiped her body roughly with a sheet and mumbled, "Bitch."

When she came to, Newman's face felt sticky and she saw semen between her breasts. The semen was "confirmation that this really did happen," she told me. Otherwise, she might have thought it was all a bad dream.

She now had a decision to make. "It was like, *Are you going to go out there and do a whole bunch of aimless things? It's your word against somebody else's. This is an institution where there are more numbers against you. Even when you're not expecting the worst from people, you know this person works here. He's going to have favoritism here.* I just thought fast and decided I needed proof." She grabbed the bedding and her hospital gown—the evidence she felt she needed to convince anyone of the truth. She was "really mad, really upset," Newman remembers. "It's not a good feeling, to feel that you're a piece of trash like that. I didn't feel human. I felt very, very, very low."

She says she promptly told the physician's assistant what happened and that he discouraged her from calling the police. (The physician's assistant denies that he dissuaded her from reporting the assault, but he admits not passing the allegation up the chain of command as hospital protocol required.) When she was physically able, Newman left the hospital carrying a large plastic bag with her evidence, walked a half mile to her sister's home, and asked her sister to call the police.

Soon after, officers arrived and began, as Newman puts it, "interrogating" her—"Like I was making it up," she recounts. She was asked to repeat her story more than a dozen times. "The cops weren't, 'Oh my God, you poor thing.' They were like, 'Man, I don't want to get in the middle of this. It's nasty, and I think she's crazy.'

"They kept questioning me and then asking me if I was on drugs. They kept asking me, 'Do you do any cocaine, heroin? Do you do opiates or anything?'" She told the officers that, apart from the drugs administered at the hospital, she wasn't using, and didn't use, any drugs. But they continued asking the same questions. "More than enough times for you to start understanding that someone's questioning your story," she explains.

The response came as no surprise to Newman, who had expected all along that her story would be disbelieved. This was precisely why she had taken the hospital bedding, which she would later hand over to the police officers investigating her report. Soon, despite their misgivings, they escorted Newman to a different hospital for further examination and evidence gathering. Newman watched as a forensic technician used a special chemical and UV light to search for semen on the bedding that she had taken from the hospital. She had repeatedly described where the doctor ejaculated, but still no one had chemically examined her body. When the technician announced that the bedding would need to be sent to a lab for further testing, Newman had a "hunch"—she told the technician to spray the chemical on her body.

Newman recalls a collective gasp from the medical workers and law enforcement officers in the room when her face and the area between her breasts lit up from the presence of semen. Just like she had told everyone.

The DNA test results—which would ultimately show a match to the doctor—wouldn't arrive for months. In the meantime, Newman continued to fear that her story wouldn't be believed. The proof would have to be irrefutable, she knew; otherwise, people would find a way to dismiss her account. She could even predict the questions they would ask: "Were they having sex? Is she a prostitute? Was she trying to get drugs?" And she was right: "All of these allegations actually came up," she told me.

When the police spoke with the doctor at his New Jersey home the evening Newman made her report, he offered a very different story. "I am embarrassed because I 'whacked off' in the lounge," he said, "and it was possible that the ejaculate may have gone from my hands to the woman's blanket. Semen may also have transferred from my hand to her face during the time I treated her." The doctor also suggested, "She may be mistaken about me ejaculating on her face, because she was on morphine."

He wasn't arrested that night. But the accusations made their way into the press, which prompted a public expression of support—for the doctor. One physician said he felt "so bad" that the accused man was "being dragged through the mud on this." Friends and colleagues expressed strong skepticism of the allegations. One concluded that the story "absolutely reeks." Another went so far as to propose that the most "statistically likely" explanation was "the accuser has a behavior/ mental health condition (think borderline personality disorder)," and noted that, while women with these "issues" can be targets of sex crimes, "people with such conditions" are "also capable of creating a scenario to ruin someone's career." Even people who didn't personally know the doctor came to his defense, as so often happens—one commented that the man's successful career in medicine "earns him the benefit of the doubt from me."

Within a week of Newman's allegations going public, a second woman learned of these allegations and went to the police alleging that in September 2015, the same doctor had groped her breasts in the emergency room when she was being treated for a cold. It was the first time this second woman reported to the police, but she *had* already shared her account. In a group therapy session, she described how a blond doctor, who she knew only by his first name, touched her breasts. With the credibility complex in mind (albeit not by name), she said she was "freaked out" because the man was a doctor, while she was a young woman of color who had been sexually abused in the past. The group social worker relayed the woman's report to the hospital, which neither documented nor investigated the allegation.

Four months after the social worker's report went nowhere, with two complaints now in hand, the police made the arrest. And in March 2016, after two *more* women came forward, prosecutors charged the doctor—David Newman (no relation to Aja)—with sexually abusing Aja Newman and three other patients, all poor women of color. David Newman eventually pleaded guilty and was sentenced to two years in prison.

Aja Newman says she was "very, very disappointed" with the light prison sentence for her abuser, which she sees as bound up in race and class—his and hers. She also realizes that the case never would have made it to criminal court without the DNA evidence taken from the semen left on her eye and cheek, and that the other allegations helped tipped the scales.

"Women in general are at the bottom of the food chain," she said when I asked her why she had expected to be disbelieved. "I feel like we are pretty much the last, but then I also feel like, as a woman and as a minority, I am the last of the last. Not being of a certain class or financial status, I definitely do believe that's a disadvantage on top of everything, so that makes me the last of the last of the last, unfortunately." But she added, "I kind of feel like I'm a big deal and figured I'd use my voice anyway."

———

When someone makes a claim like *this happened*, the believability of that claim depends on two factors: the trustworthiness of the reporter and the plausibility of her account. To evaluate these factors, we rely on our "understanding of how the world works," as the philosopher Karen Jones has written. Alas, this understanding fails us when we're faced with an allegation of sexual misconduct. We may think otherwise, but our judgments about what to believe are frequently faulty.

Because many of us take on board a set of core misconceptions about sexual misconduct—including those myths of perfect victims and monster abusers—we're prone to dismiss allegations that are, in fact, true. In most cases, the word of a woman alleging sexual assault or harassment is simply not enough. Even if we don't reject her allegation outright, we get stuck in a state of apparent equipoise, unwilling or unable to pick sides in the "he said, she said" contest—which means we don't credit the accuser when we should, and the accused wins the day. The credibility discount often translates into demand for an unreasonable amount of corroboration—say, a mass of accusers. We are especially distrustful of certain types of accusers and certain types of claims.

When it comes to credibility inflation, we are far too willing to embrace the false denials of accused men, especially those who occupy positions of power and trust—not because we are foolish or naïve, but because we are primed by our culture and our law to rely on these men and take on faith their descriptions of reality. These are men whose authority is rarely questioned. And for these men, whose power augments their credibility, inflated credibility generates greater power. The credibility complex protects existing hierarchies, along with the sexual prerogatives that these hierarchies allow.

WE'LL GET TO HOW DISCOUNTING and boosting work when an accuser says *this happened*. First, let's unpack what we mean by "belief."

Belief falls along a continuum of certainty. It's not an on/off switch. Rather it's nonbinary, fluid, and provisional. Philosophers refer to this spectrum as "degrees of belief," meaning that "our confidence in the truth of some propositions is higher than our confidence in the truth of other propositions." For example, if I tell you I saw a dog walking on a Chicago sidewalk this morning, you'll be quite confident in the truth of my statement. If I tell you I saw an elephant walking on a Chicago sidewalk, you might still believe this is true, particularly if you have no reason *not* to take me at my word, but you'll be less certain that I saw an elephant than that I saw a dog. Your assessment of the plausibility of my account will impact how you assess my statement, as will your opinion of me. If I'm known to you as a generally trustworthy person, you'll not only tend to believe what I say, you'll also tend to possess more confidence in your belief as to my claim—and the converse is also true. With all this in mind, it can be rather confusing to speak only of "belief" without reference to the complexities it entails. Outside the legal system, we rarely acknowledge *degrees* of belief, or the spectrum of certainty on which they fall.

Within the legal system, distinct standards govern the confidence required of jurors before they can reach a verdict. Evidence that proves guilt *beyond a reasonable doubt* is needed in criminal court. In civil cases, a judgment for the plaintiff is typically allowed when a *preponderance* of the evidence supports the claim—that is, when it is more likely true than not. *Clear and convincing* evidence is another familiar legal standard, which falls somewhere between preponderance and beyond a reasonable doubt. And lower standards of evidence govern a police officer's decision to briefly detain a citizen (*reasonable suspicion*) or to make an arrest (*probable cause*). As was the case when police officers responded to Aja Newman, individual biases and misconceptions can of course influence how these standards are applied. Nevertheless, in each of these contexts, the determination at issue is pegged to a designated level of confidence that a set of facts is true.

Once we step out of legal and quasi-legal settings (like a campus disciplinary proceeding), however, there is no preset confidence level. Instead, when we respond to allegations by our friends, coworkers, and family members, we're left to our own devices when choosing a threshold for belief and then deciding whether an allegation surmounts it. How sure must we be in order to *believe* the accuser, and to support her accordingly? There is no one answer—here too, context matters. But unless we acknowledge the spectrum of certainty, we risk applying a confidence level that markedly disadvantages victims.

I'VE SEEN OVER THE YEARS how, when an accuser comes forward, whether in the court of public opinion or to members of her inner circle, and says, "I was raped—this happened" or "I was harassed—this happened," her account is often dismissed as falling short of proof *beyond a reasonable doubt*.

Outside criminal court, "beyond a reasonable doubt" is a curious standard to apply, since the consequences that flow from belief are far less weighty than those that follow a criminal conviction. For instance, when an accuser makes an abuse allegation to her friend, the friend can offer support, cut ties with the abuser, assist with finding professional help. On campus or in the workplace, belief that the abuse happened may entail more serious sanctions. Still, they are less severe than those at stake in criminal cases, where the demand for proof beyond a reasonable doubt reflects the enormity of the available punishment—liberty is on the line. When the stakes aren't nearly as significant, our insistence on such a high level of certainty is misplaced.

And this insistence spells the demise of most allegations. Our tacit selection of the highest standard of confidence virtually guarantees dismissal of accusations that surface in our daily lives, a context that is unlike the criminal system in important ways. Law enforcement officers are given the authority to draw on a range of investigative techniques not available to those on the sidelines. Subpoenas and search warrants can turn up valuable corroborative evidence that may never surface when an accuser comes forward in an informal setting.

Outside criminal court, when we demand a level of certainty that almost no allegation on its own can surpass, and where we lack the wherewithal to gather additional evidence, we will almost invariably find a reason not to believe.

DEFAULT TO DOUBT

Many of us overestimate by a long shot the likelihood that an accuser is lying or mistaken when she comes forward. Most people "start from a position of not wanting to believe that it happened," as described to me by a lawyer with decades of practice handling criminal and civil cases of sexual abuse. You too might adopt an initial stance of disbelief. Over the years, I've heard from well-meaning friends and colleagues with a wildly skewed sense of the frequency of false reporting. We default to doubt.

While law enforcement officers are surely not alone in this regard, their attitudes about false rape complaints have been measured more than others'. In one survey of nearly nine hundred police officers, more than half stated that anywhere from 11 to 50 percent of sexual assault complainants lie about being assaulted, while another 10 percent of the officers surveyed thought the rate of false reporting is somewhere between 51 and 100 percent. A study of a different set of police officers found that a majority of the detectives believed 40 to 80 percent of sexual assault complaints are false. In keeping with this distrustful mindset, one Midwestern police officer told researchers, "I don't know what percent it would be, but I would say definitely over a third, probably approaching you know 40 or 45% . . . have *very* serious questions of the veracity." And in 2016, an Idaho sheriff asserted, "The majority of our rapes that are called in, are actually consensual sex."

Attitudes like these are reinforced when police officers see their colleagues dismissing similar reports. The confirmation bias leads people to "seek out and attend to information that already confirms their beliefs," as psychologist Jennifer Eberhardt at Stanford explains. "Once we develop theories about how things operate," says Eberhardt, "that framework is hard to dislodge." Accusers regarded as discredited bolster a sense that accusers *shouldn't* be believed.

This invisible feedback loop is not confined to the police setting. We are all shaped by the reactions of those around us when we judge credibility. We watch to see how accusers we know are treated, how high-profile accusers fare, and what happens when accusers turn to formal systems—the criminal law, campus tribunals, workplace HR. Whenever an allegation is deemed false, the myth of the untrustworthy accuser is reinforced, making it more likely that the next allegation will also be considered false. Disbelief begets disbelief, across all walks of life.

THE INCIDENCE OF FALSE REPORTING is much, much lower than most of us assume. Studies using the most reliable research methods, those that look beyond the police classification, find false reporting rates between 2 and 8 percent. A recent meta-analysis puts the rate at about 5 percent.

Apart from overestimating the odds that a report is false (often by a lot), we tend to doubt the wrong kinds of allegations. Research suggests that the reports most likely to be considered false—those involving acquaintances and those involving intoxication—are the most likely to be true. This makes sense. As the psychologist Kim Lonsway says, "Someone filing a false report is likely to describe a scenario that conforms with the cultural stereotype of a 'real rape.' It would thus involve a stranger with a weapon and perhaps even a ski mask. The rape would take place in an alley, with extreme violence by the rapist and utmost physical resistance by the victim. The victim would respond hysterically and report the crime immediately." Lonsway adds, "This stereotype of a 'real rape' is exactly the opposite of the type of sexual assault that tends to raise suspicion in the minds of most people." Based on academic research, journalistic accounts, and documented exonerations, one recent analysis concluded that "every part" of the conventional narrative about false reports is incorrect.

The conventional narrative warps our initial starting point when we're faced with an allegation of abuse. We begin from a place that is overly skeptical: we approach the accusation with an exaggerated sense that it's false. We then compound this error by insisting on an unrealistic quantum of evidence to supplement the accuser's account. Survivors like Aja Newman expect to confront this collective tendency—it's why she took the bedding from the hospital. She knew that the standard of corroboration required for people to reach their designated confidence level is unreasonable at best, and impossible at worst.

THIS UNREASONABLE DEMAND FOR CORROBORATION recently materialized in the world of opera. In August 2019, the Associated Press published a story reporting multiple allegations of longtime sexual misconduct by the singer and conductor Plácido Domingo, which he then denied. (He later apologized for his misconduct, but subsequently disavowed his apology and once again disputed the women's claims.) The story detailed the accusations of eight singers and a dancer who said that Domingo sexually harassed them over the course of three decades, including at opera companies where he held top managerial positions.

Patricia Wulf, a mezzo-soprano, was the only woman who allowed her name to be used in the story. The others requested anonymity, fearing retaliation from their employers and harassment from members of the public. To corroborate the accusations, reporters spoke with "many colleagues and friends" in whom the women confided, and also confirmed that the alleged victims would have overlapped with Domingo at the times and places named in their accounts. The story also mentioned a "half dozen other women" who said "suggestive overtures by Domingo made them uncomfortable."

In the weeks following publication of the allegations, eleven *more* women came forward with reports of past sexual harassment by Domingo (which he also denied). One accuser, Angela Turner Wilson, allowed her name to be used; the rest were unnamed in a second Associated Press story. At the time of the alleged abuse, Wilson, like Wulf, said she was afraid that she wouldn't be believed, and so she never reported her claims to management. When she eventually spoke with reporters, Wilson provided the journal she kept at the time of the events in question. The journal included an entry about Domingo that read, he "has told me several times how happy he was with my singing" but "he hits on me all the time," and added, "Please God don't let it get any worse."

Weeks after the two sets of allegations were published, the general manager of the Metropolitan Opera convened a meeting with the chorus and orchestra to explain why Domingo had not been suspended or released from his upcoming performances. The Met later issued a statement that included the manager's explanation for the opera's inaction: despite the twenty accusers, "there was currently no corroborated evidence against Mr. Domingo." (Soon after, following a meeting at which members of the orchestra and chorus expressed their opposition to the opera's response to the allegations, the Met announced that Domingo would immediately step down from all future performances.)

AN UNREASONABLE NEED FOR CORROBORATION is par for the course in sexual misconduct cases. Alaleh Kianerci is a veteran sex crimes prosecutor in Santa Clara, California, who has handled many complex cases, including that of Brock Turner, the Stanford swimmer convicted of sexually assaulting Chanel Miller in 2015. Kianerci is very familiar with the high standard of persuasion in criminal court. Remember that in every single case, prosecutors must prove guilt beyond a reasonable doubt to convict. Kianerci emphasizes that, as a practical matter, this burden is even higher in sex crimes cases. When it comes to sexual assault, "people think there needs to be more evidence. This is something that we know from our experience talking to jurors and picking juries." Many people expect DNA to establish guilt, an impossibility in cases where the defense is not that the accused didn't have *intercourse* with the victim, but that she *consented*. Or people "want it on video," explains Kianerci. "Of course we all want those things," she adds. "But that's not how human life is. Not everything is caught on video. Not everything leaves some sort of scientific trace."

Evidence collected in a sexual assault kit (also known as a "rape kit") can sometimes help to satisfy the demand for corroboration. It's not always possible to collect this type of evidence, however, particularly with the passage of time. And rarely is this evidence seen as definitive in a "consent defense" case. Remember that Abby Honold's sexual assault examination surfaced abundant physical proof of a horribly violent rape—and still, after hearing the accused man say the sex was consensual, the investigating detective interpreted Abby's physical injuries as evidence that "kids are into kinky shit these days."

"HE SAID, SHE SAID," HE WINS

At its most extreme, the credibility discount consigns an accuser's word to its own inferior category: *not evidence.* This treatment of the accuser's version of events makes little sense. Consider that in the courtroom, victim testimony about what happened *is* evidence—often, it is the most powerful evidence of all. Outside the courtroom, in life, evidence is any information that rationally changes the odds that a proposition is true. Evidence of that proposition can be stronger or weaker; it can be sufficient or insufficient to prompt belief. But to classify an accuser's word as something *less than evidence* is to mischaracterize it, and to ensure that the allegation will be dismissed.

Downgrading an accuser's word is especially pronounced when the accused tells a different story. Faced with competing versions of events, we resort to framing the dispute as a "he said, she said" contest that "she" is destined to lose. We dismiss the entire mess as unresolvable: a deadlock that, on its face, cannot justify action. When the accuser's account is pitted against the accused's, there seems no way to break the tie. And so we preserve the status quo, which allows everyone to proceed like nothing happened, shielding the abuser from any consequence for his actions. "He" wins.

LAUREN TEUKOLSKY IS A LOS ANGELES lawyer with extensive experience bringing sexual harassment claims on behalf of low-wage workers and others. She finds that in cases where "it's purely just a female narrative versus a male narrative, typically, the woman is not believed" when she comes forward. Teukolsky told me, "Very often, HR for the company will kind of throw up their hands and say, 'well, it's a "he said, she said," and because we don't have any corroborating evidence, we're just going to call it a draw . . . and everyone is just going to sort of go on as they were without any repercussions.'"

Even the terminology "he said, she said" offends Teukolsky. "It's thrown back against me all the time to say, 'There's really no evidence,'" she notes. Teukolsky has seen, time after time, that when an accusation is relegated to the status of "she said"—one-half of a "he said, she said" dispute—the allegation is doomed.

There is one final way that we default to doubt about an accuser's version of events. It is to reject a contested allegation outside the courtroom by simply observing that the man accused is "presumed innocent." The presumption of innocence is a bedrock principle of criminal justice; it mandates that unless the state's evidence rises to the requisite threshold, the accused can't be convicted. The presumption of innocence can be overcome by evidence—including, as I've said, a victim's account from the witness stand. In our daily lives, the accuser's description should function in similar fashion: a credible account should change our thinking. But this requires us to *reason* about the allegation and the denial, resisting the many traps set by the credibility complex.

The problem is that we don't recognize when an account is credible. We fail to trust where we should. We dismiss as implausible allegations that are, in reality, the exact opposite. We make these mistakes in part because even the best of us draws on a firmly rooted mythology of the false accuser.

THE ACCUSER IN OUR MIND

The woman who lies about sexual abuse is a cultural mainstay. In the Bible, Potiphar's wife accuses Joseph of rape after he rejects her advances, and this archetype has persisted across the ages. In 2016, Donald Trump harnessed the very same "woman who cries rape" archetype in order to defend himself against multiple allegations of sexual misconduct. "Every woman lied when they came forward to hurt my campaign," he said at a campaign rally, adding, "If they can fight somebody like me, who has unlimited resources to fight back, just look at what they can do to you." In 2018, addressing the sexual misconduct accusations against his Supreme Court nominee Brett Kavanaugh, Trump volunteered, "And it's happened to me, many times, where false statements are made and, honestly, nobody knows who to believe." Trump described this as a "very scary time for young men in America," when you can be "perfect your entire life" and "somebody could accuse you of something." The Kavanaugh allegations also propelled #HimToo, which went viral after a tweet bemoaned "the current climate of false sexual accusations by radical feminists with an axe to grind."

Many people would disavow this worldview. Nonetheless, all of us are shaped by a culture that casts sexual misconduct accusers as unreliable sources of information. Without always realizing it, we absorb the message that women cannot be trusted when they recount rape or harassment. This orientation can lead us to misjudge those who allege abuse. When we are prone to see accusers in general as liars, we are too quick to decide that a particular accusation is untrue.

The ready availability of certain stock representations of lying women makes it easy for us to disbelieve. One figure who looms large is the "gold digger." Within the legal system, plaintiffs of all kinds can be questioned about their financial interest in bringing suit, and lawyers who represent accusers in civil cases are well versed in this line of attack. But sexual misconduct accusers are even more susceptible to such treatment than others. "The victim is viewed as someone who is basically just trying to make a fast buck," explained Robert

Vance, the plaintiff's lawyer from Philadelphia, adding that sexual harassment allegations are often seen as "just a money grab."

Sex crimes prosecutors must also contend with the "gold digger" stereotype, which the defense can deploy in criminal court. At Bill Cosby's retrial on sexual assault charges after his first trial ended in a hung jury, Cosby's lawyer said of the accuser, "What does she want from Bill Cosby? Money, money, and lots more money." Outside the legal process, accusers are besmirched in the same way. One study of how Twitter users respond to sexual assault accusations against high-profile men found that users frequently selected the hashtag "#golddigger" to digest their reactions. The gold digger desires fortune above all else; if need be, she will even concoct an allegation of abuse regardless of what she must endure when she comes forward.

Other caricatures of lying accusers distort our judgments about whether to believe. The *woman scorned* seeks revenge on the man who rejected her. The *regretful woman* rues consensual sex. The *political tool* is willing to be used to advance a partisan agenda, or perhaps is motivated by an agenda of her own. The *attention seeker* craves the spotlight. (Women whose sexual identity is perceived as "an 'act' for attention from straight men," including bisexual women, are particularly likely to be seen as attention-seeking liars.)

The lying woman is not the only archetype that fosters disbelief. Rather than intentionally deceiving anyone, the *mistaken woman* is confusing what actually happened. Debra Katz is a leading civil rights lawyer who has spent decades representing women alleging sexual misconduct, including Christine Blasey Ford. When I spoke with Katz, she observed that the "narrative of denial" has shifted. Increasingly, it now features a different kind of accuser—one who is not lying, but instead is misinterpreting or misremembering what happened. Whether it is her perception or her memory that is deemed faulty, she may be a "nice lady, but she's wrong."

Women are dismissed as untrustworthy because they're viewed as lacking the competence to discern, recall, and make sense of facts about their lives. This incompetence is different from deceit, but the upshot is the same. An accuser who is cast as mistaken or lying (or both, however illogical) is of course unbelievable. Regardless of why she's considered untrustworthy, her accusation will be dismissed.

When this happens, we're likely to become even more skeptical of future allegations that come our way. Remember the confirmation bias, which causes us to search for evidence that confirms our preexisting beliefs, and then to interpret this evidence in a manner that further solidifies these beliefs. Whenever we regard an accuser as discredited, it buttresses our impression that she *shouldn't* be trusted. Once we've witnessed the dismissal of an allegation, or we've dismissed one ourselves, the confirmation bias contorts our credibility judgments about all subsequent allegations.

This effect is magnified when a false allegation is well publicized. Duke lacrosse. *Rolling Stone.* These cases captivate the popular imagination in large part because they resonate with entrenched beliefs about lying accusers and the misogyny that animates these beliefs. The "lying accuser" cases have come to represent a false reality—an inverted world where sexual assault accusations are normally false. Sheer outrage at the women whose stories crumble under scrutiny inhibits our capacity to discern a more complicated picture. The stories that fall apart and our responses to them often revolve around a cultural preoccupation with aberrational violence. "The truth about rape is that it's not exceptional. It's not anomalous," writes commentator Jia Tolentino in her discussion of the *Rolling Stone* accusation. "And there is no way to make that into a satisfying story." We are drawn to extraordinary cases because they obscure the unbearable ordinariness of sexual violence.

SOME ACCUSERS ARE PERCEIVED FROM the get-go as less trustworthy than others. For these accusers, the barriers to belief are even higher. "We have cases where drug-addicted homeless women are sexually assaulted," the prosecutor Alaleh Kianerci recounts, "and right off the bat, they're fighting an uphill battle." Kianerci says the same is true of women in the sex industry, recalling a case that involved multiple Asian American women who were raped while working at brothels. The most vulnerable victims are also the most unbelievable, Kianerci stresses. "Whether it's drugs, alcohol, homelessness, career choices, people just don't want to believe them."

Another impediment to trust is poverty. Emily Martin, the vice president for education and workplace justice at the National Women's Law Center, notes that poor people are less likely than others to be found credible when they tell their story. Low-wage victims of sexual harassment, in particular, face dauntingly high barriers to belief.

Sandra Pezqueda's story is typical. In 2015, Pezqueda was hired as a dishwasher and chef's assistant at a luxury resort in California. Soon after she began working, she says, her supervisor at the staffing agency began to harass her. According to Pezqueda's account, the supervisor commented on her good looks, repeatedly asked her out on dates, called her at home, switched her schedule so she would be working alone with him, twice tried to kiss her in a storeroom, and took her off the schedule for weeks after she rebuffed a direct advance. Pezqueda says that when she complained to another supervisor, he maintained that nothing could be done—it was her word against his, she was told. Months later, Pezqueda was fired.

VICTIMS OF WORKPLACE SEXUAL HARASSMENT confront many of these same challenges when they sue in civil court. Compared to criminal court, here the burden of proof is much lower—all that's needed is proof by a "preponderance of the evidence," or proof that makes the plaintiff's claims more likely true than not. Yet even this lower standard is often too high for sexual harassment plaintiffs. Just as listeners default to doubt when accusers come forward outside the courtroom, jurors discount accusers' credibility when they become plaintiffs. As ever, race matters, class matters, sexual identity matters.

One less obvious characteristic that bears on trustworthiness is appearance. In the realm of belief, societal standards of beauty work against women in very particular ways. Whether she is conventionally attractive or not, a woman's looks can undermine her believability—a specific instance of what the legal scholar Deborah Rhode referred to generally as "the injustice of appearance." Ari Wilkenfeld, an experienced D.C. civil rights attorney, told me that women who are perceived as unattractive are easily discredited as improbable targets of sexual advances. At the same time, attractive women are often seen as inviting advances, which prompts disbelief when they describe the behavior as unwelcome. When we spoke, Wilkenfeld bemoaned this appearance-based twist on yet another perverse Goldilocks scenario. To be credited when she alleges sexual harassment, a woman must look "just right." Otherwise, she will tap into deeply seated myths about accusers.

BELIEVABILITY IS NOT ONLY ABOUT trusting the source of the claim; it's also about seeing that claim as plausible, or in line with our intuitions. Every time we decide whether to believe *it happened*, we draw on our impressions of how the world works. This is where myths about stranger rape, perfect victims, and monster abusers come into play, leading us down the wrong path. Accused men often tell a story that's consistent with our preconceived notions, however off base, while most accusers advance a narrative that's at odds with what we mistakenly think we know about abuse.

The plausibility of a claim also rests on our sense of whether the accuser behaved like the victim in our mind—a victim who doesn't match up with reality. When an accuser acts differently from this imagined victim, her allegations seem untrue and we dismiss them. We've already seen some ways that deviation from the ideal victim script can undermine an accuser's believability. When she didn't resist, when her emotional response isn't what we expect, or when she maintains contact with her abuser, her account is readily dismissed.

Our plausibility calculus is tainted in another important way. Because we misunderstand how victims react to trauma, we're far too quick to distrust accusers when their memories of the incident are incomplete or otherwise flawed. In one rather typical case, a college student reported her sexual assault to campus authorities only to watch the case collapse at a later hearing. A small detail in her account had changed. Eight months earlier, the accuser had described sitting and looking at her phone before she was assaulted. At the hearing, she again described sitting and looking at her phone before the assault, but her exact location in the room had changed. "The hearing officer took this to be a major inconsistency that undermined her credibility such that she must have been completely inventing the entire incident," the woman's lawyer, Brenda Adams, told me.

Commonplace intuitions about what victims should recall about their abuse are mostly contradicted by neuroscience. Trauma experts understand that many victims are unable to remember the details of what happened just before or just after the assault. Victims can also find it difficult to provide a neat chronological account. But most people don't know about potential neurological explanations for these limitations, which presents unfair barriers to belief. "No one will accept the story unless it's linear," says Adams.

The demand for an exhaustive narrative is misguided. When we remember an experience—whether or not it's traumatic—our encoding of that experience is partial. Jim Hopper, who teaches in Harvard University Medical School's psychiatry department and consults nationwide on the neurobiology of trauma, notes that a key concept in memory research is the distinction between central details and peripheral details. Even under ordinary circumstances, we pay most attention to central details, which are more likely than others to be encoded—the first step in creating a memory—and stored once encoded. For example, you're more apt to remember where you ate the last time you went out to dinner than you are to remember who sat at the adjacent table. Details that we don't notice or find significant may not be converted to a storable memory. "Central details get prioritized for encoding and storage," Hopper explains. "Right there, that tells us that all of our experiences are memories that are going to be incomplete and fragmentary—we're only going to selectively remember some. Even some of the central details are going to fade over time. That's just the nature of human experience."

The brain is more taxed by threatening situations. Bessel van der Kolk is a leading expert on the physiological effects of trauma. His book *The Body Keeps the Score* shows how trauma is imprinted on both the body and the brain. One important finding is that traumatic memories are disorganized. A systematic study by van der Kolk and his colleagues showed that victims of terrifying experiences "remembered some details all too clearly (the smell of the rapist, the gash in the forehead of a dead child) but could not recall the sequence of events or other vital details (the first person who arrived to help, whether an ambulance or a police car took them to the hospital)."

As Jim Hopper states: "In situations of stress and trauma, there tends to be a narrowing or focusing on parts of the experience that the brain is appraising as really essential to survival and coping. That zeroing in of attention, the collapsing in on central details and the ignoring or non-processing of peripheral details—that is accentuated." As a result, memories of traumatic experiences are more fragmented than others.

In addition, we have only a limited amount of time to create memories when we're under stress. The hippocampus plays a critical role in encoding information into short-term memory and storing it as long-term memory. When our brain detects a threat, the hippocampus operates in an unusual manner. After five to twenty minutes in "superencoding mode," when central details are strongly encoded, the hippocampus enters a "minimal encoding" phase, "in which the encoding and especially the storage of details—even central ones— are severely limited or not happening at all." The biology of superencoding means that it can't be sustained for long without permanently damaging the cells. So our bodies have adapted, burning into memory the information that's most likely to be needed for future survival, while protecting our hippocampus.

In her testimony before the Senate Judiciary Committee at Brett Kavanaugh's confirmation hearing, Christine Blasey Ford was asked by Democratic senator Patrick Leahy about "the strongest memory you have, the strongest memory of the incident, something you cannot forget." When she answered, it was almost as if she was again a teenager reliving what allegedly happened with Kavanaugh and his friend in the room. But because Ford is a research psychologist at Stanford's medical school, not only could she describe her recollection; she could also channel her professional expertise to explain it. In recounting her strongest memory of the night, Ford managed to also capture the workings of the brain under stress. "Indelible in the hippocampus is the laughter, the laugh—the uproarious laughter between the two, and their having fun at my expense," she said.

The remarkable exchange continued:

SENATOR LEAHY: You've never forgotten that laughter. You've never forgotten them laughing at you.

CHRISTINE FORD: They were laughing with each other.

SENATOR LEAHY: And you were the object of the laughter?

CHRISTINE FORD: I was, you know, underneath one of them while the two laughed, two friend—two friends having a really good time with one another.

Dahlia Lithwick was one of the reporters who witnessed this testimony. In her account, Lithwick says Ford was "quiet," "authoritative," "utterly authentic and vivid and true." Lithwick adds that Ford "was so scrupulous about word choice and about correcting even tiny slips of imprecision, that the effect was surgical." "Everyone believed her," Lithwick writes. "Everyone."

When Kavanaugh testified and denied everything, that consensus, if it ever truly existed, dissipated. Less than a week after the hearing, a nationwide survey found stark disagreement among the general public about whether to believe the accuser or the accused. "Who do you think is telling the truth about what happened at the party in high school?" respondents were asked. Just under half believed Ford, a third believed Kavanaugh, and about a quarter felt "unsure."

Many who didn't believe Ford pointed to gaps in her story. Rachel Mitchell, the lawyer for the Republican senators on the Judiciary Committee, wrote in her assessment, "Dr. Ford has no memory of key details of the night in question," including who invited her to the party, how she got to the party, or where and when exactly the party took place. But "perhaps most importantly," urged the lawyer, "she does not remember how she got from the party back to her house," which "raises significant questions."

The science of traumatic memory suggests otherwise. In an essay published shortly after the hearing, psychologist Jim Hopper noted that "gaps and inconsistencies in peripheral details—as well as the inability to pinpoint when and where a long-ago assault occurred— are totally normal and to be expected." Under stress, once Ford's hip- pocampus entered the minimal encoding phase, the encoding and storage of her memories would be impaired. What might seem suspi- cious about the holes in Ford's testimony is entirely consistent with a traumatic response. As Hopper wrote, Ford's "relief at having escaped and her fear that someone might realize she'd just been attacked" count as "highly significant central details"—details that would be "among the last to get in before her hippocampus, entering its own self-protective mode, lost its ability to store indelibly any of what came next."

Incomplete memories are a common by-product of trauma, which means we err in the wrong direction when we hold imperfections in an accuser's account against her. This mistake is easily explained. While trauma experts recognize the origins of dissociated memories, most of us are not trauma experts. "Ignorance of how memory works is a major reason why sexual assault is the easiest violent crime to get away with," Hopper concludes. Because we don't know better, we become incredulous when an accuser's account is missing details. Or when it's not linear. Or when it includes facts that seem less im- portant than those that are excluded. Without warrant, partial stories become fodder for disbelief.

The effects of trauma on memory extend beyond encoding and storage to retrieval. A traumatic memory is more accessible in a com- fortable setting—one where the listener appears open to believing.

When an accuser is met with evident suspicion or judgment, she is less likely to surface traumatic memories. Hopper explains, "If you're stressed, it impairs your ability to retrieve information that is stored in your brain." Even if an accuser *can* retrieve this information, she might not feel secure enough to share it with a listener bent on disbelieving.

MISUNDERSTANDINGS THAT SURROUND TRAUMA HELP explain why police officers tend to approach rape allegations with undue skepticism. Rachel Lovell is a sociologist whose research focuses on law enforcement's response to gender violence. Lovell told me that many police officers "scrutinize sexual assault cases more intensely because they don't understand victims' responses." She added, "They're seeing deception when in fact it's trauma." In a study of untested rape kits funded by the National Institute of Justice, Lovell and her colleagues examined thousands of police reports in cases that were not pursued. In one report, the officer wrote, "The victim is laughing. She's obviously being deceptive, but she appears to be in pain." Lovell says this kind of confusion on the part of the officer is pervasive. "For people who understand the neurobiology of trauma, all those things seem within the typical range of victim behaviors." But if the officers' framework for assessing the accuser's account doesn't reflect the impact of trauma, they may leap to conclude that an accuser is lying.

I heard a similar explanation from Rebecca Campbell, a psychologist who is among the nation's leading experts in law enforcement's response to sexual violence. Campbell was the head researcher for another National Institute of Justice–funded study of rape kits—this one in Detroit. The study found that a primary reason for officers' dismissal of allegations was that the accuser's response deviated from their preset notions. "They're expecting the proverbial hot mess," Campbell told me. "They're expecting crying, they're expecting really visible signs of distress . . . If the victim doesn't exhibit what they believe to be the one way to act, they often make an inference that the victim isn't credible." (Again, perceived overemotionality is held against victims in much the same way as perceived underemotionality.)

As Campbell emphasizes, the science can't determine that an accuser is being truthful. But science does suggest that police officers—like the rest of us—should be cautious about deciding, based on demeanor alone, that an accuser is lying. "Science tells us there's a variety of reactions to trauma," Campbell says, "and it is not for police to evaluate whether one reaction is right or wrong. It is to say, well, that is how they react." Campbell notes that, rather than fixate on the victim's response, officers who are aware of the science can "actually do an investigation."

In most cases, an adequate investigation never unfolds. Instead, officers unwittingly rely on myths about how victims behave in order to justify the dismissal of allegations that might with effort be corroborated. When sexual misconduct accusers come forward, investigations are prematurely cut short, leaving additional evidence ungathered. This is a recurring pattern. Across police departments big and small, officers too quickly decide that a case is without merit, resulting in the dismissal of rape allegations at disproportionately high rates.

One way that officers can close an investigation is to designate the complaint as "unfounded," which means it's considered baseless or false. Many law enforcement agencies rely heavily on this unfounded classification to "clear" sexual assault reports without an arrest. High "clearance" numbers, which are used as a measure of how effectively police are solving crime, can instead camouflage low arrest rates. Consider just several examples. In Pittsburgh, over 30 percent of rape cases were unfounded in 2017. In Prince William County, Virginia, that figure was nearly 40 percent in 2016. And an earlier analysis found similarly high rates: between 2009 and 2014, 34 percent of rape reports were unfounded in Baltimore County, 46 percent were unfounded in Scottsdale, Arizona, and more than half were unfounded in Oxnard, California. These numbers starkly contrast with the actual incidence of false sexual assault reports—again, researchers estimate a rate of about 5 percent.

A ProPublica investigation of sixty-four law enforcement agencies found that fifty-four made arrests in fewer than a third of their cases. Fourteen police departments—including Chicago, Seattle, San Diego, Phoenix, Portland, Tucson, Nashville, and Sacramento—reported figures in the single digits. (Salt Lake City's was the lowest rate, with arrests in only 3 percent of its cases.) "No matter the jurisdiction," found a recent study of law enforcement agencies across the nation, "sexual violence seldom results in an arrest."

Credibility discounting at an early stage portends an allegation's eventual dismissal. When officers promptly discredit accusers, they overlook potential corroborative evidence—evidence like texts, voice mails, photographs, social media posts, forensic reports, witnesses to the lead-up or aftermath, and, on rare occasion, eyewitnesses. Although older allegations are more difficult to corroborate, many of the same investigative techniques can lead to relevant evidence. Yet police tend to short-circuit their investigations, dismissing allegations that could, with effort, be bolstered. The "he said, she said" contest might well be avoided if officers would suspend their tendencies to distrust, blame, and disregard women who report abuse.

Rebecca Campbell emphasizes that distrust of accusers corrupts the entire investigative process. "It's been documented in research study after research study," Campbell explains, that when victims report to police, "more often than not, they are not believed, they are not deemed credible, and there is no quality investigation done in the case." During her law enforcement trainings, Campbell is clear that she's not advocating for an arrest in every sexual assault case. Rather, she tells officers, "The key here is to try to move forward with investigations. It's just that simple. The facts of the case will sort themselves out." As she said to me, "the problem has been that the police will not do the investigation."

IN 2011, LARA MCLEOD WAS arrested for falsely reporting her rape—a charge that was later dropped. From the very beginning, the detective who first interviewed McLeod appeared to doubt her claims, asking her why she didn't try to escape her attacker (who had a gun) and why she didn't keep her arms down to prevent him from taking off her shirt. This distrustful orientation set in place a lax investigation that would doom her allegation.

Police officers could have tried to obtain security footage from the 7-Eleven where McLeod said the accused man had taken her before the incident while the two argued about whether she would have sex with him. Officers could have reviewed McLeod's medical records from after the incident. And officers could have checked their database to see if the man had ever been accused of rape or other crimes. But investigating officers took none of these steps. A subsequent examination of internal police documents and recordings underscored "how grievously the police botched their investigation from start to finish, allowing their beliefs about sexual assault to influence the way they pursued the case." Although the false reporting charges against McLeod were eventually dismissed, along the way she spent $50,000 in legal fees to defend herself. The man she accused was never even arrested.

Shelved rape kits epitomize law enforcement's failure to pursue investigative leads. More than one hundred thousand of these kits sit untested around the country, prompting a nationwide grassroots effort to "end the backlog" through laws that mandate testing and allocate the resources necessary to do so. Rape kits require an invasive physical probe—a trained nurse collects and preserves evidence from the victim's body that can include hair, fibers, semen, saliva, skin cells, and blood. In her study of the Detroit police department, Rebecca Campbell learned why police officers don't test the kits. She and her colleagues found that the evidence languished because the police had decided early on not to pursue the complaints. Even before available leads were pursued, the allegations were dismissed. Campbell and her colleagues concluded, "In many respects, the untested kits were a tangible sign about the dispositions of these cases—the case had been shelved, figuratively; the kit had been shelved, literally."

BENEFIT OF THE DOUBT

While the credibility complex prompts undue distrust of victims, it also bestows unjustified benefit of the doubt on the men who deny their allegations. Most men are granted an automatic presumption of competence and reliability when they assert innocence—they are deemed trustworthy. At the same time, their version of events often aligns with our impressions, however ill-conceived, of how the world operates—their story is plausible. Those accused of sexual misconduct tend to receive a *surplus* of belief.

John Clune is a Boulder, Colorado, lawyer who has worked for more than two decades pursuing sexual misconduct cases, first as a prosecutor and now as a civil rights lawyer. Clune's clients have included several women with allegations against high-profile men, and many more women whose cases never make the news. Clune emphasizes that, in his experience, as compared to their female accusers, most accused men are perceived as "more logical and more rational human beings." Men in positions of leadership or respect are considered especially worthy of belief.

Consider this: the first time Hollywood mogul Harvey Weinstein came to the attention of law enforcement officials was in 2015, when model Ambra Battilana Gutierrez walked into a New York police precinct and reported that he had just groped her breasts and tried to put his hand up her skirt. Gutierrez's decision to complain immediately was an anomaly. "Being from another country—I'm Italian—made me less understanding of his level of power," she would later explain. "Also, I really don't like to be touched, and knowing that someone invaded my space that way, it was way too much for me. And I just believed in the system."

The following day, detectives arranged for Gutierrez to wear a wire, and she recorded an exchange with Weinstein that included a damning admission. When asked why he had touched her breasts in his office the day before, Weinstein answered, "Oh, please, I'm sorry," adding, "I'm used to that," and, "I won't do it again."

Two weeks later, prosecutors announced they were closing the case against him. "After analyzing the available evidence, including multiple interviews with both parties, a criminal charge is not supported," said a spokesperson for the Manhattan District Attorney's Office. According to Gutierrez, the prosecutor "interrogated me like I was the criminal, with questions like, 'Have you ever been a prostitute? Or, 'Have you ever gotten gifts?' Or, 'Have you ever asked for a movie role?'" Gutierrez also remembers the savage media coverage, which included press accounts "saying I was a liar and putting my bikini photos on the front page."

The defense team claimed that Weinstein touched Gutierrez's breasts to determine whether they were "real," which was said to bear on her future as a lingerie model. Gutierrez alleged that Weinstein not only groped her breasts, which he acknowledged on tape; she also described him reaching a hand up her skirt and asking to kiss her. But Weinstein insisted he simply touched her breasts, only for professional reasons, and *these denials turned out to matter more than the accusation*. Prosecutors concluded they would not be able to establish that Weinstein touched Gutierrez for the purpose of sexual gratification, as required by the New York law that prohibits forcible sexual touching. As one former prosecutor–turned–defense lawyer later remarked to the *New York Times*, "The idea that Weinstein's criminal intent was unprovable because of his stated 'professional need' to personally inspect her breasts doesn't pass the laugh test." Still, Weinstein's version of events prevailed.

ANOTHER ACCUSED MAN TO RECEIVE the benefit of the doubt after telling law enforcement his side of the story was the former athletic trainer and USA Gymnastics national team doctor Larry Nassar. When first questioned about allegations of sexual abuse by a former patient, Nassar convinced investigators that he was engaging in legitimate medical practice, and the investigation was dropped. Many dozens of girls would be molested after Nassar first came to the attention of the police. Fourteen years later, more than 150 women would detail their abuse at the former doctor's sentencing hearing in criminal court.

Much or all of this could have been prevented: Back in 2004, Brianne Randall, a high school athlete in Meridian Township, Michigan, made an appointment with her mother to see Nassar, who was then a prominent osteopathic physician and athletic trainer. They wanted help with Randall's scoliosis. On the first visit, with her mother in the room, Nassar performed a series of routine tests. On the second visit, without her mother there, the examination was entirely different.

Nassar began the exam by massaging Randall's spine. From there, he pulled her underwear to the side and began "pressing on the outer area all along her vagina." He then tried to put his finger in her vagina (unsuccessfully because she was wearing a tampon). He continued massaging her vagina for about twenty minutes before reaching under her gown and placing his hands on her breasts, "rubbing around" and "squeezing" while she lay on her stomach. After telling her that he wanted to see her once a week for an hour a visit, Nassar asked Randall for a hug. He had not worn gloves during the exam.

Randall felt "scared" and "uncomfortable," and she promptly told her mother about what Nassar had done that "freaked her out." The next day, Randall and her mother walked into the police station to lodge a complaint.

About a week after the police interviewed Randall, they spoke with Nassar. Notes of this conversation are brief. Nassar claimed he was performing a procedure to relieve Randall's lower back pain, and it required him to "touch" and "palpate" the region near her vulva. He described the technique as the Sacrotuberous Ligament Release and told the investigating detective that "this technique has been published in medical journals and training tapes instructing the same are available to physicians throughout the United States." Nassar provided the detective with a twenty-six-page PowerPoint presentation that accompanied the report.

The interview notes contain no indication that Nassar was ever questioned about fondling Randall's breasts or attempting to penetrate her vagina with his finger. Nor was he asked about why he didn't wear gloves during the exam. Their absence is only mentioned in reference to a later conversation with Randall's mother, who said she was "troubled by the fact that Dr. Nassar did not wear latex gloves"—leading the detective to respond, "I would not be able to affect whether or not the doctor wore gloves or if he had another person present during the procedure, however, I would pass her concerns along to Dr. Nassar." The report concludes by noting that the officer informed Randall's mother that the case would be closed "due to the facts presented to me by Dr. Nassar."

The PowerPoint presentation contains no reference whatsoever to touching or palpating the vagina, much less penetrating it. It says nothing about rubbing a patient's breasts, or the need for bare hands. But police officers didn't pursue any of these discrepancies (if they even identified them). Nor did they seek the opinion of any other doctor in the field. Instead, Nassar's far-fetched explanation was taken at face value.

Fifteen years later, when asked to explain this decision, the investigating detective—who had since been promoted to sergeant—said simply, "Nassar explained the procedure as being legitimate, therefore, not a crime." The detective chose not to proceed with the case because he believed this fiction—the only time in his career he closed an investigation without forwarding it to prosecutors.

If the Meridian Township Police Department were just an outlier, Nassar would not have been left to abuse his patients for decades. Girls and women came forward repeatedly during these years—they reported to parents, coaches, doctors, psychologists, and USA Gymnastics. Each time, the accusations were dismissed as less believable than Nassar's claim of medical justification, however preposterous. This was how Michigan State University (where Nassar was employed for many years) responded to an official complaint filed in 2014 by a twenty-four-year-old former cheerleader. The woman recounted that when she visited him for hip pain, Nassar massaged her breasts and, over protest, touched her vagina. School investigators found that the doctor's actions were "medically appropriate."

No one is immune from the effects of cultural forces that upgrade the believability of men accused and downgrade the believability of the accuser—not even victims.

WAS IT REALLY ABUSE? THE NORM OF SELF-DOUBT

We have already seen that accusers come to expect *others* to dismiss their account. But the credibility discount is not just anticipated—it is also internalized. At least initially, many accusers doubt the truth of their experiences, blame themselves, or minimize the incident. When any of this happens, it can seem pointless to make a formal complaint. From the victim's vantage, any official response would probably mirror her own or, worse, reflect an even steeper discount. Silence can appear the only option for those immersed in a culture that distrusts, faults, and disregards victims, who then distrust, fault, and disregard themselves. At its most covert, the credibility complex leads victims to elevate the perspectives and interests of their abuser above their own. I call this tendency to downgrade one's own credibility the *internalized credibility discount*.

Let's look at how this self-discounting works in the realm of trust. When it comes to believing that what happened did, in fact, happen, survivors often second-guess whether they experienced abuse. This results from a dynamic that can be understood as a form of collective gaslighting.* Philosopher Kate Abramson is at the forefront of efforts to explain what gaslighting is and how it harms victims. When she presented an early draft of a paper on the subject, the response was overwhelming. Abramson remembers "almost all the women in the room saying, 'Oh my God, I recognize that.'"

Gaslighting is a form of emotional manipulation that leaves the victim feeling as if she has become unmoored from reality. Abramson

---

* The word comes from the 1938 play *Gaslight*, which depicts a man who tries to deceive his wife into believing she has lost her mind. One of the man's ploys involves dimming gaslights throughout the house while insisting that his wife is imagining the darkness.

writes that a gaslighter "tries (consciously or not) to induce in someone the sense that her reactions, perceptions, memories and/or beliefs are not just mistaken, but utterly without grounds." As Abramson explained when we spoke, there are many ways to accomplish this. "There's the version that straightforwardly says, 'No, he's right, and you're acting crazy,' and there's the version that just says, 'It's not that big of a deal. Why are you making a fuss about this?'"

And gaslighting can be a group exercise. "There are lots of different ways in which people who aren't the gaslighter but are surrounding the gaslighted woman choose whose version of reality they're supporting," Abramson says. Even people "who just don't want to be having the conversation" with an accuser can effectively side with the accused, validating the notion that her abuse didn't happen, that she brought it upon herself, or that it wasn't so bad. Without realizing it, those around the victim reinforce the abuser's denials.

Victims of sexual misconduct are also conditioned to adopt the gaslighter's perspective about facts and their interpretation. As Abramson observes, girls and women are socialized to believe that, as compared to their male counterparts, they are more likely to be wrong. This "norm of self-doubt" manifests as "gendered-deference," in which survivors distrust their experience and afford men undue credence. *Was it harassment, or just workplace banter? Was it rape, or just a misunderstanding? Was it really abuse?*

———

Marissa Hoechstetter lives in western Massachusetts with her husband and school-age twin daughters. She works in higher-education fundraising, and volunteers in her community. Before moving to New England, she lived in New York City, where her daughters were born.

After Hoechstetter became pregnant in 2010, she interviewed several doctors before settling on Robert Hadden, a man with decades of practice in obstetrics and gynecology. Hadden seemed like a good choice. Not only was he the uncle of a good friend, but he worked at what Hoechstetter describes as the "well known, well-respected" NewYork-Presbyterian Hospital. She saw the doctor throughout her pregnancy.

When we spoke about these visits, Hoechstetter recalled a number of "red flags" that were visible to her only in hindsight. Hadden asked questions about her sex life and orgasms for no apparent reason; he performed unusually long breast exams and very frequent Pap smears. Hoechstetter once realized, "I don't think he was using gloves." But, she adds, the idea of being sexually abused by a doctor "is so far outside the realm of something that you think possible . . . you tell yourself that you must be mistaken."

A year after her daughters were born, Hoechstetter returned to Hadden for a follow-up appointment. This would be her final visit. "The time he assaulted me and licked me was the last time I went," she told me. Hoechstetter remembers feeling the doctor's beard on her vagina, and she "definitely, very clearly" knew she was being violated. "I just froze. He left the room, and I never went back to the office."

Still, she kept wondering and questioning herself. "Honestly, you think something is wrong with you," she says. "I knew something happened, but I kept thinking about it. I kept turning it over in my head, like, 'You must be wrong. That didn't happen. But it did. But it didn't.'" She explains, "Your brain just can't reconcile it."

For years, Hoechstetter didn't tell a soul about what happened. She continued to doubt whether her suffering mattered. "I told myself that it wasn't violent. I wasn't physically hurt. I wasn't violently raped by a stranger." Like most working moms, she was also busy and tired, focusing on her young children and her job, and didn't feel she had the bandwidth to fully process her experience.

In 2015, Hoechstetter discovered that Hadden had been indicted for the sexual abuse of six women. More women would later come forward publicly with similar allegations—the dozens of former patients included Evelyn Yang, a former marketing executive and mother of two who is married to the politician Andrew Yang. (Many of these women have sued the hospital for allegedly allowing the doctor to continue his pattern of abuse.) Hoechstetter describes learning that "Doctor Bob" was a serial predator. It was terrible and overwhelming, but also a "moment of validation." "You're not crazy," she recalls feeling. "It's not a weird memory. It definitely happened."

For many victims, this realization can be hard to come by. Remember Kimberly Lonsway, the psychologist who explained that we are widely motivated to doubt the occurrence of sexual abuse. Accepting what happened, Lonsway said, requires us to rethink "gender and sexuality and our past experiences." Doubt, even self-doubt, can seem the better alternative.

DOUBT BAKED INTO LAW

Distrust of sexual assault accusers is formalized in the law. Within the criminal law, skepticism has been the official rule for much of this nation's history. In sexual assault cases and only in sexual assault cases, accusers faced several unduly burdensome requisites. While these rules have largely been abandoned, they persist in new guises, reflecting and reinforcing a cultural inclination to dismiss women who allege rape.

First among the legal hurdles in sexual assault cases, a victim's testimony alone could not possibly prove guilt. Without further corroboration, a witness who recounted her rape could never have her allegation reach a jury for deliberation (unlike a witness who described, say, his robbery). This unique corroboration requirement, as it is known, was expressly designed to protect men from the archetypical lying woman.

When New York first enacted its corroboration requirement in 1886, it did so to shield defendants from what one court characterized as "untruthful, dishonest, or vicious" accusers. This approach was soon adopted by other states, including Georgia, whose Supreme Court proclaimed that without a corroboration requirement, "every man is in danger of being prosecuted and convicted on the testimony of a base woman, in whose testimony there is no truth." By siding with "every man" against his accuser, our laws buttressed the prevailing stereotype of lying women.

The "prompt complaint" rule likewise lays bare the law's distrust of rape accusers. The rule allows only allegations reported soon after the incident to proceed. Like the special need for corroboration in sexual assault cases, this requirement rests on a presumptive distrust of rape allegations. Writing in 1900, the Utah Supreme Court expressly equated delayed reporting with falsehood: "The natural instinct of a female thus outraged and injured prompts her to disclose the occurrence, at the earliest opportunity, to a relative or friend who naturally has the deepest interest in her welfare; and the absence of such disclosure tends to discredit her as a witness." From the vantage of law, women who did not report "at the earliest opportunity" were not to be believed.

Yet another instance of the criminal law's distrust of sexual assault accusers is the so-called cautionary instruction. At trial, jurors were explicitly warned by the judge to evaluate the complainant's testimony with extra suspicion. These instructions were meant to ensure that, in every sexual assault case, jurors would remain distrustful of the version of events offered by an accuser. In the parlance of one representative warning from California, since a rape charge "is one which is easily made and, once made, difficult to defend against, even if the person accused is innocent . . . the law requires that you examine the testimony of the female person named in the [charging document] with caution." To protect innocent men from false rape allegations in particular, jurors were ordered to be extra vigilant when judging the testimony of accusers. This added caution was layered on top of the high standard of "proof beyond a reasonable doubt" required in all criminal prosecutions.

In 1962, an official posture of disbelief was enshrined in the Model Penal Code, an influential guide for lawmakers around the country looking to reform their state's criminal statutes. The Code's section on sexual assault includes all three rules that traditionally disadvantaged accusers: a corroboration requirement, a rigid "prompt outcry" rule, and cautionary jury instructions. The Code describes these rules as necessary safeguards against women who falsely allege rape. To support the exceptional requirement of corroboration, the Code notes "the difficulty of defending against false accusation of a sexual offense," while stressing that "the corroboration requirement is an attempt to skew resolution of [word-on-word] disputes in favor of the defendant." To justify a hard "prompt outcry" rule—that the accuser must report a sexual assault to authorities within three months of the offense—the Code mentions accusers who are "vindictive," as well as the "dangers of blackmail or psychopathy of the complainant."

This defense of the "prompt outcry" rule was updated in 1980, although the rule itself stayed unchanged. The new explanation rests on "a fear that unwanted pregnancy or bitterness at a relationship gone sour might convert a willing participant in sexual relations into a vindictive complainant," and suggests the outcry rule is needed to limit "the opportunity for blackmailing another by threatening to bring a criminal charge of sexual aggression." Last, to rationalize the instruction that tells jurors in a sexual assault case "to evaluate the testimony of a victim . . . with special care," the Code cites "the emotional involvement of the witness and the difficulty of determining the truth with respect to alleged sexual activities carried out in private."

The 1962 model rules on sexual assault remained untouched until 2012, when the American Law Institute began a process of revision.* Still today, for all to see, the criminal law continues to incorporate intense distrust of rape complainants. More than a dozen states impose a "prompt outcry" rule or a corroboration requirement, while a handful of states and the federal courts allow for a cautionary instruction in rape cases. Doubts about sexual assault accusers, while formally on the wane, remain lodged in the criminal law.

———

Like criminal law, sexual harassment law advances a view of accusers as not credible when they delay reporting, embedding the myth that when women are assaulted or harassed, they disclose it immediately. Here too, the legal requirements placed on victims are disconnected from how most experience abuse and its aftermath. The law exacerbates a widespread misperception that women who wait to report misconduct are to be disbelieved.

Most sexual harassment cases that happen in the workplace hinge on the liability of the employer rather than the harasser, since supervisors and coworkers cannot be individually sued under Title VII, the statute that prohibits discrimination in the workplace (or under many analogous state civil rights acts). Under Title VII, an employee has less than a year—just 300 or 180 days, depending on where the complaint is initiated—to file a claim with the Equal Employment Opportunity Commission; otherwise, the claim is time-barred. But the time period for most employees who have been sexually harassed is even shorter than for other workplace plaintiffs.

In two cases from the 1990s, the Supreme Court held that a worker who experiences a hostile work environment must behave "reason-

---

* This process is still underway, and I am a participant.

ably" in response to the harassment; otherwise, the employer can use this "unreasonable" response against her. By creating this defense, the Court turned the focus to the accuser, whose failure to complain in a timely manner can spell the demise of her case. Indeed, the defense "indirectly imposes a prompt complaint requirement on harassed employees," as legal scholars Deborah Brake and Joanna Grossman explain. "The failure to complain is almost always fatal to the plaintiff's case," they add, "since courts have been relatively unwilling to accept excuses and tend, instead, to assume that such a failure is always 'unreasonable.'" Lower courts have considered unreasonable a delay as short as one week and, in another case, seventeen days.

An insistence on prompt complaint is a poor fit with the realities of abuse. Victims of sexual harassment rarely come forward when the harassment begins. Ari Wilkenfeld, the D.C. civil rights attorney who has worked with hundreds of harassment plaintiffs, describes "stages that a person normally goes through to process what happens to her." "The time limits to report are far too short," Wilkenfeld notes.

Robert Vance, the Philadelphia civil rights lawyer, underscores that low-wage workers are especially disadvantaged by prompt complaint rules. These are workers who "tend not to complain until the 'last straw' moment," Vance says, "because, economically speaking, it's a job they need." Many of his clients have "bills to pay and mouths to feed," and they endure prolonged abuse before finally reaching their limit. When these women do come forward, they are asked to explain themselves, and their reporting delay may well disqualify them from ever obtaining relief.

As Lauren Teukolsky, the employment law practitioner in Los Angeles, told me, "I frequently have women or men come to me and say, 'Look, this terrible thing happened. I've been too scared to come forward, but now that I'm in therapy, I'm in a much better place. I feel like I have the strength to come forward.' Then I have to say to them,

'You know, you're too late. You would have had a great claim a year ago, but you just waited too long.'" Teukolsky also observes the skepticism faced by her clients—"If sexual harassment victims don't come forward right away, they must be lying." The short window for pursuing a legal claim cements this understanding, however inaccurate. If "real victims" don't hesitate to complain, dictates the conventional wisdom, accusers who fall short of this ideal cannot be credible.

Pretrial discovery compounds the sense that imperfect victims (all victims) are not to be believed. Both sides rely on the discovery process to gather evidence that might be relevant to trial. In sexual harassment cases, the defense is permitted to explore a vast range of topics said to bear on a woman's credibility, and the law gives wide latitude to defendants intent on probing an accuser's past. Discovery is often used to "dig into women's mental health, sexual, and family history," Ari Wilkenfeld says, in order to advance what is colloquially known as the "nuts and sluts" defense. You may recall that Anita Hill, the lawyer who publicly accused Clarence Thomas of sexual harassment, was widely portrayed at the time as "a little bit nutty and a little bit slutty." Belief outside the courtroom shapes belief inside it, and vice versa.

In a typical case, defendants are able to unearth mountains of evidence meant to destroy an accuser's credibility if it doesn't persuade her to settle the case. Joseph Sellers, a leading civil rights attorney, describes how he prepares his clients for discovery. "Expect a thorough inspection of every aspect of your personal life," Sellers tells women—psychological history, abortions, first sexual encounter, past sexual abuse. Social media records are fair game. Many judges and arbitrators are unwilling to limit the scope of this intrusion. Accusers' pasts are pried open for scrutiny, and whatever is found there can undermine them. Perhaps this is why the second woman to come forward against the doctor who also abused Aja Newman worried that her past sexual abuse would be used against her.

Discovery works very differently for accused men, who regularly shield evidence of previous harassment from exposure. Any confidential settlements and nondisclosure agreements involving the alleged harasser mostly remain off-limits to accusers. Discovery in sexual harassment cases re-creates a lopsided world. In this world, accusers are suspect from the get-go, and all facets of their lives can be used to discredit them. Accused men are buffered from their misdeeds and remain, as ever, credible.

I've outlined the ways in which the credibility complex influences our beliefs about what happened. But belief is more complicated; it also includes our response to the second part of an accuser's claim: the abuser is to blame for his conduct. We don't ordinarily think about credibility in this more expansive manner—but we should. Belief that the abuser—not the accuser—is at fault is a critical, if overlooked, component of our credibility judgments. Unless we are willing to allocate responsibility for the abuse *on the abuser*, we will dismiss the accusation. Like distrust, blame-shifting preserves a world where, as a matter of course, sexual misconduct is justified.

4

BLAME-SHIFTING

HOW VICTIMS ARE FAULTED

Until she left Northern California to attend the University of Arizona in 2005, Jillian Corsie had seldom been away from home. She met one of her first college friends in math class. Like Corsie, the young man struggled to understand the material, and the two bonded over extra study sessions. About a month into the school year, Corsie's friend raped her. When we spoke, she didn't dwell on the details. "We were at a party together and we went back to my dorm room to order pizza and he assaulted me. That's kind of the gist of that," she says.

There was no question in Corsie's mind this was an assault—she knew exactly "what was happening as it was happening." She remembers telling her rapist that she had a boyfriend and she "wasn't interested" before he forced her to have sex. She immediately disclosed to her suitemates that she'd just been raped, and she mentioned the possibility of reporting the assault to their residential advisor. Corsie recalls her suitemates saying, "No, no, don't do that," but nothing more about the conversation.

Corsie returned to her own room and called her boyfriend back home to tell him what had just happened. She recalls him asking whether she had been beaten or tied up, and she understood the thrust of his question—she could have done more to fight back if she was truly unwilling to have sex with this man. Many years would pass before Corsie would return to this conversation with her then-boyfriend, and he would admit that he hadn't believed her. "I think it didn't line up with what he thought a rape was; therefore, it wasn't rape and I just slept with someone and regretted it," she explains. It's difficult for her to remember the aftermath of the rape in detail—"It was such a crazy time," she remarks.

She knows that for the next two weeks, she mostly stayed in bed, finding comfort in all-hours chats with her best friends from high school. When Corsie's parents saw her phone records, they called and confronted her, wanting to know why she was spending hours talking to old friends rather than adjusting to life in college.

Corsie ended up "blurting out what had happened." When I asked why she hadn't told her parents sooner, she was clear: "You don't want your parents to know anything about any kind of sex life whatsoever," she says, "but especially something like that. It's the worst part of this whole thing. I told my mom, 'I wish I could hold up a veil in front of all of your eyes, so that you wouldn't have to know any of this. But I can't.'"

When she heard about the rape, Corsie's mom started crying and handed the phone to Corsie's dad, who promptly called his daughter's local police precinct. Soon after, Corsie met with two male police officers. "I remember having to use really graphic words like penis and vagina, which is just humiliating anyway and especially in this context," she says. She remembers staring at a calendar on the wall while relating "detail for detail what happened."

They asked her what she now thinks of as "the usual questions"— "'What were you wearing?' 'How much did you have to drink?'" And then the officers left the room to make a phone call. When they returned, they told Corsie that under Arizona state law, what happened to her was considered consensual. They also told her: "'Don't mix alcohol with beauty.' And that was it."

The stretch ahead was very difficult. Corsie wondered, "Did I give the wrong signals? Was I leading him on? Is this my fault?" She is careful to add, "I rationally knew this wasn't my fault." But her disclosure had prompted a complete nonresponse—from the police, and also from her boyfriend and many of her friends. This collective dismissal colored her understanding of the assault. No one acted as if her rapist was blameworthy. Instead, Corsie was treated as the culpable party. She "felt disbelieved by everybody, regardless if they believed me or not."

"I kind of went off the deep end," she describes. She started drinking heavily and, she says, "put myself in really dangerous situations." Corsie adds, "I think the reason I did that, partially, was because I was willing something else to happen to me that could actually be credible and be perceived as a bad thing."

She managed to return to math class, where she was forced to see her rapist three times a week. She did what she could, and moved from her regular spot in the front of the classroom to the back row.

On some level she knew that what she'd described was a profound violation, and yet no one seemed to think she had been wronged. "That's what really fucks you up in the future," she explains.

Corsie told me she sometimes regretted reporting her rape—she's clear that the aftermath was even worse than the incident itself. "If I could have just been assaulted and figured it out on my own, that would have been better than having to go through all of that reporting and essentially being blamed for it."

Corsie graduated from college and moved forward on her path to becoming an award-winning documentary filmmaker. She describes the fallout from her assault as "shelved" and "kind of done." Yet she thought "constantly" about the damage inflicted—not by the rapist, but by a system that failed her.

More than a decade later, she went back to the University of Arizona to meet with the police officer who had warned her not to "mix alcohol with beauty." The two had exchanged several emails and phone calls over the preceding year—prompted by Corsie's outreach—and she saw that the officer had come to regret his handling of the case. Corsie now describes him as "kind and supportive"—a "wonderful person." But she was furious when, several months after their meeting in Tucson, she saw the police report for the first time. The report stated that "a sexual assault did not occur." And at the end, it read, "I then gave her some advice on how to prevent this from happening again."

In 2016, Corsie made a short documentary film about her experience, which she titled *Second Assault*. "The film is about my journey to confront a system that failed me, and also to confront the culture that we live in—and how that supports this idea of a second assault, which isn't necessarily just what happens when you report, but also what happens when your friends and boyfriends and people around you don't believe you," she told a reporter.

By coming forward, Corsie made this claim: she'd been wronged. But, with few exceptions, the people she turned to for help remained unconvinced. "When nobody believes you, where do you go? You're locked in your own brain."

Only after she began publicly telling her story did this change. Once people started believing that the rape happened and it wasn't her fault, Corsie started to heal. Looking back now, she understands that people blamed her so they didn't have to blame her rapist. By judging her, everyone around her could avoid holding him to account.

———

A primary function of the credibility complex is to deny the blame-worthiness of the accused while manufacturing blame on the part of the victim. Together, law and culture advance a view of women as inviting sexual overtures unless they do enough to demonstrate otherwise. Simply by *being*, a woman can activate these blaming impulses. And when we hold accusers responsible for their abuse, even partly, we absolve the abuser of responsibility. This preserves familiar structures—however hierarchical—in which the collective, particularly its most powerful members, is deeply invested.

You'll recall that an allegation of abuse involves a trio of claims. An accuser who comes forward not only asserts that the misconduct happened; she also insists that it was wrong. This second part of the claim is what drives her to disclose; implicit in the act of reporting is a declaration that the abuse was a violation—a violation for which the abuser is responsible.

A credible sexual misconduct allegation moves us to attribute fault to the wrongdoer. And the opposite is true: when we reject the accuser's assertion of blame, her accusation goes nowhere. She is discredited, as she would be if we rejected the *this happened* part of her allegation. The end result is the same, although the discounting mechanism is quite different.

When we attribute "some level of blame" to the accuser and "less than complete blame" to the accused, we let the accused off the hook. By deciding that the accuser invited the misconduct, we can dismiss her report. This penchant for blame-shifting is well documented. Research participants who are presented with scenarios involving a description of rape consistently see victims as culpable. Study after study shows that sexual assault victims are "often blamed and denigrated for their role in the rape, even to the extent whereby the victim is held responsible for the assault." Whether we deny the occurrence of the misconduct outright or justify it implicitly, we side with the accused.

The blame-shifting impulse is rooted in a familiar archetype—the perfect victim, as we saw earlier—and the mythology surrounding it. Indeed, researchers have consistently found that higher levels of rape myth acceptance are associated with greater victim blaming. But cultural ideals of victimhood are only part of the reason we hold women responsible for their abuse. We're also psychologically motivated to shift blame.

The "just world" theory sheds light on our victim-blaming ways. According to this theory—which originated in the mid-1960s and has since been supported by a stack of empirical research—we long for the stability that comes from believing that people normally get what they deserve. Yearning to live in a just and orderly world motivates us to interpret events to confirm this version of reality. "If others can suffer unjustly," observes a seminal paper by the psychologists Melvin Lerner and Dale Miller, "then the individual must admit to the unsettling prospect that he too could suffer unjustly." Rather than acknowledge this possibility, we decide that a crime victim deserves her fate, because of her "'bad' character" or because she engaged in bad acts that can be condemned as "careless or foolish."

Our bias toward believing that good, well-behaved people will not suffer leads us to fault accusers who come forward to claim they were hurt. When one of Harvey Weinstein's lawyers, Donna Rotunno, was asked in early 2020 if she had ever been sexually assaulted, her response was revealing. "I have not . . . because I would never put myself in that position," Rotunno said. She continued, "I've always made choices, from college age on, where I never drank too much, I never went home with someone that I didn't know. I just never put myself in any vulnerable circumstance ever."* Rotunno may well have

---

* After the interview aired, many sexual assault survivors reacted on Twitter using the hashtag #WhereIPutMyself.

had strategic reasons for saying this—the interview took place in the midst of Weinstein's trial. But it's also quite likely that Rotunno was expressing her genuine belief. For someone who views herself as capable of staving off rape, the world is a much safer place. In this more secure, more just world, anyone who is raped must have somehow brought it upon herself. And since she is at fault, her abuser is not.

When an allegation threatens our sense of security, the lure of victim-blaming can be overwhelming. Research suggests that when we identify with a rape accuser, we may "dissociate" ourselves from her in order to "reduce the cognitive dissonance that is produced by the possibility of also becoming a victim of rape." We put distance between ourselves and the victim, finding ways to sever any emotional connection between someone who is too much like us for comfort. One way we protect our psychological well-being is to focus on what the accuser did to bring the abuse upon herself. If she is different from us, we can feel safe.

For all of us, the world can seem less frightening when victims are responsible for what befalls them.

"WHAT IS WRONG WITH ME . . . ?": SELF-BLAME AND SHAME

The idea that victims are to blame for their abuse is so deeply ingrained in our culture that many survivors internalize it. Remember how Jillian Corsie asked herself, after she was raped, "Did I give the wrong signals? Was I leading him on? Is this my fault?" Even though Corsie "rationally knew" she wasn't to blame, she couldn't help but wonder. Looking back more than a decade later, she emphasized that she was "barely eighteen" at the time of her rape—that she had changed a lot since then.

Most accusers I've spoken with over the years have struggled to place blame entirely on the perpetrator. This is a manifestation of the "norm of self-doubt" that the philosopher Kate Abramson explores. *What did I do to tempt him? Could I have done more to stop it?* For many survivors, like Corsie, self-blame is inseparable from the blame imposed by others.

Blame-shifting by the outside world and blame-shifting from within give a pass to abusers, whose credibility in the realm of fault gets an enormous boost. One woman I spoke with perfectly captured this dynamic. She was sixteen and, for the first time, drunk at a party. A self-described "theater dork," she found herself locked in a bedroom with a group of varsity football players, who forced her to perform oral sex on them. "I begged them not to take my virginity, and they didn't," she told me. "But I went to school on Monday and I was suddenly known as the 'blowjob queen.'" Her best friends sat her down and insisted that she needed to "behave" herself in the future.

Now in her thirties, the woman explains, "I was shamed and blamed from the get-go, which is why I didn't realize it was assault when I was younger." It was only when she watched Christine Blasey Ford testify at Brett Kavanaugh's Supreme Court confirmation hearing that she suddenly experienced the shock of recognition. Decades later, this woman understood *for the first time* that the football players were responsible for her sexual assault, and she was not.

"IF I WAS TRULY HONEST, I still blamed myself for not screaming or kicking. For going there in the first place," writes Chessy Prout, whose sexual assault by a fellow student at St. Paul's School in New Hampshire resulted in his conviction on several misdemeanor charges. "I was too trusting, too naïve," says Prout. "I felt like it was all my fault. It would take me years to accept what now seems obvious: rape is not a punishment for poor judgment."

Research confirms that many women see themselves, rather than their abuser, as responsible for or even deserving of their sexual victimization. Nicole Johnson, the psychologist who specializes in the treatment of sexual assault victims, see this "all the time" in her practice, she told me. Johnson says that when survivors come forward, the first questions they're often asked—still—are "How much did you have to drink?" or "Did you go home with him?" In these vulnerable moments of disclosure, survivors are told, "There was something you did that put yourself in this situation." It's no wonder victims spend time thinking about what they could have done differently— this response perfectly mirrors the way others are assigning responsibility.

Johnson adds that self-blaming may also serve a protective function. Victims want to "figure out what they did to make this happen" in order to "prevent it from happening again." This mindset can feel less terrible than admitting the abuser was in control, or that a person who was trusted betrayed that trust. In her exposé of sexual assault in Missoula, Montana, the investigative reporter Katie J. M. Baker describes an undergraduate remarking, "We'd rather blame ourselves for the situation than believe our 'friends' could ever do something like this to us."

From a therapeutic perspective, the coping mechanism has a downside. Research shows that self-blaming delays healing. In her practice, Johnson tries to help survivors "keep that protection but also move the blame to the responsible party." Internalization of responsibility is also harmful from a legal point of view: self-blame can hurt survivors in litigation. As one experienced trial lawyer notes, when an accuser has faulted herself for not preventing the abuse, she's later "hit over the head with those statements" if she chooses to pursue a claim.

Blame goes hand in hand with shame. Donna Freitas, the author of the memoir *Consent*, chronicles years of harassment by her graduate school professor and how he altered her life course. Throughout the abuse, and after it ended, Freitas not only gave her harasser the benefit of the doubt at her own expense; she also faulted herself for his unwanted attention. On one level, the level of rationality, Freitas knows that the blame is not hers. Even so, like many victims who channel blame inward, Freitas says that she continues to "look for the reason for what happened" by "looking within myself." She ponders what many victims ask themselves: "What is wrong with me, what failure was there in my upbringing, what shortcomings in my character, what crack in my self-understanding, my sanity, what thing or things did I do to cause this man to prey on me, specifically? What about *me* turned him in my direction? What about *me* made me tolerate something so palpably repulsive for so long?"

No woman is immune from the kind of scrutiny that leads to misplaced attributions of blame. But certain women are prime targets.

"BAD" VICTIMS

Even today, women are expected to forestall whatever sexual abuse comes their way—we demand nothing less. A woman must avoid being too appealing as a target. This ideal stems from the enduring cultural stereotype of the "good girl," which women can never outgrow. Our expectation accepts the male urge to assault and harass as a given. The good girl never drinks to the point of impairment. The good girl doesn't dress or act in ways perceived as too sexual. The woman who fails to redirect that male urge is complicit in her violation— in essence, she's not a victim.

Women who drank alcohol before they were assaulted are special fodder for judgment. While intoxicated rapists are seen as less responsible for their actions than sober rapists—"The bottle may grant a pardon to the perpetrator," as one set of researchers put it—the opposite is true of victims, who are perceived as *more to blame* for the rape when they are intoxicated.

Nancy Hogshead-Makar, the Olympic swimmer–turned–civil rights lawyer, tells me that, in her practice, she sees harsh judgment directed at victims who were drinking. "People look at drinking almost like she let him down," Hogshead-Makar says. "She wasn't able to fend him off the way she would have if she'd been sober."

Many women who are assaulted under the influence of alcohol internalize this message. Typical is the account of one twenty-one-year-old woman who drank too much and awoke to her cousin's boyfriend raping her. This woman felt that "it was her own fault for getting drunk and passing out at her cousin's house." She chose to tell no one what happened.

The journalist Vanessa Grigoriadis spent years investigating sex and sexual assault on college campuses around the country. In her book, *Blurred Lines*, she writes, "The assaulted girl takes others' doubt to heart, analyzes every detail of the night, then berates herself for the way her one-shouldered dress showed skin or for her decision to have that fifth vodka shot."

WOMEN'S OBLIGATION TO FORESTALL ABUSE also entails not dressing or acting in ways considered "sexy." Victims perceived as sexual are often thought to have tempted their abuser—to have "asked for it." This belief is critical to what legal scholar Duncan Kennedy describes as an "ideology of sexual relations." "In this narrative," Kennedy writes, "a woman wears provocative clothing and suffers sexual abuse," while the abuser "is exonerated or excused on the basis of what *she* did." By her conduct or appearance, the "sexy" woman signaled that she was interested in sex or sexual overtures. So she deserves what came her way. In her memoir, Rose McGowan writes she was told many times that men "just can't keep their hands to themselves," and that she "drove them to it" with her beauty.*

The cultural obligation to keep men at bay is imposed on women early in life. As Peggy Orenstein explains in *Girls & Sex*, teenage girls are warned about provocative attire and given dress codes that prohibit clothing deemed unacceptably revealing. "This isn't the place for your short shorts or your tank tops or your crop tops," the student body was instructed at one high school welcome meeting. As a student who attended the assembly told Orenstein, school officials assumed "a connection" between the girls' dress and sexual harassment—"Like maybe if you don't 'respect yourself' by the way you dress you're going to get harassed, and that's your own fault because you wore the tank top." Orenstein writes, "Boys run afoul of dress codes when they flout authority: 'hippies' defying the establishment, 'thugs' in saggy pants. For girls, the issue is sex. Enforcing modesty is considered a way both to protect and to contain young women's sexuality; and they, by association, are charged with controlling young men's."

Even more than their white counterparts, Black girls are told to hide their bodies in order to avoid abuse. In *Pushout*, Monique Morris chronicles the double standard imposed on Black girls whose very existence is sexualized. "One Black girl after another felt barred from wearing clothing that other girls could wear without reprimand," Morris writes, adding that the girls she spoke with "pointed to popular characterizations of Black women's bodies as part of the problem." One student described how the adults in her school would tell her, "You're Black. You can't wear those because you're showing much more skin because your body weight and your body shape is

---

* On college campuses around the country, sexual assault survivors have installed art exhibits aimed at "reclaiming the four words often used to discredit them: 'What were you wearing?'"

different . . . But they automatically think that other race girls can wear it because it's not, like a sexual thing."

The rampant sexualization of Black girls translates into constant harassment. "No matter what a Black girl does, no matter her age, and no matter how small or big she is, a man is going to always look at her sexually," Morris observes. Because Black girls are assigned the impossible role of preventing their abuse, many will be blamed for their violation.

Research shows that when Black girls grow up, they will experience much the same: Black women are often harassed with racially charged, sexualized comments about their clothing. As compared to white women, their attire is "held to a higher standard."

Black women are also at greater risk of being blamed when they are sexually harassed. Based on her personal experience as a graduate student and her work in the field, the psychologist Carolyn West says that Black harassment victims are frequently seen as having invited their abuse. She explains that because of deep-seated views of Black women as "naturally lascivious, and always seeking sexual contact," they are ready targets of blame.

Among the cluster of stereotypes that have long oppressed Black women is the image of the Jezebel, which originated under slavery and served "to relegate all Black women to the category of sexually aggressive women." The Jezebel was thought to possess "excessive sexual appetite"—a fiction used to justify "the widespread sexual assaults by White men typically reported by Black slave women." To this day, when Black accusers come forward, they are especially likely to be held responsible for their abuse. "If Black women are perceived as inherently promiscuous," write the psychologists Roxanne Donovan and Michelle Williams, "then regardless of the situation, they are at greater risk of being blamed when they are raped." Many Black survivors realize this, anticipate it, and act accordingly. Psychologists have found that "fear of being blamed and reinforcing the Jezebel stereotype" keeps Black women from disclosing their abuse.

For Black survivors, the Jezebel image can also steer blame inward. Vanessa Grigoriadis spoke with Karmenife, a senior at Wesleyan at the time, who said she was assaulted as a freshman, but for years didn't see the incident as rape. "You know, women of color, particularly black and Latino women, are often categorized as unrapable because we're hypersexualized," Karmenife explained. "Supposedly, we're always asking for it. So when this happens to you as a woman of color, you have all this institutionalized oppressive shit in your mind going, 'Oh, you were asking for it because of your body, the way you're shaped. This is just how it is.'" Karmenife later created a series of photographs taken in and around fraternities on campus, including the house where she was assaulted. The series was titled "Reclamation," and Karmenife said it helped her to heal. "I needed to take these spaces that had so much power over me, over my community, over everything, and then have that power completely switched and have it rest on my shoulders," she explained.

—

Rape and harassment are bound up in power, gender, and sex—all of which are loaded with cultural meaning. In a patriarchal society, female sexuality is uniquely threatening, which is why, throughout history, it's been "a thing to be stolen, sold, bought, bartered, or exchanged by others"—always, in one way or another, controlled by men. These mechanisms of control have softened over time. More women than ever embrace their sexuality as a source of pleasure and power. Yet still today, women of all stripes are judged against what sociologists refer to as the "sexual double standard," which activates blame, along with self-blame and shame.

Paula England is a sociologist who has spent many decades researching norms of sexuality and gender. England is a leading expert on the sexual double standard, which she says continues to disadvantage women. "One piece of evidence that there is this shaming in the culture around women's sexuality is that there's such an abundance of words that are negative to denote a sexually active woman," England explains. The same is not true for men. When England asks her undergraduates at New York University to generate words that describe sexual women, they quickly create a list of pejoratives that include "slut," "whore," "ho," and other terms. By contrast, when she asks for descriptors of sexual men, her students normally suggest "player." England tells me, "And then I say, okay, if we compare whore and player, which has a more negative connotation?" England and a colleague also found empirical evidence of a double standard by examining a large data set of college students. Their conclusion: "the evidence suggests that women risk much more disrespect than men for casual sex."

Other research on the sexual double standard has exposed its accordion-like qualities. It turns out that women need not actually engage in sex to be penalized for their sexuality. One team of sociologists led by Elizabeth Armstrong spent an academic year studying "slut shaming" on a university campus they refer to as Midwestern. The sociologists write that "the practice of maligning women for presumed sexual activity" is commonplace among boys and men, but also among women—the subjects of the study. "Slut stigma," the sociologists add, "is more about regulating public gender performance than regulating private sexual practices."

For the college women studied, slut-shaming reinforced class distinctions. This was true whether or not the behavior coded as "slutty" was overtly sexual. A "desirable, classy appearance," for instance, was often contrasted with an "undesirable, trashy appearance." Women were judged for wearing the wrong clothes or makeup. Women were judged for simply drawing "inappropriate attention" to themselves.

Regardless of precisely how they did it, women who departed from conventional, class-based notions of acceptable femininity were labeled "sluts."

On or off campus, a chief way to discredit an accuser is to call her a "slut," which conveys not necessarily that she's lying about what happened, but that she deserved to be assaulted or harassed. Because female sexuality is awash in stigma, we are culturally primed to see sexual misconduct accusers as having invited their abuse—by their dress, by their appearance, by living in the world.

Erica Kinsman is a former Florida State University student whose rape allegation against football player Jameis Winston was featured in the documentary *The Hunting Ground*. Winston said the encounter was consensual, and prosecutors declined to pursue charges. The film depicts Kinsman, who settled a civil suit against Winston in 2016, recalling, "All these people were praising him . . . and calling me a slut, a whore."

This treatment is not cabined to culture. We also find it in law, where blame-shifting takes many forms—like assigning fault to women who don't fight back hard enough. Remember Edna Nethery, who saw the conviction of her rapist undone by the Wisconsin Supreme Court in 1906 because she didn't do enough to stop him. Over one hundred years later, many women are denied the law's protection because they fall short—they drank too much, they behaved too provocatively, they dressed "too sexy" . . . For any number of reasons, they're seen as unworthy victims—in the end, not victims at all.

LEGAL BLAME-SHIFTING

Charlotte can recall only bits and pieces of the night. The thirty-five-year-old woman, a mother of two, attended a wedding in Minnesota with her aunt, where she drank a beer and three glasses of wine. She remembers dancing before suddenly losing coordination. She remembers meeting the wedding photographer. She remembers lying next to him on the grass and a security guard helping her up. She remembers struggling to walk. The rest of the night is a blur. The next day, Charlotte awoke in a motel room, sore, and went to the hospital, where a sexual assault nurse examiner found injuries consistent with an assault.

The wedding photographer was questioned by police officers and admitted that he digitally penetrated Charlotte and she performed oral sex on him in his parked car. He claimed this was all consensual. But based on Charlotte's account, the security guard's observations, and video footage from the wedding facility, the photographer was arrested and charged with sexual assault. At trial, he was found guilty of the most serious charge—sexual penetration of a person known to be "mentally incapacitated" or "physically helpless."

On appeal, the conviction was reversed. Writing in 2014, the appellate court found insufficient evidence that Charlotte was impaired to the degree required by law. (A lesser charge of nonconsensual sexual contact was affirmed.) Charlotte was "physically impaired," said the court, but not enough to be considered "helpless." Nor did Charlotte's condition satisfy the definition of mentally incapacitated.

Although being under the influence of alcohol or any other substance can qualify, the law sets forth a colossal proviso. Only if the alcohol or substance was "administered without the person's agreement" is the victim's incapacitation recognized. Since Charlotte had chosen to consume alcohol, the resulting impairment was considered her own fault, which meant that the photographer would not be held accountable for capitalizing on it.

Reflecting on the court's ruling, a Minnesota prosecutor explained in 2020 how the law works against intoxicated victims. "We have to turn a bunch of these cases down presently, because we don't have someone who in essence was passed out," said the prosecutor, adding, "It's making it near impossible to successfully prosecute cases"—cases where a woman is responsible for her alcohol consumption and so, in the eyes of the law, her assault.

The law's reproach of voluntarily intoxicated women is not new. The 1962 Model Penal Code—the highly influential guide for lawmakers around the country—prohibits sexual intercourse with a woman who is *involuntarily* intoxicated. But the drafters specifically rejected the idea that a man would be barred from having intercourse with a woman who, as a result of self-induced intoxication, cannot "control or appraise her conduct." If the intoxication is her fault, so too is any nonconsensual intercourse that results. The rule is justified by reference to "the social context of romance and seduction," where alcohol and drugs are "common ingredients of the ritual of courtship." When "relaxation blurs into intoxication and insensibility," both parties share the blame when the man forces sex on the woman. As the Code drafters maintained, "where this progression occurs in a course of mutual and voluntary behavior, it would be unrealistic and unfair to assign to the male total responsibility for the end result."

The singular treatment of voluntarily intoxicated victims permeates the law today. More than half the states distinguish between voluntary and involuntary intoxication. In these states, when an abuser administers a substance without the victim's knowledge, he can be held to account. Otherwise, nonconsensual penetration becomes the intoxicated victim's responsibility.

This is what happened to Audrey, a woman from North Carolina who was celebrating New Year's Eve of 2005 with three friends. After spending the night eating and drinking at several bars and restaurants around town, she wound up back at the apartment of one of her friends, a man named Kinsey, although she was too impaired to know her whereabouts. She fell asleep on the bed, at which point, as a jury later found, Kinsey raped her. When she awoke, Audrey quickly left his apartment and went down to the lobby of the building, where she sprawled out on the floor in a very intoxicated state. Police officers were called, and they took Audrey to the hospital, where she was evaluated for possible injuries arising from "excessive alcohol consumption and from sexual intercourse," as a court would later describe.

Kinsey was charged with second-degree rape, which is defined by the statute as intercourse with a victim who was either "physically helpless" or "mentally incapacitated." But under North Carolina law, again as is true in many states, only involuntarily intoxicated victims can be considered incapacitated. The jury wasn't told this—the trial judge made a mistake. As a consequence, Kinsey's conviction was overturned. The sexual assault statute, explained the appeals court, does not cover "a person who voluntarily and as a result of her own actions becomes intoxicated to a level short of unconsciousness or physical helplessness."

If Kinsey—or anyone other than Audrey, for that matter—were responsible for Audrey's intoxication, he could be found guilty of rape. Audrey's decision to drink meant that Kinsey couldn't be convicted. *Even if* she was "substantially incapable of either appraising the nature of her conduct or resisting the act of vaginal intercourse," she was not the victim of rape.

This legal blame-shifting corresponds to widespread biases about intoxicated accusers. Researchers have consistently demonstrated that intoxicated women are seen as "more responsible" for their victimization than sober women. In one study, mock jury participants read a summary of a first-degree rape case ("first degree" meaning a case with considerable physical force) involving a man and a woman who met at a concert. The victim drank either four sodas or four beers throughout the night depending on the scenario the participant was assigned. In some scenarios, she purchased the drinks herself, and in others, the man purchased them for her. A mock trial summary included the prosecutor's case, the defense case, and the judge's instructions—the only facts that varied were the amount the accuser had to drink and who purchased the drinks. Participants were then asked to rate the woman's credibility.

As predicted, both male and female mock jurors perceived intoxicated women as less credible than their sober counterparts. What also stands out about the study is that credibility was downgraded more dramatically if the woman bought the alcohol herself. When a victim is considered responsible for her intoxication, she is "viewed by jurors as more responsible for sexual assault," the researchers found, making jurors less likely to convict the accused man. Because the rest of the "evidence" in the rape case was held constant, the mock trial results show that the victim's discounted credibility was connected to attributions of fault, rather than just to believability. The study suggests that when women engage in behaviors considered "risky," like consuming alcohol, they are more likely to be seen as blameworthy actors and less likely to be perceived as victims. The accuser's conduct is condemned because she left herself vulnerable to attack—so the thinking goes. At the same time, the abuser is given a pass. She becomes the target of blame, and he escapes it altogether.

TOO SEXY FOR THE LAW

Melissa Nelson was twenty years old when she was hired to work as a dental assistant for James Knight. Nelson had worked in his Fort Dodge, Iowa, office for over a decade before he fired her in 2010.

The problems began a year and a half earlier. On several occasions, Knight complained to Nelson that her clothing was too tight, too revealing, and "distracting." Knight occasionally asked Nelson to wear a lab coat over her clothes, which he viewed as necessary because, he said, "I don't think it's good for me to see her wearing things that accentuate her body." According to Nelson, her clothes were not tight or in any way inappropriate for the workplace.

Nelson viewed Knight as a friend and a "father figure." She was a parent, as was Knight, and the two would sometimes text each other with updates on their children and mundane happenings. Nelson's messages were not flirtatious. Knight, however, began a one-sided exchange of sexual commentary, in person and by text. A court would later offer this summary of their interactions:

> Dr. Knight acknowledges he once told Nelson that if she saw his pants bulging, she would know her clothing was too revealing. On another occasion, Dr. Knight texted Nelson saying the shirt she had worn that day was too tight. After Nelson responded that she did not think he was being fair, Dr. Knight replied that it was a good thing Nelson did not wear tight pants too because then he would get it coming and going. Dr. Knight also recalls that after Nelson allegedly made a statement regarding infrequency in her sex life, he responded to her, "[T]hat's like having a Lamborghini in the garage and never driving it." Nelson recalls that Dr. Knight once texted her to ask how often she experienced an orgasm. Nelson did not answer the text.

One day in early 2010, Knight called Nelson into his office. He had arranged for a pastor from his church to "observe" the conversation, and in the pastor's presence, Knight told Nelson she was fired. Knight's wife apparently viewed Nelson as a "big threat" to the marriage. Reading from a prepared statement, Knight told Nelson that "their relationship had become a detriment" to his family.

When Nelson's husband heard that she had been fired, he called

Knight, who arranged for the two men to meet with the same pastor present. That evening, Knight stressed that Nelson had done nothing wrong, and that she was "the best dental assistant he ever had." But he said he worried that he was getting too attached to her, and he feared he would "try to have an affair with her" if he didn't fire her.

Nelson sued Knight. Like federal law, the state's antidiscrimination statute prohibits an employer from basing an adverse employment decision on a worker's sex. Knight's defense was straightforward if strained. Nelson was not fired because she was a woman—which would have been illegal—but because she was a temptation. In response, Nelson pointed out that sexual harassment is prohibited by law. Although she didn't include a harassment claim in her suit, it would not be right, she urged, for Knight "to avoid liability for terminating her out of fear that he was *going to* harass her."

The Iowa Supreme Court disagreed. Knight may have "treated Nelson badly," but he didn't unlawfully discriminate against her. As the court saw it, Knight's actions could be justified as a necessary means to keep him from sexually harassing Nelson. "Even if the reasons for termination are unjust," said the court in 2013, firing Nelson *before* she was subjected to a hostile work environment "by definition does not bring about that atmosphere." Although Nelson did nothing wrong, even by Knight's account, she paid the price for his sexual attraction to her. Yet the law sided with Knight.

Women are regularly held responsible for controlling men's sexual urges. Misconduct becomes the fault of the victim rather than the abuser. The legal scholar Lynne Henderson has called this an "unspoken 'rule' of male innocence and female guilt in law." The rule holds that men are "entitled to act on their sexual passions, which are viewed as difficult and sometimes impossible to control." For their part, women are expected to "avoid stimulating" men if they "do not wish to have sexual intercourse" or to be sexually harassed. If a man's lust finds an outlet, goes the thinking, the fault belongs to the woman who drove him "wild." Women who *do* next to nothing may nonetheless be blamed for their abuse, since their existence alone is seen as temptation enough. Victims are faulted for getting in a car, running with headphones on, falling asleep on a couch, smiling, engaging in casual conversation, not finding a way to stop the workplace overtures, and so forth.

Sexual harassment law reinforces this cultural fixation on women who invite their abuse. The leading case on "unwelcomeness" is *Meritor Savings Bank v. Vinson*, which the U.S. Supreme Court decided in 1986. The story begins more than a decade earlier, when nineteen-year-old Mechelle Vinson was hired to work as a teller trainee at a small bank in Washington, D.C. Vinson, who is Black, had grown up poor and surrounded by violence. Her previous employment experience was limited to temporary work in an exercise club, a grocery, and a shoe store, which made the steady bank job even more appealing.

A few months after Vinson began working at the bank, her manager, Sidney Taylor, demanded she have sex with him. She later recounted that when she refused, Taylor threatened her. "I said, 'I don't want to go to bed with you.' And he says, 'Just like I hired you, I'll fire you. Just like I made you, I'll break you, and if you don't do what I say then I'll have you killed' . . . And that's how it started."

Over the next two and a half years, Taylor subjected Vinson to "repeated outrages of sexual attention," including "40 or 50 episodes" of forced intercourse. Several times, she said, he raped her so violently that she sought medical attention. Vinson also described how Taylor fondled her, exposed himself to her, and barged in on her in the bathroom, and how she, over and over again, asked him to stop.

She chose not to file a formal complaint because she couldn't risk losing her job. "This man would fire me," she recalled thinking, "and my God I need my job." When the stress from the harassment and assaults forced her to take sick leave, Vinson was fired. At a meeting with a matrimonial attorney about pursuing a divorce from her husband, she happened to describe her suffering at work and was referred to an employment discrimination lawyer. She later sued the bank and Taylor—and everyone fully denied the accusations.

The case was tried before a judge, who allowed the defendants to introduce evidence that Vinson wore "low-cut dresses," "low-cut blouses," and "extremely tight pants." The judge also permitted a coworker to testify that Vinson "had a lot of sexual fantasies" and "talked quite a bit about sex." The judge heard from Vinson and from several coworkers who witnessed repeated incidents of her abuse and experienced similar misconduct themselves. At the end of the trial, the judge found for the defendants. Any "intimate or sexual relationship" between Vinson and Taylor was "a voluntary one by plaintiff having nothing to do with her continued employment," concluded the judge. Put simply, Vinson "was not the victim of sexual harassment and was not the victim of sexual discrimination."

Why wasn't Vinson credible when she claimed that Taylor's sexual advances and abuse harmed her? Evidence admitted at trial about her dress and sexual fantasies tapped into long-standing beliefs about Black women's promiscuity. "All too often," wrote her lawyers when appealing the decision, "it is Black women like Ms. Vinson who have been specifically victimized by the invidious stereotype of being scandalous and lewd women, perhaps targeting them to the would-be perpetrators."

Vinson was cast as a woman who deserved her abuse "because she asked for it, we know she asked for it, because she is a temptress, a seductress, a lascivious woman," her trial attorney had objected. As the legal scholar Tanya Hernández emphasizes, "stereotypical presumptions of African American women very likely contributed to the outcome."

VINSON'S CASE EVENTUALLY MADE ITS way to the Supreme Court, posing the question whether sexual harassment in the workplace violates federal antidiscrimination law. In a landmark victory for victims, the Court held for the first time that sexual advances constitute a form of unlawful discrimination when they create a "hostile work environment." The Court wrote: "The gravamen of any sexual harassment claim is that the alleged sexual advances were 'unwelcome,'" instructing that the "correct inquiry" is whether Vinson *by her conduct indicated* that the alleged sexual advances were unwelcome."

The creation of the unwelcomeness test tempered Vinson's win. The focus would now be trained on her and on all accusers going forward. What mattered was how Vinson showed Taylor that his sexual overtures were not welcome. To this end, the Court blessed a searching inquiry into the victim's conduct and appearance. Vinson's "sexually provocative speech or dress," was said to be "obviously relevant" to whether she found the sexual advances unwelcome. This legal framework—which the Supreme Court handed down to the lower court resolving Vinson's claim—remains in place today.

The framework disadvantages some women more than others. Regardless of what they wear, Black women are more likely to have their clothes considered "inappropriate" for the workplace—for instance, one Black employee was told she was dressing "too sexy" when she wore tan pants and a loose-fitting shirt. "The mere fact that it is a Black woman or woman of color wearing it can subject the apparel to a characterization as overly sexual and offensive," Tanya Hernández concludes. This cultural bias is aggravated by sexual harassment law, which expressly connects what courts commonly refer to as "sexually provocative speech or dress" to the idea that an accuser welcomed the advances. Regardless of her race, courts "repeatedly apply the unwelcomeness requirement in a manner that encourages stereotypical thinking about how a plaintiff 'asked for it.'"

Joseph Sellers is the D.C. lawyer who represented Mechelle Vinson after the Supreme Court remanded her case and before the parties ultimately settled in 1991, thirteen years after Vinson sued. This final phase of the litigation was shaped by the Court's newly announced unwelcomeness standard, which Sellers immediately realized would impose an unfair burden on Vinson and countless victims going forward. One particular incident captures this burden, Sellers told me. As he recalls, Vinson described having been "summoned" by Taylor during her lunch break to a nearby motel and told to take off her clothes. She had already informed her boss that she didn't want to have sex with him. But Taylor had said words to the effect of, "Look. I'm in this industry. If you're not going to cooperate with me, I can be sure that you will never get another job in the Washington area, in this industry, again."

Vinson was a young "single mom and terrified at the prospect of disappointing or upsetting Taylor," who had enormous control over her ability to make a living. But in that motel room, "Nobody locked the door. Nobody put a gun to her head," Sellers says. This could have been held against his client, who submitted to intercourse with Taylor that day. "The question was whether she had shown—and it was viewed as a burden on her to show—that the conduct was unwelcome." If Vinson didn't do enough in this regard, the blame was on her.

Since handling Vinson's case, Sellers has spent many decades representing victims of sex discrimination. He views the unwelcomeness test as a poor fit for the workplace with its myriad power imbalances. "In my experience, it's very rare that, where an overture is made by somebody with considerable power over the woman's future, the person says something as direct as, 'Please don't do that. That makes me uncomfortable.' Instead, they make excuses. 'Well, I'm sorry, I'm busy tonight. I'm busy tomorrow night.'"

The question for a jury, if a case makes it that far, is whether the victim's conduct was "sufficiently clear to show unwelcomeness," Sellers notes. This inquiry readily lends itself to blame-shifting. Particularly when the relationship between the harasser and his target is hierarchical, an accuser may not be positioned to *do enough* to be seen as a victim rather than an enabler. As Sellers puts it, the Court's unwelcomeness standard is "behaviorally unrealistic in many settings." When victims are especially vulnerable, they are unlikely to satisfy the legal burden imposed on them. Without power in the workplace, a woman will find it difficult to directly confront her abuser about the unwelcomeness of his behaviors, leaving her a prime target for whatever comes her way. "And that's the nature of harassment," Sellers explains. "People typically do it to women who they think are vulnerable, otherwise they wouldn't do it."

———

An accuser's sexuality is often weaponized by the legal process to this end: she, not he, will be blamed for what happened to her. In civil cases, pretrial discovery rules allow intrusive examinations into the lives of plaintiffs, and accusers may be subjected to broad questioning about their sexual lives in preparation for trial, where this information may or may not be allowed.

In one typical case, filed in federal court in 2013, a teenage restaurant worker who alleged she was harassed and raped by her thirty-five-year-old supervisor sued the restaurant chain for damages. The defendant wanted to inquire about a huge swath of the young woman's sexual history. Over objection, the court granted the defendant's request and ordered the accuser to do the following:

> Identify all dating or sexual relationships (both consensual and nonconsensual) that you have had, including the dates

of each relationship and the names, dates of birth, and current contact information, including addresses and telephone numbers, for each individual with whom you have had a dating or sexual relationship, and as to any physical relationship describe the nature. State whether, prior to you being 16 years old, you have communicated with any individuals over the age of eighteen for the purpose of beginning or continuing a dating or sexual relationship. If so, state the names, dates of birth, and current contact information, including addresses and telephone numbers, for each individual with whom you have such communications as well as the dates of each such communication. State whether you have ever become pregnant and if so, state the dates of the pregnancy. State whether you have ever contracted any sexually transmitted disease and if so, state the date(s) and name(s) of the disease(s).

On the criminal side, a rape accuser who testifies can be cross-examined with her sexual history. "Rape shield" laws are meant to protect victims from just this kind of attack, which pervaded rape trials until the new rule emerged in the 1970s. But the protection of the rape shield is not absolute. Women may be punished by an exception that, in several states, allows evidence of past consensual sex that doesn't conform to a judge's idea of acceptable female sexuality. Even with the rape shield rule in place, accusers have been asked at trial about past sex work, group sex, sex in public, sex outside monogamy, sex with perceived frequency, teenage sex, and woman-initiated sex.

The admission of sexual history evidence "increases the blame people assign to a woman who has been raped and decreases the blame they assign to the defendant," writes the legal scholar Michelle J. Anderson. Still today, victims "who have stepped outside of the traditional bounds of feminine sexual modesty" are unlikely to receive the benefit of our doubt, or the protection of our laws. When their sexual pasts are harnessed against them, accusers are readily portrayed as unworthy victims—victims who deserved, at least in part, their abuse.

By coming forward, accusers place themselves under a sexist microscope—often to be dismissed. One lawyer I spoke with described a typical "heavy victim blaming" defense in a case he was handling at the time. By disparaging the accuser for her sexuality and a supposed lapse in judgment, the defense was banking on "enough 'bad behavior' on the part of the victim" to turn jurors against her even if they believed the alleged conduct occurred. In other words, the defense centered on blame (*he's not responsible*) rather than distrust (*it didn't happen*). This strategy is effective because it taps into commonly held beliefs about women's accountability for their abuse and widespread unwillingness to hold men answerable for their misdeeds. "Don't mix alcohol with beauty," Jillian Corsie was warned—not because the officer didn't believe her account, but because he held her alone responsible.

———

The law's preoccupation with the victim's conduct increases the odds that complaints of harassment will be settled on the cheap, dropped, or dismissed. The story of a woman named Crystal shows how seemingly strong cases for liability can devolve. Several of Crystal's coworkers saw a male coworker "pinch, kiss, poke, and hug" female workers, including Crystal. They also heard the harasser "direct explicit sexual propositions and vulgar remarks at Crystal" and at other women. Crystal complained to her employer at least once following a "hard smack on the backside," but to no avail. She ultimately quit her job despite the financial stress this entailed—Crystal was a single mother who wasn't receiving child support payments. She decided to take legal action because, as she put it, "someone has to take a stand; they can't treat people this way."

As her lawyer would later recall, "this was not the usual 'he-said-she-said' case; at his deposition, the harasser did not deny making the sexual comments or engaging in the physical touching." But that admission was not enough. Without disputing the truth of Crystal's factual allegations, the employer's defense was that the misconduct was welcome. To advance this defense, "the employer turned a searchlight on Crystal's behavior," however unrelated to the workplace abuse. Pretrial discovery was wide-ranging. Crystal had two children with different fathers, one of whom she never married. She met her current boyfriend online, and he quickly moved in with her and her young children. She discussed her personal life with coworkers and offered unsolicited advice on relationships. She distributed Valentine's Day cards at work. Questions were asked about "how often Crystal went out with coworkers after hours—leaving her children at home—how many drinks she had imbibed and whether in that setting she had responded in kind to sexually charged jokes and comments."

Her lawyer recalled that Crystal was hurt and humiliated by this treatment. "She became fearful and angry when I counseled her that I did not know whether a judge or jury would understand that discussing personal lives or laughing at racy jokes over drinks after work did not constitute an invitation for a coworker to engage in sexual vulgarity and shoulder-rubbing on the job," Crystal's attorney wrote. "I knew intuitively that her tight jeans, low necklines and bleached hair would not help." All this had a tangible impact on Crystal and her willingness to pursue the claim. Her lawyer recalls, "Crystal had been prepared to handle unemployment, financial uncertainty, litigation and even cross-examination as to the story she had to tell. She was not willing to be attacked, innuendoed and mislabeled; therefore, she accepted a settlement. . . . She ended the case with a sense of bitter enragement that her former employer had turned her story of righteous whistle-blowing into a tale of a workplace tart who brought trouble onto herself."

When a sexual harassment victim proceeds beyond discovery, a common defense at trial is that she welcomed the abuse. One analysis of the case law concludes, "The result is an inquiry into what type of person the plaintiff is, and whether that type of person would have wanted to be propositioned, touched, or spoke to in the way that the defendant chose." To show that the accuser was not a real victim, courts over the years have admitted evidence that the accuser was molested as a child. That she was assaulted as a teenager. That she had a troubled marital history. That she raised a daughter with significant problems. That she allowed nude photos to be published. That she did not wear a bra under her T-shirt. That she used crude language. That although "she continually asked" the harasser not to touch her and "attempted to avoid his hugs," "her requests were not delivered with any sense of urgency, sincerity, or force."

Without evidence to the contrary, women are assumed to invite whatever sexual advances come their way. Our culture and our law require accusers to displace a presumption of welcomeness. When they can't satisfy this burden, we blame the accuser. Her harasser, meanwhile, is seen as yet another hapless victim of female sexuality. He escapes without consequence. And, as we'll now see, she falls into the *care gap*.

5

THE CARE GAP

HOW VICTIMS ARE DISREGARDED

Vanessa Tyson aims to make the world a better place. It's important to start there. She doesn't define herself exclusively as a survivor of sexual violence. "One difficulty about coming forward is that this isn't what I want to be known for," she says. "This happened to me. It certainly affected me. But it's not the entirety of who I am, nor has it ever been."

Tyson teaches politics at Scripps, a prestigious women's college in Claremont, California. In the summer of 2004, when the Democratic National Convention came to Boston, where Tyson was a twenty-seven-year-old graduate student at nearby Harvard University, she volunteered as a logistics coordinator, helping to ensure the event ran smoothly. There she met Justin Fairfax, who was also attending the convention as a campaign staffer. The two quickly realized they had a close mutual friend from Fairfax's days at Columbia Law School. Tyson remembers that she and Fairfax "laughed about what a small world it was, particularly for African Americans at elite institutions." On the third day of the convention, when Fairfax asked Tyson to accompany him to retrieve papers at his nearby hotel room, she had no reason to hesitate. She would enjoy a few minutes of fresh air and sunshine after days holed up in the convention hotel, where she was staying.

When the two arrived at Fairfax's room, Tyson stood in the entryway while he looked for his papers. He then walked over and kissed her—an advance she recalls as "not unwelcome"—and she kissed him back. This is where it should have ended, she insisted when we spoke, adding that she was "fully clothed in a pantsuit and had no intention of taking my clothes off or engaging in sexual activity." But "what began as consensual kissing quickly turned into a sexual assault," she wrote in a statement released to the public in February 2019. Tyson describes how Fairfax pulled her toward the bed, put his hand behind her neck, and forcefully pushed her head toward his penis. "Utterly shocked and terrified," she recounts, "I tried to move my head away, but could not because his hand was holding down my neck and he was much stronger than me. As I cried and gagged, Mr. Fairfax forced me to perform oral sex on him."

Afterward, she just wanted to return to her hotel, which felt safe. "I was stunned," she says. "I don't think I had words for it. I mean, maybe this is luck . . . that most of the men I dated were physically respectful of boundaries. Nobody had ever used physical force against me in that way. I kept trying so hard to lift my head and I couldn't."

She managed to avoid Fairfax for the remainder of the convention, and she told no one what happened. She was humiliated and ashamed. Not only did she volunteer at a Boston rape crisis center, where her mission was to empower survivors of sexual assault. She was also, as she emphasized, a "Harvard graduate student who prided herself on intelligence." She felt she should have known better than to "walk into a trap." She says, "It takes a long time to come to terms with the fact that the punishment for 'trusting' shouldn't be oral rape."

Tyson kept her silence for over a decade. Then, in October 2017, when she learned that Fairfax was running for lieutenant governor in

Virginia, she began quietly telling friends about her encounter with him. Later, in February 2019, she would come forward with her allegation widely, but only after she had been awarded tenure at her university. When I asked Tyson if there was any link between that tenure grant and her decision to publicly accuse Fairfax, she was clear: "I had security." She explained, "Look, I grew up with not a lot of money. I was raised by a single mom who didn't get a dime from my father. . . . My mother never went to college. Growing up, I understood I had nothing to fall back on." As Tyson saw it, tenure was a "job for life," and this "privileged position" allowed her to finally divulge her account of abuse.

Fairfax denied the allegations and claimed his sexual encounter with Tyson was consensual. "At no time did she express to me any discomfort or concern about our interactions," Fairfax maintained.

Soon after Tyson went public with her story, a second accuser came forward to allege that Fairfax raped her when the two were undergraduates at Duke. (Tyson didn't know the second accuser.) Fairfax denied her accusation as well.

He also compared himself to a lynching victim, and Tyson found this association "disgraceful, irresponsible, and manipulative." "Never was it two black women lynching black men," she told Gayle King on *CBS This Morning*. "One need only look at history to try to understand that, in fact, the role of black women had always been leading anti-lynching campaigns. You know, black women were lynched specifically trying to protect black men."*

---

* Fairfax later sued CBS for defamation and intentional infliction of emotional distress based on the network's broadcast of King's interviews with Tyson and the second accuser. The suit was dismissed by a federal district court, and Fairfax—who announced his run for Virginia governor in September 2020—has appealed.

During our conversation, Tyson cried only once: when she talked about her life in the months after her allegations made national news. "I didn't know what was going on. I was so scared," she says. She worried about her safety and the safety of her loved ones—not for fear of Fairfax himself, but of those who sided with him and sent threats her way. Although Tyson and the second accuser both called on the Virginia General Assembly to hold public hearings where each woman would testify, no hearings ever took place, and Fairfax kept his job despite calls from some Democrats for him to resign. The status quo was preserved, as is typical.

In hindsight, Tyson feels less that her allegation was disbelieved than that it didn't matter. "One thing that I notice about sexual violence is that a lot of people would like to glance away from this," she has remarked. She understands why survivors ask themselves whether coming forward will "do any good," because often it doesn't.

But Tyson would make the same decision to report, even knowing that Fairfax would never face public hearings and that he would remain in office—knowing that the man she says sexually assaulted her would suffer no consequences whatsoever. She returns to her privilege as a tenured professor that enabled her to come forward, and cites the many survivors who don't have the economic security to face the likely backlash. Although the entire experience has exhausted her, she nevertheless believes coming forward was "the right thing to do."

People with power protect others with power, she says, and sexual assault victims become "collateral." For all of us, caring about survivors and their needs is destabilizing—it disrupts our lives and the societal structures that order them. To preserve the status quo, we must disregard allegations of abuse, no matter how believable. We overlook the women who suffer, and their worth.

———

In the realm of care, the credibility discount and the credibility bump work together to ensure the protection of the powerful. By "care," I have in mind concern, regard for the plight of another—what *matters* to us. It turns out our care is distributed unevenly and predictably: the suffering of an abuser who could face accountability for his misdeeds matters far more than the suffering of his victim. The disparity between inadequate regard for survivors and excessive regard for offenders reflects what I call the *care gap*.

The care gap reflects structural inequalities while covertly bolstering them. This gap actually consists of many asymmetries, which track hierarchies that include gender, race, class, and more. In other words, the odds that a person's suffering will matter correlates with privilege and status—we tend to care less about some victims than others, and more about some abusers than others. As the writer Rebecca Traister notes, "This is the *truly* grotesque factor: It is power itself that renders people recognizable to us, affords them our sympathy and empathy."

Because care is distributed along lines of power, marginalized accusers are the most readily dismissed. When we spoke, Fatima Goss Graves, the head of the National Women's Law Center, observed, as "#MeToo went viral, and millions of people were saying 'me too,' I don't think it was an accident that it was celebrities who captured the nation's attention." The actress Ashley Judd and accusers like her—mostly white women with considerable social capital—were able to jump-start a movement because, as Graves says, "we're conditioned to care more about people with power and influence."

For men, power and influence provide a buffer against allegations of misconduct. Those in positions of professional and social dominance are permitted to maintain their status without the upheaval brought about by accountability. This is a privilege long granted to revered male elites. The culture that supports and affirms these men exerts a powerful gravitational pull toward protecting them. "Women's careers and psyches have been torpedoed by male exploitation for centuries," writes Jia Tolentino in the *New Yorker*, "but it is a shame, apparently, for the men who exploited them to have to answer for what they've done."

When we assess credibility, as a rule, our concern flows away from accusers and in the direction of the men they accuse. Philosopher Kate Manne has suggested that this allocation of credibility "serves the function of *buttressing dominant group members' current social position*, and protecting them from *downfall* in the existing social hierarchy: by being, for example, accused, impugned, convicted, corrected, diminished," or otherwise held to account. A "disposition" to side with the men against the women who accuse them can feel "like simply being fair to the men who stand accused, rather than being *unfair* to the women who are making these accusations," Manne notes. This ostensible neutrality disguises a systemic safeguarding of powerful men and their array of entitlements.

OUR CULTURAL TENDENCY TO DISMISS allegations of abuse aligns with the very human impulse not to intervene. This general preference for circumstances to remain the same is referred to in the field of behavioral economics as the "status quo bias." The psychologist Daniel Kahneman, who won the Nobel Prize for his efforts to integrate insights from cognitive psychology with economic science, explains that we are intensely motivated to defend the current state of affairs. This bias, also known as loss aversion, is a "powerful conservative force that favors minimal changes from the status quo," Kahneman writes. Research in this area has largely focused on financial decision-making, but it clearly has broader import, as noted by Kahneman and others. The studies tell us that we are pushed in the direction of decisions that settle rather than destabilize.

"All the perpetrator asks is that the bystander do nothing," says the psychiatrist Judith Lewis Herman. "He appeals to the universal desire to see, hear, and speak no evil. The victim, on the contrary, asks the bystander to share the burden of pain." A credible accusation of sexual assault or harassment is profoundly unsettling. Herman observes that, by coming forward, "the victim demands action, engagement, and remembering." And if we reframe what was done to her as unworthy of consequence, we can avoid the disequilibrium that would follow if we did the opposite: care.

The care gap is widened by our selective propensity to feel others' pain. "Empathy is biased," writes the psychologist Paul Bloom, who cautions against overreliance on empathic decisions. Although often viewed as an unmitigated good, empathy "distorts our moral judgments in pretty much the same way that prejudice does."

When an accuser comes forward, the credibility of her account and of the accused's denial is bound up in whose suffering matters. And while empathic tendencies vary from person to person, as a whole, our culture is oriented to the pain of the powerful. This orientation can lead us to mete out care unfairly from the beginning—but even if we start from a less biased place, the credibility complex often leads us to the very same, dismissive end. Our concern is apportioned along axes of power, accentuating the gap between victim and abuser.

"CAN'T YOU TAKE A JOKE?": LAUGHTER AS DISREGARD

Sexual assault and harassment are often repackaged as humor, guaranteeing that an accusation won't elicit our concern. When abuse becomes a joke, we need not care, so we need not act. What may seem like harmless fun is in fact further violation.

Consider the case of Leticia Vallejo, who for nearly two decades worked as a housekeeper at a hotel in Southern California. As she would later allege in her lawsuit against the hotel, Vallejo was subjected to sexual harassment in the form of comments from men who would leave the hotel bar to use the lobby restroom while she was cleaning it. She says that she repeatedly complained to management and asked for a sign that would allow her to keep people out while she was working, but her requests were denied. In the summer of 2017, Vallejo was cleaning the restroom when a seemingly intoxicated man groped her breasts, rubbed his erection against her, and offered her $50 in exchange for a sex act. She immediately fled.

When Vallejo shared her account with her supervisor, she recalls that his response was to laugh. "He should have offered you $100," the supervisor remarked. Vallejo says that hotel management never investigated her complaint. "There's no protection," she observes. "Somebody needs to listen to us."

Lauren Teukolsky, the Los Angeles lawyer who specializes in employment discrimination cases (and also represented Vallejo in her suit against the hotel chain), told me that, whether the abuser is a patron, a coworker, or a supervisor, she sees a "high tolerance" for a "constant drum beat of sexually inappropriate behavior at work." If Teukolsky's clients complain to their human resources department or to a supervisor, the response is often, "Oh come on, can't you take a joke?" or "You just need to lighten up. This is your problem for not being able to see how funny this is." When harassment is framed as innocuous workplace banter, perhaps even flattery that ought to be appreciated, women's claims of harm are dismissed.

The abuse of marginalized and vulnerable workers is particularly likely to be trivialized as innocent fun. Like many of the thirty women employed at Ford Motor Company's Chicago factories who would eventually sue the company, Suzette Wright is a Black woman who says she endured ongoing sexual harassment. After ignoring repeated overtures and crass comments from male coworkers, Wright finally complained to her union representative after a man she considered a mentor offered to pay her $5 for oral sex. The official took the man's side, not because he didn't believe Wright's allegation, but because he considered the harassment harmless.

Wright would later describe how she was diminished by the harassment she endured—it made her feel like she was "getting smaller" until she was "just like a shell of a person." The union representative recast Wright's suffering; if it existed at all, it was inconsequential, silly. Wright says the official told her, "Suzette, you're a pretty woman—take it as a compliment." When another employee at the Chicago factory reported to a union representative that her manager had pressed his groin against her, she was given a similar directive: *you should be flattered*. In 2000, Ford agreed to pay $9 million in damages to the women while denying liability.

Across industries, accusers find their abuse mocked and trivialized when they come forward. Jenna Ries is a Michigan woman in her thirties who sued McDonald's for enabling a "culture of sexual harassment" at its franchises. Ries alleges that a restaurant swing manager routinely grabbed her outer vaginal area, breasts, and buttocks, and that he once forced his penis into her hand. Ries says she frequently came home from work crying; she felt physically ill; she was anxious; and she dreaded her shifts while also fearing that she would lose her job, which paid the rent and bills. Other women who reported similar harassment to their general manager also say he did nothing to address their ongoing abuse. Instead, they describe him insisting that the accused man was "just joking," and they were "being dramatic." The women's ordeal was of no concern. Quite the opposite—all of it was made to seem amusing. Ries alleges, "On the numerous occasions that workers reported that the swing manager had smacked a woman's buttocks in view of the security cameras, the General Manager would often laugh alongside the swing manger even after reviewing the tape." This was not distrust; this was disregard. They didn't care.

In *Boys & Sex*, Peggy Orenstein recounts several well-publicized stories in which humor was deployed as a means of dismissing sexual assault. For example, a high school boy from Steubenville, Ohio, was caught on video joking about how his friends assaulted an unconscious girl at a party. "She is so raped," the boy said, laughing. When someone suggested that rape wasn't funny, he replied, "Rape isn't funny—it's *hilarious*." Orenstein observes that those who view assault as "hilarious" can dismiss it—"They don't have to take it seriously, they don't have to respond: there is no problem." This also helps explain why abusers sometimes describe their assault as "funny." As Orenstein explains, "in order for a morally reprehensible act to be seen as a joke, it has to be considered harmless by the perpetrators; they have to resist identification with the subject, ignore pain."

Finding humor in abuse is commonplace among offenders and those who surround them, to this end: indifference to a victim's suffering benefits abusers who escape consequence. And it further disempowers those they hurt. Nevertheless, those most disadvantaged by this dynamic can also fall prey to it.

THE CARE GAP INTERNALIZED

No one remains untouched by the cultural forces that cushion powerful men from accountability—not even survivors. When a victim internalizes the care gap, righting the wrong that was done to her seems less important than preserving the abuser's impunity. This dynamic has repeatedly surfaced in conversations I've had over the years with accusers, who dwelled more on how disclosure would harm the abuser than how *they* were harmed by the assault or harassment. A culture that routinely downgrades the worth of victims in relation to perpetrators is a culture that muzzles accusations of abuse.

BEGINNING IN CHILDHOOD, A PREMIUM is placed on self-sacrifice for girls, who learn that their self-worth is attached to caring for others. Girls are "trained from an early age to take men's needs and desires more seriously than their own." This training cultivates what the legal scholar Robin West has called "the giving self"—an individual who defines herself by the care she provides to others.

Girls grow up likely to perform far more than their fair share of emotional labor in intimate relationships and even in professional settings, as "work wives." For many women and girls, caring for others takes priority over their own "interests, ambitions, projects, and independence." This lack of regard for the self—a failure to "give oneself one's 'due,'" as West describes it—is "harmful and injurious."

Women's "disproportionate embrace of the giving self" does not emerge by chance, but as a central feature of subordination. The philosopher Kate Manne writes, "Patriarchal ideology enlists a long list of mechanisms" to ensure that women adhere to an ethic of selfless care. The list includes distinct narratives about women's "proclivities and preferences." It also includes "valorizing depictions of the relevant forms of care work as personally rewarding, socially necessary, morally valuable, 'cool,' 'natural,' or healthy (as long as women perform them)." These "enforcement mechanisms" are what Manne calls "the functional essence of misogyny."

The giving self takes responsibility for her abuser's continued success and well-being while magnifying what accountability would entail. Research shows that under circumstances where gender is salient, women are further prompted to see the needs of others as paramount. As the philosopher Kate Abramson told me, in the typical case of sexual misconduct, gender is *quite* salient, which makes an accuser even more receptive to the message, "Oh, have some sympathy" for the man who did this.

This "over-regard" for the abuser means that consequences, however minimal, are deemed an unacceptably high price for him to pay. Many women are reluctant to come forward because they don't want to "ruin a man's life." Nicole Johnson, the psychologist with expertise in treating sexual assault survivors, sees this regularly. She remembers one particular client whose rapist belonged to a fraternity with close ties to the victim's sorority. Members of both organizations banded together to discourage the victim from reporting to the university. And they gave her the familiar warning—it "could really ruin his life."

LAURIE PENNY IS AN AUTHOR who has written about surviving a relationship that involved sexual, physical, and emotional abuse. "I've been that person struggling not to prioritize a man's pain," she says, "and I know how hard it is to break out of that mindset." She recounts how her abuser used a "combination of threats and performative weakness" to convince her and his other victims "that he was both too powerful to be crossed and too weak to survive being held accountable." Women are susceptible to this logic, Penny notes, "because most of us have been raised with the understanding that when men get upset, bad things happen." She adds, "Men, too, even decent and nonsexist men, have grown up with this understanding—that male suffering simply matters more."

WHILE PRIORITIZING THE AVOIDANCE OF any suffering on the part of the accused, survivors tend to minimize their own experience of violation. Psychologists and social workers regularly watch victims take to heart the message that they are less important than the accused. "So many people who've gone through a sexual assault say it's not that big of a deal," or "it could have been so much worse," says Johnson.

Many decide not to report because they think the assault wasn't serious enough to warrant perceived escalation.

Just as the stranger rape paradigm distorts how responders evaluate the credibility of victims, it twists how victims assess their own experience. Victims often measure their abuse against the stranger rape archetype; in comparison, their own attack may not seem all that bad. For some survivors, what makes their assault "not rape" is that the perpetrator used his fingers or an object for penetration rather than his penis, or that there were no outward injuries. For others, what matters is that they knew their assailant as a friend or an intimate partner. "It didn't even occur to me that this would be considered sexual assault," explained one survivor after a man she was dating forcibly penetrated her when she tried to end the relationship. "I thought this was a 'domestic violence dispute.'"

Even victims of unusually violent sexual assaults may trivialize their violation. Abby Honold, the University of Minnesota student who was raped by a man she just met, was severely injured, both internally and externally. When Honold reflected on her decision to call the police, she explained, "Well, he raped me *two* times. If he'd only raped me once, I probably wouldn't have called." Many survivors respond to their violation, at least initially, in a way that echoes the cultural indifference to sexual misconduct and its victims.

Of course, setting aside one's experience of abuse can prove impossible. Johnson describes her clients wondering why they're experiencing emotional distress if nothing terrible happened. Over time, those who first minimized their sexual assault may come to understand that it matters, as they matter. But unless this happens, a survivor will not feel entitled to report what happened.

Decades ago, on the night that Donald Trump allegedly raped her in a dressing room at Bergdorf Goodman, the journalist E. Jean Carroll recalls resisting her friend's repeated suggestion to call the police. As Carroll recounts, her friend said several times: "'E. Jean, I don't think this is funny,' because—and this is one of the strangest facts of all—I could not stop laughing."

THE URGE TO PLAY DOWN one's sexual violation is especially forceful in the workplace. Many victims who weren't physically attacked point to this fact as reason to overlook the misconduct they endured. Others trivialize their abuse as funny or innocuous, taking on board the cultural tendency to find sexual misconduct amusing. As one participant in a study of humor and harassment explained, it was best not to "take anything personal," since "if you do, you'll be in tears all the time." When asked to describe her workplace conditions, which included crass jokes about her body and other gendered insults, the woman began to cry.

Research shows that even when unwanted sexual advances offend victims, and even when their work or mental health suffers as a result, they *still* may not feel entitled to a workplace free of abuse. For many women, sexual harassment remains something to live through without complaint. When harassment is pervasive, it stretches the limit of what's considered acceptable—including by its victims. Unless an employee understands what happened to her as worthy of concern, she will not report the misconduct. This understanding is hard to come by, since survivors—like everyone else—are implanted in a culture that overlooks or trivializes harm to women. Workers who internalize the cultural directive not to prioritize the interests of victims will stay silent about their abuse.

Women of color who belong to racial groups that are widely fetishized for their sex appeal are less likely to perceive their harassment as worthy of complaint. Stereotypes of Latinx women, for instance, "not only impact their experiences with sexual harassment," but diminish their odds of reporting. Rather than speak out, many Latinx women resign themselves to what seems inevitable. Comedian Anna Akana has suggested that racial stereotypes likewise contribute to the pervasive harassment of Asian American women, who come to almost expect it. Akana says, "When you're so used to being hypersexualized, you don't even register it that much anymore as a violating thing." When harassment is normalized, it becomes a feature of existence.

The tentacles of the credibility complex reach farthest when they keep victims from seeing their sexual violation as worthy of redress. Across a range of workplaces, women commonly deal with sex-based harassment by avoiding the harasser, dismissing the incident, or downplaying it.

A good illustration comes from the medical setting, where harassment rates are high and women who are training to be physicians "learn to normalize their experiences of mistreatment and abuse, to see it as 'routine' and even a necessary rite of passage for a prestigious and demanding occupation." In a study, researchers spoke with medical residents about their experiences with workplace abuse. One surgical resident was standing near the sink with her freshly scrubbed hands held high, in a "kind of vulnerable" position, when the anesthesiology attending physician "patted" her on the butt. She recalls, "The first time I thought, maybe he was just slipping me a hand, or that, *maybe I was just being too sensitive*, but then it just went on and it went on and on like several times and I really felt uncomfortable and I didn't know what I should do, what should I say?" If she said something, she feared, "they're going to go, 'whooa, she's a real bitch, she's sure uptight, she's sure sensitive.'"

Another resident recalled a different attending anesthesiologist commenting on the shirt under her scrubs in the recovery room—"What's that sexy thing you're wearing underneath your shirt?" he asked. When she ventured that she thought this remark was inappropriate, he added, "Oh, come on, I meant it as a compliment . . .

Lighten up." When she was interviewed for the study, the resident second-guessed her own reaction to the doctor's comment, questioning the researcher about whether she was "being oversensitive," and querying whether the remark would have bothered the researcher. The resident admitted, "God, it just offended the hell out of me," and then added: "I don't know if I'm wrong."

Many sexual abuse victims absorb a cultural directive to minimize the severity of their abuse. In *Consent*, Donna Freitas describes having been stalked for more than two years by her graduate school professor, who—against her wishes—flooded her mailbox with letters, phoned her daily, appeared outside her apartment, and insinuated himself into her family. Throughout this period, Freitas wondered, and wonders still, whether she was overreacting to her professor's behavior. "Am I making too big a deal over it? Is it really innocent after all?" she writes. "You begin to doubt your judgment about everything," she observes. "I assumed the best about him, presumed any nagging feeling was my own fault, that I was just imagining things, inventing the unease that came to reside inside me . . . and never left me again."

THE LAW'S CARE GAP: SEXUAL HARASSMENT

When victims of workplace sexual harassment sue for damages, their allegation is often dismissed as insufficiently serious. Many women lose—not because their account is disbelieved, but because, in the eyes of the law, their violation doesn't matter. By setting an extremely high bar for what counts as actionable, sexual harassment law ignores real harm to victims. These victims fall into law's care gap, and we shield their harassers and their employers from liability.

One reason for this is that the law of private harms, otherwise known as tort law, traditionally overlooked sexual harassment. Until a new legal claim was created in the 1980s to recognize sexual harassment as sex discrimination, most women who suffered harassment on the job were without a legal remedy. The law as it existed until then failed to account for a societal backdrop that included gender inequality, both within the workplace and outside of it. These limitations inspired the feminist legal scholar Catharine A. MacKinnon to pioneer the claim of sexual harassment. Along with other activists and lawyers, MacKinnon persuaded the courts to place sexual harassment in context. "Practices which express and reinforce the social inequality of women to men are clear cases of sex-based discrimination," she declared in 1979. Less than a decade later, the Supreme Court would endorse this bold insight.

In *Meritor Savings Bank v. Vinson*—the case brought by Mechelle Vinson, who alleged harassment by her bank manager—the Court held that sexual harassment is a violation of Title VII, the federal law that prohibits sex discrimination in the workplace. But the victory for victims was qualified. According to the Court, writing in 1986, harassment is only legally actionable if it reaches the level of "severe or pervasive." It does not suffice for the worker to experience her environment as hostile or abusive. Instead, the law's hypothetical "reasonable person" must also perceive it this way. The legal standard puts judges and juries in the position of deciding whether, in their view, the harasser's conduct was egregious enough to count. If not, from the vantage of law, the abuse doesn't matter.

Three decades after *Meritor Savings Bank v. Vinson*, an analysis found "case after case where federal courts ruled that conduct is not sufficiently serious to be considered discrimination." By channeling the widespread impulse to minimize the toll of harassment, the "severe or pervasive" requirement often dooms a victim's claim. Cases have been dismissed when "women allege that their bosses or their coworkers repeatedly touched their breasts or buttocks, supervisors regularly asked employers on dates or for sexual favors, or employees were continually the victim of unwanted sexualized comments and gestures." Unless it makes work "hellish for women," as the legal standard was articulated as recently as 2002, the toll of sexual harassment is not the law's concern. Although the "hellish for women" test has since been formally disavowed, in practice it remains a fair description of what victims must suffer in order to receive the law's protection. Old legal definitions maintain their hold when they align with tenacious cultural understandings.

Courts tend to discount harassment that doesn't involve physical assault, however abusive the conduct. One woman said she endured a workplace where the CEO commented on the size of a female employee's rear end, asked about a female employee's pubic hair, remarked on a female employee's "hickey," noted that he liked "dark skinned women," told a female employee that she needed to get a new haircut because she looked "butch," cited Bible scripture maintaining that men are superior to women, and suggested to the plaintiff that he could "take her from her husband," in exchange for money. Writing in 2018, a federal court held that the women's allegations "simply do not rise to the level of severe or pervasive sufficient to sustain a sexually hostile work environment claim."

To support this conclusion, the court cited an earlier case holding that the victim's allegations fell "well short of the level" required to qualify as actionable sexual harassment. In that case, as the court described it, the woman testified that her supervisor told her, "'I'm getting fired up,' rubbed his hip against hers while touching her shoulder and smiling at her, made sniffing noises while staring at her groin, and constantly followed and stared at her for eleven months." The dismissal of allegations as insufficiently severe or pervasive can have "a kind of domino effect, leading to the dismissal of later cases," as the legal scholars Sandra F. Sperino and Suja A. Thomas observe. "After one judge deems a case with significant evidence of harassment as not severe or pervasive enough to be called harassment under the statutes, other judges believe they must dismiss later cases with similar or less evidence of harassment."

Throughout the law, verbal abuse is trivialized. Employers are not liable for what courts have countenanced as "off-color comments, isolated incidents, teasing, and other unpleasantries that are, unfortunately, not uncommon in the workplace." This tolerance for verbal harassment licenses a range of abuse. A supervisor who, over the course of months, commented that the victim "had a cute ass," requested that she wear dresses so he could stand at the bottom of a ladder and look up her skirt, and inquired about her menstrual cycle. A boss who regularly rubbed or grabbed his crotch in the victim's presence, stared at her breasts, told her she smelled good, and commented that she should "wear low-cut blouses and short skirts." A supervisor who repeatedly asked the victim if she was "'getting enough' lately," told her she looked "young and beautiful," and propositioned her for sex. In each of these cases, the allegations were dismissed as beneath concern before the victims had a chance to prove them.

Even when the harassing conduct is physically assaultive, time and time again it falls short of the legal standard. One victim, a cashier at a parking facility, described having suffered repeated incidents of physical and verbal abuse by her manager during her eighteen-month employment. According to the woman's account, he once touched her breast and sexually propositioned her. On a separate occasion, he "made several suggestive comments" and offered to pay her if she would date him. On a third occasion, he offered her a drink and asked her to join him at a hotel where they could have a "good time." In a final incident, he "patted" her breast and buttocks. Throughout this period, the woman said, the manager would remark on her lower socioeconomic status. Yet her allegations didn't meet the legal standard. While the manager's "purported behavior is loathsome and inappropriate," the court wrote, the victim "has at best demonstrated sporadic and isolated incidents of harassment."

The court pointed to a string of cases that were also dismissed— all because the harassment was deemed not severe enough, or not pervasive enough, to count. A supervisor's "ten incidents of harassing conduct over two years" were "not frequent enough" to create a hostile work environment. A supervisor's "rubbing employee's shoulders, grabbing employee's buttocks, and offensive touching were not severe enough to create" a hostile work environment. A supervisor's "four incidents of unwelcome contact with subordinate's arm, fingers, and buttocks, along with repeated sexual jokes aimed at subordinate," were not severe enough to create a hostile work environment. A supervisor's "repeated requests for a date, kissing subordinate without her consent, and touching her face" were not severe enough to create a hostile work environment. On and on, yet none of these allegations would amount to sexual harassment under the law.

Nor would it be actionable harassment for a supervisor to rub a victim's shoulders and back, call her "baby doll," and tell her she should go to bed with him. For a manager to bombard a victim with "sexually suggestive comments" and leering looks, phone her at home to say he missed her, and "inappropriately" touch her breast. For a supervisor, over time, to touch a victim's knee, rub his hand along her upper thigh, kiss her until she pushed him away, and "lurch" at her from behind the bushes "as if to grab her."

Sexual harassment victims are degraded, objectified, demeaned, humiliated, tormented, diminished, dehumanized—and still their suffering does not matter. One woman said she was repeatedly subjected to comments about her breasts, requests to lick whipped cream and wine off her body, solicitations for dates, and unwanted touching of her shoulders, arms, and buttocks by male employees. Another woman recounted ongoing abuse by her supervisor, who told her she was only there "because we needed a skirt in the office," asked her to spend the night with him in a hotel room, asked her to "blow" him, unzipped his pants in front of her, and referred to women as "bitch," "slut," and "tramp." One woman described harassment by her supervisor that included him asking her out on dates, inquiring about her personal life, calling her a "dumb blond," touching her shoulder repeatedly, placing "I love you" signs at her workstation, and, on several occasions, attempting to kiss her. The law did not recognize these women as victims.

Federal civil rights law is not alone in perpetuating this neglect. State tort law is designed to redress civil wrongs that cause damage. But it also defines the harm of abuse narrowly and in ways that are incompatible with the realities of abuse. This disconnect was one of the main reasons that activists and scholars argued for a reframing of sexual harassment as sex discrimination. Yet many victims of workplace harassment cannot turn to federal civil rights law for relief. Only employers of a certain size—in the private sector, those with fifteen or more employees—and workers who satisfy a narrow definition of "employee" are subject to the dictates of Title VII, the law that prohibits employment discrimination based on sex and other protected characteristics. And because supervisors and coworkers cannot be individually sued under Title VII (or under many analogous state civil rights laws), a victim who seeks damages from her harasser must assert a tort claim, which presents a distinct set of obstacles.

In order to prove "intentional infliction of emotional distress," a plaintiff must show that the offending conduct was "extreme and outrageous." This standard ignores behavior that is wrong and harmful, but also normalized. Conduct that has long been permitted in the workplace may not seem extreme or outrageous to judges, who often find that sexual harassment does not qualify—even if it meets the stringent federal law definition of "severe or pervasive." When courts dismiss a claim for failure to satisfy the standard of outrageousness, they do so not because the allegation is disbelieved, but because it's considered too trivial to matter.

One supermarket employee said she was subjected to "sexual propositions, vile and filthy language, off-color jokes, physical groping, and the posting of sexually suggestive pictures." Her claim was dismissed because the evidence did not "establish the requisite outrageousness." In another case dismissed as insufficiently outrageous, the plaintiff was fired after confronting the company president about his harassing behavior, which was said to include "hugging and refusing to release her in spite of her resistance, rubbing her breasts with the back of his arm repeatedly, and making sexually explicit jokes and suggestive comments." One court found that an airline maintenance worker named Valerie failed to satisfy the test for outrageousness despite allegations that she suffered months of harassment. Pornographic pictures were repeatedly placed on her desk in her absence. Sexually loaded, derogatory comments were posted in public places and directed at her in person. On a separate occasion, the woman was mentioned on the office attendance board, which noted that a coworker was "Sick—Due to lack of blow jobs from Valerie." The misconduct was "not civilized behavior," conceded the court, which nevertheless concluded that "the acts described in the complaint do not reach the level of outrageousness required."

CERTAIN WOMEN ARE TREATED WITHIN law as especially unworthy of care—in particular, women who are tarnished by their past sexual encounters, whether consensual or nonconsensual. The law's embrace of "damaged goods" reasoning significantly expands the scope of pretrial discovery in sexual harassment litigation.

Courts have allowed inquiry into a victim's sexual history to show that the abuser didn't cause her mental or emotional injury. (A tort plaintiff must prove that she was damaged by the defendant's actions.) For instance, one defendant sought to question the plaintiff before trial about her consensual sexual relationships in the years following her alleged sexual assault in prison. The court permitted this, finding the inquiry relevant to whether the woman had truly experienced "severe psychological and emotional distress and difficulty in participating in consensual sex since she was allegedly attacked." Evidence of prior sexual abuse is often admitted for this same purpose—to show that the victim was already damaged when she was harassed or assaulted by the defendant. Even if she was harassed, "damaged goods" reasoning holds that the victim's harassment isn't cause for concern. A woman's history is used to taint her, and it's as if she has forfeited any claim to care.

When evidence of a woman's sexual history is allowed to undercut a claim of damages, the question is not whether the abuse occurred, but whether it matters. Some courts maintain that previous consensual experiences with third parties—not the abuser—make the abuser's unwelcome conduct less offensive. On this theory, courts have admitted sweeping evidence—evidence of a victim's extramarital affair with a coworker, evidence of sexual molestation by a victim's father, evidence that a victim's "many sexual relationships caused her to express concerns of shame, guilt and lack of self-esteem," and the like.

WOMEN WHO WORKED IN A Minnesota coal mine were the first to join together as a group to bring a sexual harassment class-action suit. When the case made its way to court, the testimony of the miners was vivid and powerful. One woman recounted stalking by a coworker and several incidents of abuse, including having her pants slit open with a knife. She described the anxiety, humiliation, and stress that she experienced as a result of the ongoing harassment.

On cross-examination, the defense attorney was given wide

latitude to interrogate this woman about her past. The point wasn't to deny the harassment, but rather to suggest that she hadn't been injured by it. The woman was forced to recall incidents dating back nearly five decades. When she was six years old, an uncle sexually abused her. When she later married, her husband was physically abusive to her and to her son. When her back was turned, her son climbed on the stove and burned himself. When she tried to leave her husband and bring her son to her mother's home, her mother turned them away. When she reported her husband to the police, he shot himself in the head. When she remarried, her second husband was even more abusive than the first. He sexually abused one of her daughters. The questioning went on and on, plumbing the depths of this woman's terribly difficult life, all in an effort to show that the harassment she endured at work didn't matter. By the time she finished testifying, she felt she had been "raped on the stand."

"THE MEASURE OF INJURY IS a telling expression of a culture's deeply held values," write the legal scholars Martha Chamallas and Jennifer Wriggins. Several lawyers representing victims of sexual harassment have mentioned to me how valuations of damages, which are inevitably subjective, are skewed by bias. Since poor women and women of color are often devalued, so is their suffering. Those who don't seek therapy, however unaffordable it may be, seem unharmed. Those who endure the abuse for as long as humanly possible seem unaffected. Those who return to work, if only because they depend on the paycheck, seem undamaged. These are the workers whose compensation is likely to be most diminished. These are the victims who are most disregarded.

The law's restricted use of money damages to measure the harm of sexual harassment further devalues victims. Research (and common sense) tells us that workplace abuse can cause productivity to decrease, which limits opportunities for promotions and transfer. But these costs can remain hidden, and are not easily quantified if they are exposed. Losses that are noneconomic and nonphysical tend to disappear altogether from legal view. Harassment can reinforce a victim's inferior status in the workplace. It can sexually objectify, isolate, and alienate her. It can "stigmatize and dehumanize" her, along with other workers who share her identity. These "distinctive harms" of sexual harassment are not easily captured by conventional legal understandings of injury or readily measured in dollars, as Martha Chamallas observes.

Even if juries were inclined to care about these harms, the law establishes caps on damages that can be awarded for noneconomic injury. Under federal law, limits on sexual harassment damages available to workers have not increased since 1991. (Depending on the size of the employer, the range is $50,000 to $300,000.) Many states also cap damages for noneconomic losses, including pain and suffering. In this "hierarchy of value," harms routinely suffered by victims of sexual harassment are the least conducive to compensation.

Caps also serve a "screening" function, limiting "the number and kind of cases that plaintiffs' attorneys are willing to accept." This disadvantages workers with smaller economic losses—those at the lower end of the pay scale, who are also most vulnerable to harassment. The suffering of marginalized victims is devalued when the law privileges market-based loss.

In 2011, a New York court reduced the damages awarded to a young woman who was sexually harassed while working at a franchise sandwich shop. The woman, Carolan Henninge, was a high school student at the time. The owner of the shop, also her supervisor, subjected Henninge to "touchy feely" interactions, sexually loaded remarks, and "constant pressure" to visit him in his apartment. When she ultimately did so, the man raped her.

Henninge returned to work without reporting the incident—she was frightened and she needed the job. When her abuser once again ordered her to come to his apartment and she refused, he "swore at her, sent her a series of angry, insulting text messages, and told her that he understood her refusal to mean that she was quitting her job."

On appeal, the court held that punitive damages in the amount of $500,000 for "mental anguish and humiliation" was excessive. The conduct "including, among other things, forcible sexual intercourse with a high school student—was unquestionably reprehensible," wrote the court. But Henninge apparently did not suffer enough to warrant the compensation, which an administrative law judge had set. The court acknowledged that Henninge felt "violated" and frightened; she "wept as she testified that, more than a year after the events in question, she still experienced difficulty in trusting others." When she worked in the sandwich shop, she seemed "distressed and irritated, withdrew from friends and family, and lost interest in activities she had previously enjoyed," according to her mother. And Henninge "sought medical testing for communicable diseases as well as counseling." Yet the court was unconvinced that this qualified as the kind of damage that merited $500,000. Henninge "attended only two counseling sessions, apparently required no further medical or psychological treatment, and within several months was able to return to work for a different employer," stated the court before reducing the young woman's damages to $50,000.

THE LAW'S CARE GAP: RAPE

Rape law has long denied protection to the most vulnerable victims. This absence of law is an offshoot, and a driver, of asymmetrical care. When Black women were slaves, their rape—whether by white masters or by Black men—was lawful. In keeping with this approach, when the Mississippi Supreme Court dismissed charges against a male slave in 1859, it made clear that the rape of a young Black girl was not a crime. "Masters and slaves can not be governed by the same system or laws; so different are their positions, rights and duties," wrote the court. Other state courts reached the same conclusion, dismissing indictments where the victim was not white.

Change was slow and incomplete. In 1860, the Mississippi legislature criminalized the rape of a Black girl under the age of twelve by a Black man, while still allowing the rape of Black women and the rape of Black girls by white men. Rape statutes finally became race neutral after the Civil War. But the criminal justice system remained steadfastly hostile to Black women and their claims. In a sentiment that encapsulated prevalent attitudes toward Black accusers, one judge remarked in 1974, "With the Negro community, you really have to redefine the term rape. You never know about them." Harm to Black survivors went untouched by law.

By defining what's illegal, we designate the injuries that most matter. Despite over a century of reform, rape law continues to side with abusers when it places certain types of harm outside its boundaries. The law overlooks sexual violations that don't fit a narrow definition, excluding victims and harming them in untold ways. "It is extremely damaging to be raped or sexually abused," writes Robin West. "But it is made all the more so by virtue of the sure knowledge that *you have to take it*: that one is *not entitled* to redress for these harms; that one has no *rights* in the face of their occurrence." Victims who learn their injury isn't important enough to be recognized by the law confront a devastating truth about how little they matter.

Jenny Teeson, a hospitality sales associate, had been married to her husband for more than a decade when she came across a collection of videos that he had recorded two years earlier without her knowledge. One clip revealed her getting dressed. In another, Teeson and her husband were having sex. As upsetting as this footage was, Teeson discovered more. According to a criminal complaint filed soon after she found the video, her husband had forcibly penetrated Teeson with an object while she was sleeping with their four-year-old son beside her. The couple's New Year's Eve party had ended a few hours earlier, just as 2015 was ushered in. After viewing the violation of her motionless body, she wondered if she had been drugged prior to the assault.

Teeson reported the crime to police. She had every reason to believe that the case was a strong one. Since the assault had been caught on video, typical concerns about believability would seem to fall away. But Teeson's husband was not prosecuted for rape. Instead, he was charged only with two misdemeanors—one for criminal sexual conduct in the fifth degree (meaning a nonconsensual touching with sexual intent absent aggravating factors), and the other for interference with privacy (based on the nonconsensual recording). Under the terms of an agreement with prosecutors, the sex crime was dismissed; the defendant pleaded guilty to the privacy violation and was sentenced to forty-five days in jail.

Teeson learned that criminal statutes tied the prosecution's hands. Under the law in Minnesota, which also exists in other states, because she was married to her assailant at the time of the incident, what happened to her did not qualify as rape. Even though the crime was visible for all to see, Teeson's husband was protected by a code that granted him a sexual license to do whatever he wished.[*]

THROUGHOUT OUR HISTORY, THE LAW has authorized the sexual assault of women by their husbands. Under the common law of "cov-

---

[*] Teeson subsequently worked to persuade lawmakers to repeal Minnesota's exemption, although the change came too late to alter the outcome of her case.

erture," a woman who entered into marriage became her husband's property; she ceased to exist legally. Writing in 1765, one influential treatise writer explained, "The husband and wife are one person in law: that is, the very being or legal existence of the woman is suspended during the marriage." The historian Estelle Freedman explains that, from our country's origins, a husband was entitled to control his wife's property, her earnings, and her very person. Because the husband subsumed his wife's political, economic, and legal identity, he was also seen as possessing rights to her body. He was entitled to beat her. He could restrict her movement physically. And he could access her sexually. This regime lasted through the late nineteenth century.

By entering into marriage, a woman had "given up herself" in ways that made rape by her husband a legal impossibility. Alongside coverture, the law incorporated a notion of perpetual wifely consent. In essence, women were contractually obligated by virtue of the marriage to have sex with their husbands. During the 1800s, commentators and judges would routinely refer to a wife's consent as "irretractable." Since, by definition, a wife consented to all sex with her husband, he could not conceivably rape her. Rape laws delineated what a "male person" could not do to "any woman, other than his wife." This total immunity for husbands was known as the marital rape exemption.

By the 1960s, sex outside the marital relationship had become far more commonplace. In response, the rules were changed—not to give women more rights, but to expand male prerogatives, entitling men to behave like husbands whether they were married or not. Applying the marital rape exemption to cohabitants and to so-called voluntary social companions, the law extended immunity for sexual violence. A blueprint for state legislatures—the 1962 Model Penal Code—provided a partial defense to rape where the victim was "a voluntary social companion of the actor upon the occasion of the crime," and where she had "previously permitted him sexual liberties."

Wives were no longer the only women whose sexual violation was considered lawful. Even outside marriage, within dating and intimate relationships, men were now given cover. The "improper inference of ongoing consent in sexual relationships," the legal scholar Michelle J. Anderson writes, "affects rape by intimates, regardless of the marital status of the parties."

In the mid-1970s, opponents began chipping away at rules that enabled sexual assault by intimates and acquaintances. That said, while the marital rape exemption has softened, it persists in different guises. Although it's now illegal in every state for a husband to rape his wife, most states continue to find ways to treat marital rape differently today. For example, ten states maintain special obstacles to prosecuting sexual misconduct where the victim is a non-consenting spouse. A third of the states create a spousal exemption where a victim is incapable of consenting to sex—notably, if she's unconscious.

When an exemption applies, a woman's rape allegation must be dismissed—even if she is believed. By ignoring injury, the law diminishes the victim who comes forward to say that what happened matters. For all practical purposes, her claim of worth is rejected. As Robin West explains, "The state did not and will not respond; the culture does less; it must truly have been inconsequential. It 'was nothing.' And since it was inconsequential, I too, who nevertheless *felt* harmed, must be inconsequential."

———

Absent considerable physical force, for most of our history, nonconsensual sex was not considered a crime. And after decades of reform and considerable progress, this remains the law in much of the country. In nearly half the states, penetration without consent is not outlawed unless it is accomplished by physical force or the imminent threat of it. How much force satisfies the legal definition of sexual assault? The bar is normally quite high. "Typically an excessive and unrealistic amount of it is required," writes Catharine A. MacKinnon, "often with weapons that do not include the penis, in a standard that more often seems to have in mind a fight to the death between two men than a forced sexual interaction."

As we know, cases involving weapons and serious physical injury are the rare exception. The clinical psychologist David Lisak has found that rapists routinely use "instrumental" rather than "gratuitous" violence—that is, they "use only as much violence as is needed to terrify and coerce their victims into submission." In the typical non-stranger rape, not a lot of violence is necessary to force sex. Verbal pressure and "pinning" may well suffice. But these tactics seldom qualify as legally sufficient force.

The force requirement has the effect of positioning most sexual assault as beneath the law's concern. Consider a 1992 case that is taught in criminal law courses around the country. The victim, unnamed in the court opinion, testified that she was acquainted with her rapist, Robert Berkowitz, through mutual friends. Both were college sophomores when she went to Berkowitz's dorm room to look for his roommate. Berkowitz made several overtures, which the victim rejected. He then approached her where she was sitting on the floor after declining his request to join him on the bed.

As the victim described to the court, Berkowitz "kind of pushed" her back with his body, "straddled" her, and began kissing her. The victim said she needed to meet her boyfriend, but Berkowitz ignored her protests and fondled her breasts under her shirt and bra. The victim said "no." Berkowitz "undid his pants" and "moved his body up," and tried to put his penis in the victim's mouth while she continued saying "no." She couldn't move because his body was on top of hers. Seconds later, Berkowitz got up and locked the door. Still, the victim was saying "no," and "let me go." Berkowitz positioned her body on the bed and straddled her again while he removed her pants and underwear. He put his penis inside her while she repeatedly said "no." He pulled out after about thirty seconds and ejaculated on her stomach. The victim promptly reported the assault to police.

At his trial, Berkowitz admitted that he had sex with the victim and maintained she had consented. Given how "he said, she said" cases are normally resolved, it's remarkable that the jury rejected his version of events, credited the victim's account, and convicted Berkowitz of rape. But the conviction did not stand. According to the court deciding Berkowitz's appeal, there was no "forcible compulsion," as rape law required. "Except for the fact that appellant was on top of the victim before and during intercourse, there is no evidence that the victim, if she had wanted to do so, could not have removed herself from appellant's bed and walked out of the room without any risk of harm or danger to herself whatsoever," the court wrote. The victim's "verbal resistance"—her continuous use of the word "no" to indicate an unwillingness to engage in sex—could not qualify as forcible compulsion, insisted the court. Even accepting every word of the victim's testimony as true, Berkowitz was not guilty of rape.

Still today, sexual assault allegations that lack excessive force are infrequently prosecuted. In the rare case where prosecutors move forward and persuade a jury beyond a reasonable doubt, these charges may still be dismissed by a court. In one such case, a man "placed his penis" in the victim's mouth while he "had his hands on the back of her head," and "she unsuccessfully attempted to stop the act." An appeals court reversed the conviction for lack of force. In another case, a man entered an acquaintance's home where she was sleeping with her two children next to her. The woman awoke to find the man's fingers inside of her. His conviction was reversed, also for lack of force. The same result commonly occurs when victims are intoxicated, afraid, trusting, or surprised.

"Because the law has always understood 'injury' as a broken arm or a knife wound," the psychological damage suffered by rape victims is "ignored or devalued," writes Lynn Hecht Schafran, an attorney and legal director of the National Judicial Education Program for Legal Momentum, a leading nonprofit that advocates for women and girls. All told, in nearly half the country, the force requirement reflects a very specific judgment about what kind of injuries matter. In these states, the harm of nonconsensual sex is cast aside.

"EVERYTHING SLIDING TO HIS SIDE"

Our tendency to elevate the importance of abusers exacerbates the care gap. When our concern for the accused man and the harm he'll suffer if held to account outweighs our concern for his victim, we don't act.

It will come as no surprise that powerful men benefit most from this excess of cultural regard. As Rebecca Traister observes, "The willingness to abuse power and then protect one's power by casting oneself as abused, via a fantasy of victimhood, surely has a lengthy history, but has become a particular hallmark of the post-Obama political era. The inversion of vulnerability so that it applies—nonsensically, ahistorically, yes, but too often, persuasively—to the least vulnerable is pervasive and effective."

Sexual misconduct presents a perfect case study in this inversion of victim and abuser. At its most extreme, accused men sometimes resort to lynching analogies to describe their travails. Remember that this is exactly how Virginia's lieutenant governor Justin Fairfax responded when Vanessa Tyson and a second woman came forward with sexual assault allegations against him. The strategic use of the history of racist violence "as a shield" contorts "very real history, in which (mostly fantasized or invented) claims of sexual aggressions against white women were used to justify the torture and murder of black men," Traister writes. Just as this arrangement most advantaged white men in power, powerful men continue to benefit when they reframe an abuse accusation as a metaphorical lynching.

The use of witch-hunting rhetoric is another common strategy. Throughout the sixteenth and seventeenth centuries, witch hunts "targeted the marginalized and comparatively powerless," explains historian Michelle Brock. Those executed for imaginary crimes were mostly women—indeed witch-hunting was "closely related to sex, if not solely determined by it." Today, when powerful men accused of misconduct are cast as victims of a witch hunt, this historical reality is turned on its head. "If anything," Brock suggests, these very men "resemble the authorities that drove these epidemics of persecution" of vulnerable women. The power that once enabled witch-hunting now enables sexual abuse while, at the same time, fending off accountability.

Men in positions of privilege take on outsized cultural importance, as does the potential impact of consequences for their misdeeds. Athletes. Politicians. Celebrities. Tycoons. High-status professionals. These men are granted special protection. For those already situated at the top and for those with a recognized entitlement to a "bright future," fame, fortune, and prominence confer impunity. Disrupting the lives of these men is perceived as too costly.

IN 1920, THE PSYCHOLOGIST Edward Thorndike identified what has come to be known as the "halo effect"—a cognitive bias that leads us to augment our positive impressions of others. In Thorndike's study, participants—male military officers—were too quick to correlate admirable traits that, in reality, are not correlated. Intelligence was linked to integrity, initiative to a sense of justice, and so on. Rather than independently evaluate whether, for instance, a successful person is also a loyal person, participants exhibited a tendency to "think of the person in general as rather good or rather inferior and to color the judgments of the qualities by this general feeling." One positive quality imbued a person with positive qualities down the line. As Thorndike concluded, "the magnitude of the constant error of the halo" was "surprisingly large."

Prominent men accused of sexual misconduct routinely benefit from the halo effect. John Clune, the former Boulder sex crimes prosecutor–turned–civil rights lawyer, has represented several women alleging abuse by powerful men, including prominent athletes. "Regardless of what happened," Clune told me, "if they threw for five touchdowns on Sunday or scored fifty points in a basketball game," many people seem not to care about what the accuser endured. A common reaction is to see the accused man as "a great human being because he can play sports." And "great" human beings rarely suffer consequences for inflicting sexual abuse.

When Christine Blasey Ford testified about Brett Kavanaugh's alleged assault at his confirmation hearing, one widespread response was indifference. Within the Senate and outside of it, even granting the accuracy of Ford's account, many believed that it shouldn't alter Kavanaugh's path to the Supreme Court. The legal commentator Dahlia Lithwick, who attended the hearing, wrote that Ford was told both that she was believable "and that it didn't matter a whit." She could be "the world's most reliable" witness and still what she alleged would not prevent the culmination of an apparent entitlement long in the making.

———

In 2016, Brock Turner, then a freshman swimmer at Stanford, was convicted of sexually assaulting an unconscious woman—Chanel Miller, as we would later learn—behind a dumpster in the wee hours of the morning. This kind of case would not normally result in an arrest, much less a successful prosecution. But two Swedish graduate students on bikes witnessed the assault and intervened, asking Turner,

"What the fuck are you doing? She's unconscious." Turner attempted to flee before being apprehended by the Swedish upstanders.

Their testimony, along with forensic evidence of penetration and proof of the victim's highly elevated blood-alcohol level, helped persuade a jury of Turner's guilt. When he stood before the judge for sentencing, he faced a prison term of fourteen years. Several of Turner's family members and friends had submitted letters that emphasized his promising life prospects. His sister wrote: "A series of alcohol-fueled decisions that he made within an hour timespan will define him for the rest of his life. Goodbye to NCAA championships. Goodbye to the Olympics. Goodbye to becoming an orthopedic surgeon. Goodbye to life as he knew it." His father wrote: "His life will never be the one that he dreamed about and worked so hard to achieve. That is a steep price to pay for 20 minutes of action out of his 20 plus years of life."

In her letter to the judge, Miller detailed the assault's enduring impact on her life. Miller wrote: "I am a human being who has been irreversibly hurt, my life was put on hold for over a year, waiting to figure out if I was worth something. My independence, natural joy, gentleness, and steady lifestyle I had been enjoying became distorted beyond recognition. I became closed off, angry, self-deprecating, tired, irritable, empty. The isolation at times was unbearable. You cannot give me back the life I had before that night . . ."

In 2019, Miller came forward with her more complete story. In *Know My Name*, she describes Turner's sentencing, where he received what amounted to a big break—probation with six months in jail, of which he would serve only half the time. Any harsher sentence, it seemed, would have unacceptably marred Turner's bright future—a future conditioned on privileges that included race, education, and athletic prowess. The judge adopted Turner's perspective, Miller says, "leaving me on my side and Brock to be coddled on his. . . . I finally felt the ground tilting," she adds, "everything sliding to his side."

Miller imagined sharing her dismal insight with sexual assault victims everywhere—"a system does not exist for you." Turner's sentence revealed how little they all mattered. "My lost job, my damaged hometown, my small savings account, my stolen pleasures, had all amounted to ninety days in county jail," Miller observes. She had laid bare her suffering, but it was beside the point. She writes: "The judge had given Brock something that would never be extended to me: empathy. My pain was never more valuable than his potential." (When an election two years later ousted the judge, the law professor who led the campaign against him remarked, "We voted that sexual violence, including campus sexual violence, must be taken seriously by our elected officials, and by the justice system.")

Many accusers experience this same devaluation when the men who hurt them are protected. Dozens of women have described sexual abuse by Jeffrey Epstein, the wealthy and well-connected financier whose crimes first came to the attention of law enforcement in 2005. According to the police chief who supervised the investigation in Palm Beach, one of several locations of Epstein's predations, "This was not a 'he said, she said,' situation. This was 50-something 'shes' and one 'he'—and the 'shes' all basically told the same story." Police investigators determined that, for years, Epstein had assembled and exploited a "large, cultlike network of underage girls"—some as young as thirteen, many from disadvantaged families—and coerced them into repeated sex acts. After the investigation was transferred to federal authorities in Florida, an FBI search of Epstein's mansion uncovered "hundreds—and perhaps thousands" of sexually explicit images of girls.

Instead of pursuing charges, however, the U.S. Attorney offered Epstein a jaw-dropping deal that two experienced former prosecutors described as "shockingly lenient." In 2008, the federal investigation was ended. In exchange, Epstein agreed to plead guilty in state court and serve a sentence of eighteen months in county jail. This arrangement was far outside the norm, which would typically involve substantial federal prison time. Former federal prosecutors have noted that the deal "raises every sort of red flag." The government's offer was not the result of prosecutorial overwork or neglect. Instead, it reflected a calculated decision, captured in a "non-prosecution agreement," to shield Epstein and his enablers at the expense of his vulnerable teenage victims. Prosecutors "did not want bad publicity for Epstein, they did not want other perpetrators exposed and/or they did not want the victims to object." Epstein was allowed to plead guilty to a state charge of soliciting prostitution—a "bit of legal logic that seemed to equate the coerced, abused children with adult sex workers," observes the writer Moira Donegan. During his incarceration, Epstein was permitted to leave jail six days a week to go to the office, where he continued to run his hedge fund. This jail sentence, such as it was, ended five months early when Epstein was released in 2009.

Epstein's exploitation of teenage girls was defended by a culture— and a legal system—disposed to preserve his interests. Undue regard for abusers found many outlets: the employees who helped Epstein capitalize on the desperation of marginalized girls and women; the influential friends who knew or should have known of his ongoing predations; the media that looked the other way rather than expose his crimes; the Florida prosecutors who bestowed the sweetheart deal kept secret from his victims; the jailers who allowed him to leave the grounds daily, during which time he allegedly abused at least one young woman; the New York prosecutors who recommended a downward departure from sex offender classification guidelines; the power brokers who by association legitimized his conduct. This treatment reveals "the broad cultural antipathy toward treating sexual abuse as real harm," as Donegan explains. It also shows that teenage girls matter much less than powerful men.

BLACK GIRLS AND WOMEN ARE at even greater disadvantage when their worth is stacked against their abuser's. "No one particularly cares that they are being abused," writes Moya Bailey, a feminist and critical race studies scholar who coined the term "misogynoir" to capture the racist misogyny that continues to be directed at Black females of all ages. At the same time, Black girls are often treated like fully developed adults, rather than children who require care—what researchers call "adultification." Because they are seen as less in need of "protection and nurturing" than white girls, Black girls' sexual violation tends to matter least.

Consider what we now know about singer R. Kelly. In 1994, Kelly illegally married his protégé Aaliyah, then fifteen years old and too young to legally wed. Federal prosecutors would later allege that Kelly bribed a government employee to obtain a fake ID indicating that Aaliyah was eighteen. Although their union was later annulled, accounts of Kelly preying on teenage girls continued to surface. By the late 1990s, several women sued Kelly, claiming he abused them when they were underage. In 2002, at the peak of his career, Kelly was charged with multiple counts of child pornography, discovered when a videotape was sent anonymously to a Chicago newspaper. Kelly's trial, which stretched over several years, featured a video that allegedly depicted Kelly having sex with, and urinating on, a fourteen-year-old girl who called him "Daddy." Still, despite the best efforts of prosecutors, Kelly was found not guilty—an acquittal that "concretized a message that Black girls are disposable," as the writer Ida Harris observes.

Since then, multiple women have come forward to publicly accuse Kelly of sexual assault and other violations, all of which he has denied.* "For nearly three decades," Harris writes, "R. Kelly's alleged

---

* Criminal charges against Kelly are pending in several jurisdictions.

abuse of young Black women has gone largely ignored—by the legal system that has ruled in his favor; by the media that either sensationalized or diminished these allegations; by Kelly facilitators who aided and abetted criminal and immoral behavior; and by the Black community which has protected this villain and devalued its girls." In 2019, the critically acclaimed documentary *Surviving R. Kelly* portrayed the story of Kelly's abuse and a collective failure to address it. "The fact his victims have been dismissed has everything to do with the fact they are Black girls," stresses dream hampton, one of the show's executive producers.

Music critic Jim DeRogatis broke the story of Kelly's alleged abuses in the *Chicago Sun-Times* back in 2000. For the next two decades, he worked to investigate Kelly in the hope of accountability—to no avail. "The saddest fact I've learned," DeRogatis remarks, "is nobody matters less to our society than young black women. *Nobody.*" In *Soulless*, DeRogatis identifies forty-eight victims of Kelly's abuse—women whose lives have been "significantly damaged and sometimes destroyed."

"Just as disturbing," DeRogatis writes, "I put the number of people who knew about or witnessed that damage in the thousands." Among them, DeRogatis mentions employees of record studios and labels, radio stations, magazines, newspapers, hotels, restaurants, high-end gyms, and nightclubs. Also on the list are Kelly's lawyers, accountants, drivers, security guards, and fellow musicians. "Blame a lack of empathy and morality almost as sickening as Kelly's," DeRogatis explains. "Many knew, and few did anything to stop him."

Kelly's victims were surrounded by people who didn't care enough to help. The collective indifference to their well-being was extreme. But countless survivors confront similar communal failures—failures that can be every bit as damaging as the abuse itself.

"EVEN WORSE"

WHY THE CREDIBILITY COMPLEX HARMS VICTIMS

Janey Williams grew up in the foothills of Hollywood among a diverse community of immigrants and struggling artists. The local high school was not "all about cheerleaders and athletes and who's cool and who's a nerd," she told me. Instead, the environment was kind and connected, conducive to creativity and collaboration. Williams and her friends were highly idealistic. When the tight-knit group graduated from high school, she says it "felt like the world was ours for the taking."

College was a letdown. The student body felt more homogenous and more conventional than what Williams was used to. She was an "oddball" who, for the first time, felt out of step with those around her. To escape and to see the world, she chose to spend some of her semesters abroad. Throughout college, her high school group remained in close touch, and Williams was eager to reunite with them after college. She moved back to Los Angeles in 2002.

As expected, after graduation Williams spent a lot of time with her old crew, including a young man I'll call Mark. The two were friends who had tried dating briefly before Williams ended the relationship. Mark never accepted that Williams didn't reciprocate his feelings, she says, and his behavior at times seemed obsessive. Still, she never thought he would hurt her.

The night she remembers most vividly from that period began like many others. The group met at Mark's home and drove in one car to a local bar, where Mark bought Williams a drink. Soon after she finished it, she became inexplicably sick. She ran to the bathroom and threw up, but afterward felt "fuzzy and weak," like she could "barely stand up."

Mark brought Williams back to his place, where her car was parked. When they arrived, he told her to rest and helped her to his bed. She felt "groggy and confused." At some point, she says he began to touch and penetrate her with his fingers. She said "no" and "stop" repeatedly, but he kept going. "We will never be friends," he murmured again and again. This "went on for some time," Williams recalls. She eventually managed to "push him away" and leave the apartment.

Driving home, she "suddenly felt quite sober." She wasn't ready to process the assault, she explained. "Deep down I knew immediately that there would be huge repercussions for me. That it would change everything in my life in ways that I didn't want it to and wasn't prepared for it to." She understood that her friends were "deeply invested in their friendships" with Mark. If she told them what he did, she feared they would dismiss it. And this would be unbearable. "How could I handle all of my friends knowing that he did that to me and not giving a damn? I would lose not only him, but all my friends who were like family." So she decided to keep quiet.

From the outside, life in the immediate aftermath appeared to return to normal. But Williams now found it too difficult to be around her group of friends, which of course included Mark. Soon after she was assaulted, she moved away and tried not to think about that night.

After several years and many therapy sessions, she decided she could no longer "live like that"—as if nothing happened. She realized that she would never know for certain if Mark drugged her—he would later deny this when she asked, although she says he did apologize for "losing it" and behaving the way he did at the apartment. But Williams came to understand that what happened was an extreme violation. She decided she would have to "face the repercussions" of coming forward.

All along, Williams feared that if she disclosed what happened, it wouldn't matter—nothing would change. She was right. When she told the people closest to her about what had happened that night, they acted as if there had been no assault. No one called her a liar, exactly. But they didn't actually believe her either. One friend would later tell Williams, "I thought you were telling *your truth*." It wasn't that Williams was "maliciously lying," as the friend put it. It was more that she was mistaken about the assault. This was Mark's version of events—Williams had somehow misconstrued what happened.

Of course, Williams's description left no real room for interpretation. As she would later press her friend, "What part of a girl being completely unable to move and function and you sexually molesting her while she says 'no, stop' . . . how do you think he could think there was a misunderstanding?" Still, when Williams asked her friend point-blank, "Did you believe what I was saying was true?" the friend answered, rather cryptically, "I believed that you certainly had every right to believe what you believed."

Mark's version of the incident was more convincing to their friends, Williams says, because they wanted it that way. It was easier not to take a stand, not to grapple with how someone in their midst—someone who they didn't see as a sexual predator—could do something so awful. Confronting Mark would have brought "drama." It would have required "changing their lives in some way." It might even have meant the end of their friendship with him.

When Williams came forward, she placed a burden on her

friends—a burden to act. Because they were unwilling to shoulder the load, they "buried it." Rather than "take sides," they dissected the way that Williams chose to share her story. One friend criticized her for posting the allegation on Facebook because the forum was "too public" for what should have been kept private. Another described the decision to come forward as "self-serving." Williams explains that although her friends' responses were "less obvious than traditional victim blaming," the judgment directed her way was much the same. Just as Williams had dreaded, they would "excuse him and move on."

This response was devastating, and the fallout would last long after Williams managed to move on from the actual assault, she says. She felt "deeply betrayed." Well into adulthood, she found it difficult to trust others or even to believe she was a worthy person. Her word had not been enough—no one cared that she'd been assaulted. This, she recalls, "was a hurt I couldn't name."

Time passed, and Williams created a podcast about her experience, which has helped her to better understand this hurt. She realized she was more damaged by her friends than by her abuser—because they "okayed" his abuse. One person doing "a bad thing," Williams says, "is much easier to come back from than when everyone around you sides with the person who did the bad thing." It leaves you "feeling that you're surrounded by the badness and you're trapped in it."

Williams stresses that her friends are "not bad people—they're people with consciences, they're people who loved me." This made their dismissal even worse. She explains, "We look to other people to reflect back to us what makes sense in the world, what's right and wrong. So if there's this thing inside of you that's telling you *this is really wrong* and *this is really bad*, but everyone around you is reflecting back that *you're really bad* and *you're really wrong*, that has a very powerful impact on your ability to heal. I mean, basically you can't."

When her thoughts drifted to the idea of going to the police, she quickly decided against it. "If you feel like your own friends don't want to hold the man accountable, why in the hell would you think anyone else would? They're the people who care about you most. And if they're incapable of going there, how could anyone else be capable of going there?" With everyone in Mark's corner, and no possibility of formal redress, Williams felt entirely alone. As she explains, when there's "no space or place for what happened in the world, you're left with it all inside you." She wanted Mark to be held accountable "in some small way" for what he did. But "everyone covered it right back up again," she recounts.

"Healing and moving forward from the sexual assault was a process," she told me, sixteen years after that night, while her young baby slept nearby. "But the reaction of my friends was the beginning of a new trauma that I am still working through." Finally she could identify the cause—when "what happens to you doesn't matter, you don't matter."

MANY SURVIVORS REFER TO THE aftermath of abuse as a "second rape" or "secondary victimization." Accusers who come forward only to be dismissed, like Williams, often describe fallout that is every bit as bad as—or worse than—the abuse itself. I've heard this from women who were distrusted, women who were blamed, *and* women who were disregarded. Regardless of why their report was cast aside, the credibility discount exacts an enormous toll. This is true whether the dismissal comes from a loved one, a trusted institution, or representatives of the state itself. Depending on the source of dismissal, however, "second rape" takes on a different meaning. We'll look at each harm in turn.

WHEN WE FAIL SURVIVORS

Whenever an accuser trusts us with her allegation, she puts herself in a vulnerable position. As I said early on, judging credibility is a mighty power. Our credibility judgments can validate and empower the survivor. Or they can inflict lasting damage.

Research consistently shows that when victims receive negative reactions to their disclosures—including no reaction, which comes across as indifference—they're more likely to suffer a range of mental, physical, and emotional symptoms as a result. "Betrayal, especially by a close and trusted person, can have far-reaching and damaging effects," writes the psychologist Jennifer Freyd, whose work on "betrayal trauma theory" helps explain why victims of sexual misconduct are often reinjured when they come forward to their loved ones.

Disclosure is meant to prompt a response that accepts the account as true, as a description of blameworthy conduct, *and* as deserving of care. When we credit an account, we accept this full trio of claims embedded in the accusation. By contrast, when we dismiss the allegation as false, as the accuser's responsibility, or as unimportant, we diminish the victim in a moment of great vulnerability.

In my conversations with accusers, most have mentioned that they were not only hurt, but surprised by the reaction of someone in their inner circle. These women expected more from those they trusted. This is consistent with findings that the "strength of victims' support networks," including friends, family, and romantic partners, was a poor predictor of whether accusers would receive negative reactions to their disclosure. The women I've spoken with often underscored that their loved ones were good people; the pain inflicted was surely unwitting.

Many accusers described a kind of soft dismissal: distrust was couched in benign terms, with the allegation framed as a mistake rather than a lie. Blame was subtle, pitched as supposedly helpful questions about what might have been done to prevent the abuse. Disregard was translated into advice, perhaps to "forget about what happened," or to "move on," all in an effort to proceed without further rocking the boat. Regardless of which discounting mechanism was deployed, however gently and innocently, survivors interpreted this unwillingness to disrupt the status quo as a measure of their worth. And precisely because the discounter was a trusted family member or friend, the measure had added significance.

The people closest to us should be *most* likely to believe our descriptions of reality and to care when we're hurt. When a loved one dismisses an allegation, it decreases the already slim odds that a victim will pursue a formal report. I've heard this from many women who chose not to go to the police, to their campus authorities, or to HR after someone they trusted responded poorly to their disclosure. Researchers have found this too: survivors foresee that the dismissive reactions of their confidants would be magnified by anyone without a personal connection. This is the anticipated credibility discount, as you'll recall, and it helps explain why official complaints are relatively rare. Victims also emphasize that the road to formal accountability is far too difficult to travel without the steadfast support of friends and family.

All told, personal betrayal can dictate an accuser's path forward in ways those closest to her may not intend or even realize.

MARISSA ROSS IS A WINE editor and an author. She lives in Los Angeles with her husband, dogs, and cat. In late 2019, Ross sparked national exposure of sexual harassment allegations against Anthony Cailan, a prominent sommelier. She was not a victim of his misconduct. But Ross had heard "Me Too" whispers related to Cailan that were circulating among women in the wine industry. She posted an oblique reference to the allegations on her popular Instagram account, and soon became a repository for the stories of dozens of alleged victims, whom she then connected to a *New York Times* reporter.

Ross explained to me that her decision to use her platform to help the accusers amplify their stories was influenced by her own experiences of sexual abuse and, crucially, its aftermath. When she was sixteen, a group of teenage boys forced her to perform oral sex on them. She told her friends, and they held her responsible for drinking too much. Several years later, her boyfriend violently raped her. She confronted him about it long after they had broken up, and he told her, "I was drunk, I don't remember, and you were my girlfriend." When she was in her twenties, she was attacked at a party by a coworker, who locked her in a room and tried to rip off her pants. She told her boss and coworkers, who "laughed it off" and remarked that she should have stayed away from the man.

More recently, during a night of drinking with a group of friends, she was grabbed in the bathroom, kissed, and thrown against the wall by one friend before others could come to her rescue. The next morning, the man who did this to her warned that their group of friends would be "destroyed" if she disclosed what happened. Ross stayed quiet for about six months before telling her friends and boyfriend (who is now her husband). "It did split up our friend group," she says. "And the guy who did it wrote a letter to my husband apologizing for my behavior and saying that everyone knows I'm an 'attention whore' and I came on to him, even though there were witnesses. It was so degrading, also that he was apologizing to my husband for my actions, like it was all my fault."

Throughout her career, unchecked sexual violation has been a virtual constant. Ross describes sexual harassment as an almost inevitable feature of the workplace. "Of course I've had my ass grabbed, I've had people say all sorts of ridiculous shit to me," she notes, mentioning that just a few months earlier, at a natural wine festival, a top winemaker had grabbed her breasts and informed her she had been "torturing him all weekend." She wasn't planning to tell anyone what happened, but six months later, decided to email the importer who partnered with the harassing winemaker. She had spoken to other women in the community about the winemaker and realized that this was a "pattern of behavior." "He should not be allowed to be pouring at wine events," Ross concluded, "where he can be sexually harassing and inappropriately touching women."

Ross had hesitated to officially report the winemaker because she knew firsthand—from all her past experiences—how "horrible" it was to disclose abuse. "Every time I told people, people blamed me, or hadn't believed me," she observes. "If you're getting discredited by the people around you," she asks, "why in the world would you go tell strangers and go through that again?"

Like Janey Williams and countless other women, Ross viewed the failed responses of those closest to her as a surefire sign that coming forward formally would be futile. Once her credibility was discounted by those who cared most about her—a separate violation—there was no reason to expect others to do better.

The notorious *Access Hollywood* tape that surfaced during the 2016 presidential campaign changed matters for Ross: she decided to open up about her past experiences of abuse. "When I heard [Trump] saying 'Grab them by the pussy,' I didn't just hear Donald Trump, I heard every man that's ever hurt me. It was those boys in high school, it was my ex-boyfriend, it was all those men. For me, and I imagine for many other survivors, it was not just hearing Trump, it was everyone that violated me."

Ross knows that disclosing misconduct comes at a steep price. She contemplates how her decision to report the winemaker to his importer might hurt her career. She considers whether people will stop inviting her to speak at their events, and whether she'll be blamed for outing someone whose success is lucrative for many powerful people in the wine industry. These worries are real even though Ross herself has power in this industry. Women with less financial and personal capital are worse off, she insists.

She finds it infuriating that people think accusers stand to gain when they come forward. "It's like, are you kidding me? We get dragged, just dragged."

WHEN TRUSTED INSTITUTIONS FAIL SURVIVORS

Formal institutions are integral to the workings of the credibility complex. When accusers choose to make an official report of their abuse, they are routinely failed by these institutions. The psychologist Jennifer Freyd calls this *institutional betrayal*. When I asked her why she was drawn to study the damage done by institutions, she pointed to then emerging accounts of military service members whose allegations were discredited. Many of these survivors, like Janey Williams, described the experience of coming forward as more damaging than the assault. "When people say that the way they're treated by institutions is even worse than a rape, I think we need to stop and pay attention, because that's a pretty strong statement," Freyd says.

Over the course of more than two decades of research, Freyd and other psychologists have shown that, just like victims who endure *personal* betrayal, victims whose institutions respond poorly to their disclosures tend to suffer greater psychological and physical symptoms as compared to victims whose institutions respond well. Study after study confirms: institutional failure can be more consequential than the initial violation.

PSYCHOLOGISTS EXPLAIN THAT OUR IDENTITIES are often formed in relation to the institutions to which we belong—our schools, our workplaces, our houses of worship. As we associate ourselves with our institutions, we become attached and grow to depend on them. When our institutions fail us, the betrayal can feel much like the betrayal of a loved one. For sexual abuse survivors, this betrayal comes at a time when the support of a community is urgently needed.

Trauma destabilizes victims, leaving them in a place of acute vulnerability. "Traumatized people feel utterly abandoned, utterly alone, cast out of the human and divine systems of care and protection that sustain life," writes the psychologist Judith Lewis Herman. Because a "secure sense of connection with caring people" is essential to human development, a victim of trauma "loses her basic sense of self" when this connection is "shattered." In the immediate aftermath of sexual violation, "rebuilding of some minimal form of trust is the primary task," Herman says. As a matter of course, the institutions in place to help survivors do the reverse: they demolish trust, reinforcing the victim's already diminished sense of self. Feeling disconnected, guilty, and inferior—these are "practically universal" emotions in trauma victims. A survivor whose community representatives dismiss her allegation will experience these feelings again, and often with greater intensity.

The philosopher Lauren Leydon-Hardy examines how our relationships to one another, and to our institutions, help us make sense of the world. As she said to me, "we are fundamentally social creatures . . . and all of our lives are deeply shaped by the institutions that we operate within and move between and depend on to give structure to our lives." Leydon-Hardy observes that when our institutions betray us, we "experience that as a loud signal." The signal tells us that our reality—for a victim, the reality of abuse—is misaligned with the institution's reality. The "sense of being in the upside down" is dislocating, even "horrifying," Leydon-Hardy explains.

She adds that institutional betrayal also signals that a survivor doesn't belong. When an institution sides against an accuser, it can seem like a judgment about her very worth—those who respond on behalf of the community value her so little that she is, in effect, disposable. By contrast, the abuser is valued and protected. Denigrated by the original violation, the victim is further diminished by those she trusted to right the wrong.

This devaluation is especially pronounced on college campuses, where widespread credibility discounts compound harm to accusers.

Caroline Heldman teaches critical theory and social justice at Occidental College. She is also a cofounder of the national survivor advocacy group End Rape on Campus, which was formed in 2013 as part of a larger effort to reshape how colleges and universities approach sexual assault. "We needed a national movement because we started to realize what we were up against institutionally," Heldman told me. "It wasn't simply a matter of a couple of 'bad apple' presidents, or a couple of 'bad apple' Title IX officers. It was systematic."

When leaders of this national movement began investigating how colleges were responding to sexual violence, Heldman recalls that certain patterns emerged. One was that during orientation, students weren't being educated about sexual assault on campus, reinforcing the belief that only violent stranger rape qualified, and further entrenching the traditional paradigm. If a victim of campus sexual assault later came to recognize the incident as a reportable violation, it was unlikely that she had ever been instructed on how to lodge a complaint with school officials.

Most victims who did manage to come forward met resistance at every step along the way. The message was clear: what happened, even if the accuser was accurately reporting it, was just not serious enough to warrant the university's involvement. Heldman says victims were commonly told, "I'm not sure that was sexual assault," or "I'm not sure that violates our code of conduct," or "It's just going to be really rough for you. Are you sure you want to go through this?

Your friends are going to turn on you, you're going to have to face him in a quasi-judicial setting"—in other words, a campus disciplinary hearing. This discouragement conveyed the accuser's unimportance to the institution. By disregarding her claims, campus officials were devaluing her worth.

If officials nevertheless chose to proceed with an investigation and adjudication, they consistently mistreated victims along the way. After the survivors endured that ordeal, Heldman recounts, "nothing would happen" to the accused man—nothing of consequence—even if he was found responsible. In the end, students who were assaulted on campus often learned a painful lesson about their place in the community.

Heldman, who has advised hundreds of student survivors over the years, says their school's dismissal can be pivotal. "It shatters their worldview because they really do believe in these institutions. They think that the world is better than it is, and it's that letdown that ends up stymying a lot of them professionally." Beyond the effects of the original trauma, that intense letdown is what tends to "shift their lives."

IN HER MEMOIR RECOUNTING THE experience of being sexually harassed as a graduate student, Donna Freitas writes about the lasting effects of her university's failure to act on her complaint. Although Freitas reported the abuse repeatedly, she says she never received an acknowledgment of the harassment, much less an apology for it. "That the only response I got was a demand that I pretend none of this ever happened, that I never speak of it again, had the effect of making me doubt that anything of substance did actually occur," Freitas explains. The impact of institutional gaslighting can remain even after the original trauma has dissipated.

This response is par for the course, Freitas observes. "It is an act of cruelty visited upon this person, a young woman who has just started on her way, who is at the very beginning of her professional life; an act that will hobble her for decades to come, this compelling her to pretend that all that she lived never occurred," Freitas writes.

Indeed, in the college setting, the credibility complex can leave searing marks on survivors. One study found that when accusers came forward, their academic advisors, professors, resident assistants, student government presidents, deans, campus police officers, and Title IX officials had "blamed them, stayed quiet, failed to provide support, and otherwise perpetuated institutional betrayal." These responses left survivors feeling "demoralized, mistreated, and alone."

Lynn, a first-generation college student who came from a "low-achieving" school district, was sexually assaulted during her first semester on campus. When she asked for permission to drop a class, Lynn was told by her academic advisor that perhaps she "just can't handle" college. She later said, "for a student like me" who had worked so hard to get into her college and was "told time and time again that she wasn't good enough for a top tier school, nothing could be more detrimental to my self-confidence . . . I fell apart after that."

Lynn is hardly alone in this regard. Victims who identified as lesbian, gay, or bisexual reported higher rates of institutional betrayal (even controlling for the greater frequency of their sexual violations), and they suffered worse psychological outcomes as a result. Other research supports the finding that sexual minorities are at heightened risk of institutional betrayal and its most harmful effects. In the wake of trauma, students who have been given reason to doubt their place on campus are especially wounded by the message that they don't belong.

WHEN I ASKED CAROLINE HELDMAN about changes to the landscape since End Rape on Campus began its work in 2013, she emphasized that there has been progress around the country. For the most part, school administrators have become less apt to dismiss sexual assault as unimportant, and they are more likely to address complaints that they once openly characterized as frivolous.

Of course, now some institutions simply pay "lip service" to the problem, as Heldman puts it, pointing to an "automatic assumption that the survivor is lying," and a "default" to the notion that she's not telling the truth. The credibility of accusers is still downgraded, but the typical form of the discount has mutated from outright disregard to intense skepticism.

THE STANDARD OF PERSUASION IN college disciplinary proceedings is lower than in criminal court—most schools require a "preponderance of the evidence" and some require "clear and convincing" evidence. Yet, as is true outside the college setting, student survivors often lose "he said, she said" contests; they may even lose when their allegation is supported by abundant corroboration.

Anna is one of many accusers who has been unable to convince campus officials of the *what happened* part of her claim. Two weeks into her freshman year at Hobart and William Smith Colleges, Anna says she was sexually assaulted by three students—all football players. The complaint that ultimately went to a college hearing board described repeated attacks on one night. It alleged that a senior first raped her at a fraternity house while a second student forced oral sex on her as a third student held her down. Later that night, the complaint alleged, the same senior raped her again, this time at a dance hall.

Anna's account was consistent with other evidence: Various text messages sent throughout the night. Observations made by friends during and shortly after the encounters. A blood-alcohol test indicating that, at the time of the first sexual encounter, Anna's level was twice the legal limit. Physical evidence that was discovered during

Anna's forensic exam—internal abrasions and heavy inflammation suggestive of forceful sexual assault.

The accused men denied any misconduct. The senior claimed Anna had performed consensual oral sex, but said he could not get an erection because he was tired from playing football and "a super long bus ride." Later, he maintained, Anna pulled his pants down and his "flaccid penis was rubbing up against her vagina" before he realized his conduct was "inappropriate" and pulled up his pants. A second football player said Anna performed oral sex on him while his teammate was in the room, but this was without his consent and he told her to stop. The third player said he left the room before any sexual encounter took place. According to a *New York Times* investigation, "Records show that the first two players had lied to campus officers when initially asked about Anna's allegations." The disciplinary panel, though, chose not to pursue these discrepancies. Hours after the hearing concluded, the panel found that the evidence fell short of the "preponderance of the evidence" standard (evidence that the allegation is more likely true than not), and the three men were cleared of all charges.

Like many victims, Anna came to regret reporting to campus officials. Along with the panel's dismissal of her complaint, she was subjected to students rallying in support of the football players and tormenting her with threats, obscenities, and ostracism. All of this eroded Anna's sense of self. College was meant to be her new home, a community where she could belong. When she first visited as a prospective student, she had instantly loved the campus. "This is what heaven looks like," she thought at the time, which made the school's response to her allegations even more hurtful and alienating. "I do not recognize myself—I have become someone that I hate," she has since said. "It was such a toxic environment that I needed to be home and try and find myself again."

BLAME-SHIFTING IS STANDARD FARE ON college campuses. While accused men are absolved of responsibility, blame is heaped on women who report an assault. It's not unheard-of for students who allege misconduct to be disciplined for violating conduct rules that prohibit alcohol, drugs, and premarital sex. Campus officials can penalize accusers whether they impose formal sanctions or not—for instance, one athlete claimed she was cut from the hockey team after coming forward with her allegation. (The school settled her lawsuit but denied wrongdoing.) Often when college authorities fault survivors for inviting their abuse or failing to stop it, the blame-shifting is implicit.

Annie E. Clark, an activist who graduated from the University of North Carolina and cofounded End Rape on Campus along with Caroline Heldman and others, says that, years earlier, when she went to ask about the process of reporting a sexual assault, she was told by her school administrator, "Rape is like a football game, Annie. If you look back on the game, and you're the quarterback and you're in charge, is there anything that you would have done differently in that situation?"

Clark and four other women went on to successfully sue the university for its discriminatory response to sexual assault. "I want every student to feel safe everywhere," Clark said in 2018, when the lawsuit was resolved in her favor, "but especially at school." Another plaintiff in the case, also a cofounder of End Rape on Campus, said this: "The only thing that's worse than rape is betrayal. That's something I've felt by this University time and time again."

COMPARED TO INSTITUTIONS OF HIGHER education, most elementary and secondary schools across the country are even less equipped to respond to sexual assault. "It's like the Wild West," remarks Adele P. Kimmel, a lawyer for Public Justice, an organization that represents students whose schools fail to address sexual violence. One client is a high school sophomore who says she was punished with suspension after disclosing that a fellow student forced her to perform oral sex. The girl sued the suburban school district for its alleged treatment of her complaint. According to the suit, a school resource officer asked what the girl was wearing and why she didn't "bite his penis." At a later disciplinary hearing, the district's lawyer reportedly concluded that the encounter was consensual because the accuser "chose not to scream louder and louder as this was going on." The girl was found to have violated the school's sexual misconduct policy for "participating" in sexual activities on school grounds, and she was suspended.

Suspension may be the ultimate act of institutional betrayal, and it's not an aberration. High school students are often pushed out of school when they report abuse. Research shows that Black girls in particular are most vulnerable to this treatment. The school's decision to side against them—to literally exile them from their community—is proof of how little they matter.

VIRGINIA, A HIGH SCHOOL STUDENT in Sacramento, was allegedly drugged and raped by two classmates at a party in 2016. Several students viewed a video of Virginia passed out on the bed with her pants off, and someone reported the rape to school authorities. When Virginia was called in to meet with the school's resource officer, she says she was asked a series of questions, including whether she was a virgin before the incident. This question made her feel "so bad," like "it wasn't as big a deal" that she was raped.

After she was questioned, Virginia says school administrators told her not to return to school for the remainder of the year. According to a complaint later filed against the school district in late 2018 and settled a year later, Virginia and her family were advised that because "all of the students were talking about the incident that occurred over the weekend," her presence in school was "distracting." No mention was made of the high school boys who allegedly raped her or those who shared the video of that night. To this day, Virginia says she doesn't know if any investigation was conducted. When she returned to school the following semester, she describes how "the rapists and their friends continued to harass and bully" her.

Virginia says the trauma of her rape was aggravated by how those in positions of power at her school mistreated her. After the incident, she attempted suicide, and was diagnosed with and hospitalized for post-traumatic stress disorder (PTSD) and depression. When she did finally return to school, her grades dropped from mostly Bs to Ds and Fs. She had to quit her restaurant job, which helped support her family. Her sleep habits and hygiene suffered, and she lost weight.

Because the school administration didn't seem to care what happened to her, Virginia wondered if something was wrong *with her*. When her lawsuit against the district settled, Virginia said she hoped to help survivors who also felt "like the whole world is against you."

CHANEL MILLER, THE YOUNG WOMAN who was assaulted on the Stanford campus by one of its swimmers, Brock Turner, was not a Stanford student herself. But she was raised near the university and she closely identified with the institution. In her memoir, Miller writes, "Stanford was my backyard, my community, a breeding ground for cheap tutors my parents hired over the years. I grew up on that campus, attended summer camps in tents on the lawns, snuck out of dining halls with chicken nuggets bulging from my pockets, had dinner with professors who were parents of good friends." Because of her relationship to Stanford, she had added reason to believe it would do right by her.

After her assault on campus and Turner's highly publicized arrest, Miller was not contacted by university officials for over a week. Although she wasn't a Stanford student, she had "hoped for an extended hand during that crucial period." Miller adds, "What I mean to say is I wish there'd been some display of care, some directing me to resources, some acknowledgement of what happened." Turner withdrew from the college and was no longer allowed on campus. Over time, Miller continued to feel neglected. Her assault "came and went" without an apology from the school or any apparent introspection on its part. Stanford's public statement after the trial ended was "unapologetic, almost prideful," Miller says—like "lemon wedges in the wound."

She writes, "The assault harmed me physically, but there were bigger things that got broken. Broken trust in institutions. Broken faith in the place I thought would protect me." Her assault and its aftermath seemed to fit a larger pattern, yet Stanford declined to address this pattern, Miller says, pointing to multiple failures: to conduct a systematic review of procedures, to ensure that services for victims are immediately available, to reevaluate safety on campus. In short, she explains, "They should have said, *It mattered, what happened to you.*"

———

Psychologists have identified the military's response to sexual misconduct within its ranks as a prime example of institutional betrayal. When "maintaining the cohesion of a military unit is prioritized above investigating or prosecuting reports of sexual harassment or assault," survivors suffer a separate—often more excruciating—injury. Because the military is "built upon trust, loyalty, and camaraderie," responses that discount the accuser's credibility are particularly damaging. Researchers have found that institutional betrayal following military sexual assault is associated with notable depression and PTSD symptoms.

MILITARY WOMEN ARE HARASSED AND assaulted at higher rates than their male counterparts, but many men are also betrayed by their superiors. Take the case of Justin Rose, who says he could hardly believe it when a fellow marine sexually assaulted him while he slept. The response of his superiors sealed this self-doubt. "My disorientation only worsened when I reported what had happened and the first question from my chain of command was, 'Are you sure you're not making this up?'"

The attack on Rose's credibility continued through the court-martial, where the military judge ultimately acquitted the man accused. "By the time it was over," writes Rose, "the Marine Corps had failed me three times: It had failed to take my claims seriously; then made my attacker out to be the victim and me the criminal; and finally failed to provide adequate support and resources in the aftermath of my assault (whether through access to sexual-assault counseling or something as simple as believing my story)." Rose was distrusted, blamed, *and* disregarded.

This credibility discounting caused harm that was severe and lasting. Over the years, Rose says, "I came to realize that it wasn't the assault that had the most enduring effect on me. It was people's refusal to believe that one man would assault another man. It was the mockery from leaders I had trusted and the implications that, if it had happened, I must have done something to invite it." For Rose, the military's betrayal was what he describes as a "second trauma" that was "orders of magnitude worse than the first."

A 2015 Human Rights Watch report offers this grim summary of what military accusers have suffered in the wake of their abuse: "Spat on. Deprived of food. Assailed with obscenities and insults—'whore,' 'cum dumpster,' 'slut,' 'faggot,' 'wildebeest.' Threatened with death by 'friendly fire' during deployment. Demeaned. Demoted. Disciplined.

Discharged for misconduct." "These people were supposed to be my family," says one army intelligence specialist whose supervisor discouraged her from reporting her sexual assault. She adds, "I was betrayed."

In the military environment and in other workplace settings, victims realize how little they matter to their employer when their allegations are dismissed. The recognition can be devastating—in particular, for victims whose identity is closely connected to their job. This second injury often persists long after a survivor has moved past the original violation, and it takes on a different meaning when it is inflicted on behalf of the state.

UNEQUAL PROTECTION OF THE LAW

Sexual assault victims whose credibility is discounted within the criminal justice system experience a distinct harm. When those charged with enforcing the law—police and prosecutors—decide an allegation isn't worth pursuing, the betrayal is a potent statement about the victim's worth. By protecting the abuser and not the accuser, law enforcement officers communicate to survivors that their violation does not matter. Because this dismissal comes with the state's imprimatur, it is a powerful expression of one's subordinate place in society. Whether a survivor is distrusted, blamed, or disregarded, she suffers a singular violation—one that occurs with infuriating regularity.

We know that police and prosecutors dismiss the vast majority of complaints before they ever reach the final phase of the criminal process (a trial or guilty plea)—what is called "case attrition." A 2019 study by the criminologist Melissa Morabito and her colleagues found that, around the country, police and prosecutors drop sexual assault complaints at striking rates. When it comes to sexual violence, case attrition is pervasive—most victims see their case dismissed rather than resolved.

Many survivors are dissuaded from pursuing a complaint after their initial encounter with police. Rachel Lovell, the sociologist whose research focuses on the police response to sexual violence, stressed to me that a victim's first interaction with a law enforcement officer is especially significant. "They're feeling vulnerable by telling something so intimate, and they're traumatized," Lovell explains. In this moment, survivors tend to look for signs of validation—acceptance of the trio of claims—or its opposite—disbelief along any of these dimensions. "And so that first interaction is very crucial to whether a victim continues with the investigation and prosecution," Lovell says. Lovell's research shows a "dramatic drop off" after the first encounter—survivors who feel dismissed may not pursue the complaint.

We know that more often, victims have no option, since police routinely put a premature end to most rape complaints. In the aftermath of abuse, this is a second injury, and it can leave lasting damage. This is why women are suing police departments for their allegedly biased treatment of sexual assault cases.

One of these women is Heather Marlowe. In May 2010, Marlowe and a group of her friends attended San Francisco's Bay to Breakers road race. While at the race, Marlowe was handed a beer in a red plastic cup. She drank it and, soon after, began to feel oddly inebriated. She regained consciousness inside an unfamiliar home, dazed and confused, with no memory of recent events. When she asked the man sitting in bed with her what had happened, he told her, "We had sex." At this point, Marlowe realized she had been drugged and raped. Soon after, she went to the nearest emergency room, where a nurse collected a rape kit.

The following week, Marlowe says that the investigating officer from the San Francisco Police Department (SFPD) instructed her to make contact with her alleged rapist, to "flirt with him" in order to elicit a confession, and to "set up a date" in order to prove she could identify him. Marlowe says she was told that if she refused, the police department would stop investigating her rape.

When she met with the investigating officer, she maintains that he "strongly discouraged" her from pursuing the case. According to Marlowe, the officer indicated that "it was too much work for the SFPD to investigate and prosecute a rape in which alcohol was involved." But she was not dissuaded. Eventually, Marlowe was told that the suspect's DNA sample had been collected and that her rape kit results would be available shortly.

Over the next two years, Marlowe repeatedly and unsuccessfully asked the police to test her rape kit. At one point, she says officers advised her, "because she was 'a woman,' 'weighs less than men,' and has her 'menstruations,' that [she] should not have been out partying" on the day of the incident. Soon after her kit was finally tested, Marlowe discovered that the attitudes she faced may not have been outliers. In 2014, SFPD acknowledged that "several thousand" rape kits dating back to 2003 remained unprocessed.

Marlowe sued the City of San Francisco, along with various top police officials, charging that the police department had a practice of failing to diligently investigate sexual assault allegations, as evidenced by the thousands of shelved rape kits. Marlowe could not proceed with her case—it was dismissed based on the statute of limitations and a legal hurdle facing plaintiffs who allege unconstitutional discrimination. But similar complaints against other police departments and cities have already been settled, and some are now proceeding.

In 2015, Marlowe and Meaghan Ybos formed People for the Enforcement of Rape Laws. Ybos had waited nine years for the Memphis Police Department to process her rape kit. In the meantime, her rapist assaulted five other women and a twelve-year-old girl. "Investigating and solving a rape case takes actual police work," Marlowe and Ybos write. "Detectives must find and interview witnesses, interview the victim, track down evidence, corroborate the account of events with both the victim and witnesses, and compare the case details to unsolved cases to try to detect patterns. Yet instead of doing this necessary legwork, police unfound, downgrade, and 'disappear' rape cases."

Think back to the stranger rape paradigm and the "perfect victim" archetype. Law enforcement officers often refer to "righteous victims"—women who didn't know their attacker, women who fought back, women with unblemished pasts. "If I had a righteous victim, I would do all that I could to make sure that the suspect was arrested," one police detective told the criminologist Cassia Spohn, before adding, "but most of my victims don't look like that." Spohn, an expert on the criminal justice system's response to sexual violence, calls the comment typical.

Rebecca Campbell, the psychologist who focuses on law enforcement's handling of sexual violence, encounters this same attitude in her work. "For members of society who are deemed not as important, their violence and victimization is not something that the criminal justice system is going to attend to," she says. Scarce law enforcement resources exacerbate this neglect. Campbell's research suggests that women "are treated particularly poorly by the system because of their intersectional identities." This can feel like a "second rape," she observes.

IT WAS THE SUMMER OF 2004, and Lucia Evans had just finished her junior year at Middlebury College when she met Harvey Weinstein by chance at an upscale Manhattan club. Evans aspired to be an actress. So it seemed like a break when Weinstein asked for her number.

In the coming days, when he called and invited her to meet at the Miramax office, she agreed.

At the meeting, Evans says Weinstein assaulted her. Over a decade later, she told the journalist Ronan Farrow that Weinstein forced her to perform oral sex while she said, "over and over, 'I don't want to do this, stop, don't.'" Evans recounts that she tried to escape, but "didn't want to kick him or fight him." She later wondered whether she did enough to prevent her assault. "That's the most horrible part of it . . . people give up, and then they feel like it's their fault." The shame, she says, "was also designed to keep me quiet." Weinstein denies assaulting Evans.

Evans recalls that she mostly kept silent about what happened, telling a few friends only pieces of the story. She began engaging in self-destructive behaviors, and her schoolwork suffered, as did several relationships. "It was always my fault for not stopping him," she felt. "I was disgusted with myself."

In October 2017, soon after the *New Yorker* published Farrow's article featuring Evans's account, detectives from the New York Police Department urged her to file a criminal complaint against Weinstein. Evans says this meeting with detectives felt "surreal." Unlike the other women who had publicly accused the mogul of abuse, Evans wasn't an actress—after her encounter with Weinstein, she abandoned her dream and became a marketing consultant—so she was unaccustomed to the spotlight. "And it was frightening to me," she says, "because I didn't do this for the press, obviously. I didn't do this for any kind of fame or fortune."

She was scared about the impact on her family. She was nervous about how the defense would try to destroy her credibility. "I know what criminal proceedings can be like," she explains. "I've seen a bunch of movies, and I've watched a lot of court TV. It's like, I know how this could go. And I think that the narrative has always been that victims are torn apart on the stand. And why would you do that to yourself? Why would you put yourself or your family through that?"

Detectives feared Evans would be in danger if she remained in her home and offered to relocate her. She and her husband left D.C. and temporarily moved to a house near New York City. While she considered whether to cooperate, she consulted with lawyers, family members, and friends, who all gave her similar advice: don't. "They're going to talk to everyone you've ever worked with, everyone you've ever been in a relationship with, find anything they can to discredit you," Evans was warned. "They'll go through your trash and find every single thing you've ever done in the past, and blow it up out of proportion, and shame you, and just ruin your life, basically."

When it came time to make a decision, Evans did what many of us do when faced with difficult choices—she made a list. The reasons not to participate in Weinstein's prosecution were compelling: "fear for my safety, fear for my family, my reputation, my career—everything. All these things would just be ruined." On the other side of the list, there was just one reason: "because it feels right." She agreed to cooperate with prosecutors, and, in May 2018, they charged Weinstein with her assault. Evans became a witness for the state and began the long process of preparing for trial.

Four months later, Evans learned that her allegation was being dropped. "I was blindsided," she says. "The thing that had consumed my life for the past year, that has taken its toll on my marriage, my family, my career—it's just over. I felt so abandoned. I felt betrayed." Prosecutors announced that they had learned about a conflicting witness account—one of her friends had apparently informed the investigating detective that, soon after the incident, Evans described the oral sex as consensual.

Evans disputes this version of events. But she was portrayed as a liar in the press and pilloried by Weinstein's legal team, who also questioned the integrity of the detective and his work on the entire case. According to Farrow, who continued tracking Evans's tribulations, "sources in the D.A.'s office still privately say that they found her credible, and essentially dropped her because they were being maximally conservative about safeguarding the charges associated with the other women in the case."

After the assault, Evans remembers thinking, "I just needed some type of validation, that I was okay and that I was still a good person, because I still thought it was my fault, which obviously it was not." More than a decade later, had the prosecution moved forward, had Weinstein been held to account for his alleged assault on her, this would have provided needed validation.

Instead, Evans describes feeling abandoned and betrayed. Much of what she feared when she agreed to cooperate with law enforcement had come to pass. Since the beginning, Evans worried that she was "just a tool to be used for someone else's objective." In the end, this concern proved to be warranted. "I was a pawn. I was disposable," she says. A year after her charge was dismissed, she was still processing how the experience harmed her. "I have to be honest, I haven't fully dealt with this, and it's still really a struggle."

This struggle is all too familiar—it's the struggle of survivors everywhere who suffer from the workings of the credibility complex. It falls to all of us to change this.

7

BEYOND BELIEF

WHEN SURVIVORS MATTER

Alison Turkos has talked about her rape many times. Even so, she finds it difficult to recount what happened, just as others find it difficult to listen. "I understand that my story is very hard to hear," she told me. "The reason I understand that is because I had to survive it."

In the fall of 2017, after a night out for drinks with friends, Turkos, who was in her late twenties, called a car service to take her home. Instead, she says, "my Lyft driver kidnapped me at gunpoint, drove me across state lines, and, along with at least two other men"— men who were waiting in a park—"gang raped me." The Lyft driver later dropped her back at home. What should have been a fifteen-minute drive within the borough of Brooklyn had turned into an "80-minute living nightmare."

The Lyft app recorded the extended travel time—and a $107.95 charge for what should have cost less than $20. Within a day, Turkos says she went online to report her kidnapping to Lyft, which responded by "apologiz[ing] for the inconvenience" and agreeing to refund her the charge for the trip, minus the $12 she would have paid for a ride home without the detour.

Turkos also shared her account with a close friend, who never doubted her, and together the two walked into a nearby hospital. There a rape kit was collected and, at a doctor's urging, Turkos decided to call the New York Police Department (NYPD). Later, when she signed over custody of her rape kit to officers who had responded to the call, Turkos saved every form and even took a photograph of the kit, fully expecting that her complaint would be mishandled. She had seen too many accusers dismissed over the years not to understand the workings of the credibility complex.

Although this was her first time reporting a sexual assault to the police, it was not the first time she was sexually assaulted. When Turkos was sixteen, an older boy raped her at a friend's graduation party. "There was just shame, shame, shame," Turkos recalls, and she told no one what happened. The second time she was raped was during her first week of college. Again, she didn't report the abuse to police or school officials.

Only after the third rape—the Lyft kidnapping—did she decide to call on law enforcement. Unlike her own previous assaults, this one involved strangers and a weapon—it resembled the stranger rape paradigm, which increased the likelihood that the allegation would be credited. And Turkos now had evidence that included a digital trail and a rape kit. (The kit would later be tested and reveal the semen of two men and perhaps more.)

Turkos received barely any communication from the police detective assigned the case. Six months later, after lodging an official complaint about the handling of her report, she was finally assigned a new detective. Then, the police investigation was turned over to the FBI because the Lyft driver had crossed state lines. The delays were one issue, but the case was in trouble for other reasons as well. Turkos says she was informed by a federal agent that "certain deficiencies in the way the NYPD handled the investigation initially, including a failure to obtain video evidence at the time and the botched questioning of the Lyft driver," had severely weakened the case.

Turkos also learned that Lyft was allowing her driver to continue to drive even after she had filed her formal complaints. "I did what society always says I am 'supposed' to do," she observes. "I reported to police, I reported to the 'Trust and Safety' team at Lyft. I continue to relive my trauma, share my pain, do whatever it will take to get them to help me. And yet, after all that, they couldn't even be bothered to answer a simple email. They ignored, belittled, dismissed me."

Nearly two years after the incident, Turkos sued Lyft, alleging that the company's willingness to employ her kidnapper showed "a callous disregard" for the safety of other potential victims. Several other women, most of them anonymous in court filings, have also sued Lyft, claiming that the company failed to adopt reasonable measures to prevent their assaults, and that it treated their complaints with indifference.

Turkos has become a spokesperson of sorts for the survivors. "Lyft is systematically erasing our trauma and erasing me as a victim," she says. "Their response has consistently been absolutely abhorrent to victims." She explains, "I have put my face, my name, and my reputation on the line in an effort to be taken seriously—to be heard and believed."

Turkos has also sued the NYPD, alleging a failure to protect sexual assault victims. According to the complaint, the department exhibits a "fundamental disregard for both how sex crimes occur and the debilitating, life-altering harm they cause." Women who report their sexual assaults are routinely ridiculed and mistreated, the lawsuit alleges, while their cases are "either denied any attention or so badly mishandled" that any subsequent investigation is "severely hampered." In the end, the complaint charges, perpetrators escape without consequence while victims are newly harmed.

Turkos feels fortunate to be in a position to file suit against the NYPD and Lyft. Her privilege confers credibility, she says, both in the courts and in the public sphere. She describes herself as white, "queer but straight-passing," and "gainfully employed with access to lawyers." She also notes that she's an American citizen. More marginalized survivors would find it far more difficult to push for systemic change, Turkos emphasizes. "I'm able to file a lawsuit and to say, 'I'm going to hold you accountable. Be more transparent,'" she says. "These are things that I'm able to do. These are privileges that I hold. That's how I'm spending my privilege."

She's clear that people believing her is only a starting point. The larger aim is justice, although it's much harder to pinpoint what justice looks like than to identify its opposite. "I think for me, justice has so many different definitions, and there are so many different pathways to justice," says Turkos. "I do not expect the criminal legal system to save me, or to solve everything. But it's really sad when you think about it. We supposedly rely on a system, particularly those who are most vulnerable, members of marginalized communities— that's who the system is here for, and it fails us. It fails us repeatedly."

For Turkos, the lawsuits are a way to create systemic change. She thinks about *all* the people who found themselves in a position to judge her credibility and fell short. And she realizes this wasn't a problem of "one bad actor"—not even the first detective assigned to her case. Rather, there were "many entry points" where her allegation met an audience—the friends who Turkos told along the way, some of whom responded better than others. The sexual assault nurse examiner. The multiple police officers over many months. The Lyft personnel. The FBI agents. "It's a systemic problem," Turkos says, and "not just in New York City—this is happening everywhere." It's not just the men in the park—"It's the system."

As to what would ideally happen to the men who assaulted her,

Turkos is ambivalent. She says she knows prisons are horrible places and she's generally opposed to incarceration. But alternatives to the criminal system—she mentions restorative justice in particular—are hard for her to imagine in her case. "I am nowhere near being able to sit in a room with any of the men who sexually assaulted and raped me, and to be able to say, 'I need an apology from you. I need you to go to therapy for six months.' I am not there yet."

It's been about three years, and Turkos says that some days, she still feels like a "victim." From time to time, she reflects on how she "let this happen." She wonders, "How did I get in the car with a stranger? Yes, I had been drinking, but I was not to the point of being blacked out. What did I do, to allow this to happen to me?" Other days—most days—Turkos knows she's a "badass survivor," a fierce advocate fighting the credibility complex.

———

A credible accusation is one that disrupts the status quo in a meaningful way. What counts as meaningful disruption? This depends on where the violation falls along the "spectrum of gender-based violence," as Tarana Burke has aptly described it. Disruptions of the status quo fall on a continuum of severity that should correspond to the violation.

Shortly after #MeToo exploded in October 2017, reflecting on the movement she founded a decade earlier, Burke recalled a favorite diner in her former hometown of Montgomery, Alabama, where the servers—mostly Black women—were sexually harassed by the main cook as a matter of course. Burke connected these women to Anita Hill, who "thanklessly, put herself and her career as a law professor on the line more than 25 years ago." Burke also connected the diner servers to the women who, in her words, "have been screaming about famous predators like R&B singer R. Kelly, who allegedly preys on black girls, for well over a decade to no avail." And Burke linked all these women to the "everyday" survivors who were only just beginning to tell their stories. A meaningful disruption of the status quo—what it takes to *credit* an accusation—looks different for the diner harassment victims, for Anita Hill, for an R. Kelly accuser, and for each everyday survivor.

The setting in which the accusation arises matters too, since it affects the range of available responses. For instance, support for the victim: a college administrator can provide important academic accommodations, a workplace HR department can provide a desired departmental transfer, a friend can offer emotional support. But in order to meaningfully disrupt the status quo, a response will ordinarily entail not just assistance for the victim, but consequences for the abuser. The college administrator can impose disciplinary measures, the HR officer can suspend or terminate employment, a friend can sever ties.

Across the board, a meaningful disruption of the status quo—a true finding of credibility—can restore much of what the abuser took from the survivor. Her power. Her sense of security. Her sense of control. Her ability to trust others. Her dignity. Her value as an equal member of the community. All of this is on the line each time an accuser discloses abuse. When we credit the accusation, we replenish what is rightfully hers.

Kevin Becker, the psychologist with an expertise in the neurobiology of trauma, says that a positive response from close and extended members of the community can help restore a sense of control and security, which is critical to healing. Psychologist Judith Lewis Herman likewise stresses that the people who surround the victim exert "a powerful influence on the ultimate resolution of the trauma."

How do we do this? In order to "rebuild the survivor's sense of order and justice," Herman says, members of the survivor's community must publicly acknowledge the traumatic event, assign responsibility for the harm, and act to "repair the injury." In her study of how sexual and domestic violence victims understand their violation and what it would take to "set things right," Herman found that survivors primarily sought *validation*—that is, an acknowledgment that the abuse occurred and it was harmful. "Many survivors expressed a wish that the perpetrator would confess," Herman writes, "mainly because they believed that this was the only evidence that their families or communities would credit." Some survivors cared most about validation from those closest to them, while others were interested in validation from "representatives of the wider community or the formal legal authorities."

The survivors also frequently hungered for *vindication*—"they wanted their communities to take a clear and unequivocal stand in condemnation of the offense." Denunciation of the abuse was perceived as an expression of solidarity with the victim. This, in turn, was seen as a needed corrective to the sexual violation itself. "The survivors were keenly aware that the crimes were intended to dishonor and isolate them," Herman writes. "They sought, therefore, the restoration of their own honor and the reestablishment of their own connections with the community." At the same time, the act of condemning the abuser "transferred the burden of disgrace from victim to offender."

You'll remember Nancy Hogshead-Makar—the lawyer who represents sexual abuse victims, the former Olympic gold medalist, the woman who was raped when she was a sophomore at Duke. You'll also recall that the aftermath of Hogshead-Makar's assault was exactly what she could have hoped for. She was believed. She wasn't blamed. And her community showed it cared deeply about what had been done to her. This demonstration of concern is what allowed her to move forward. While her abuser was never apprehended, this wasn't because she was distrusted or faulted or disregarded. The collective response validated and vindicated her, so that Hogshead-Makar could heal.

VALIDATION AND VINDICATION: "WHAT HAPPENED WAS WRONG"

In late 2017, as #MeToo was sparking new conversations about past abuse, Megan Ganz, a comedy writer, asked her former boss, Dan Harmon, to apologize for how he had treated her years earlier when the two worked together. Soon after, in a podcast, Harmon offered a lengthy, precise description of how he harassed Ganz when she rejected his advances. He admitted that he knew his actions were wrong. "I'll never do it again," he said, "but I certainly wouldn't have been able to do it if I had any respect for women."

After the podcast aired, Ganz tweeted, "Please listen to it. It's only seven minutes long, but it is a masterclass in How to Apologize. He's not rationalizing or justifying or making excuses. He doesn't just vaguely acknowledge some general wrongdoing in the past. He gives a full account." This was "never about vengeance," Ganz added. "It's about vindication." For Ganz, the audience for this vindication was herself as much as others.

At the time, Harmon's advances were unwanted and Ganz felt she was being treated differently from the male writers, but Harmon denied it all when she confronted him. The apology verified her reality. "We both know what happened," Ganz says, "but these were the parts of the story that only he could confirm for me." Harmon's apology also helped eliminate her lingering feelings of self-blame. She explains, "Whenever I talked to friends about it afterward, they would of course say, 'It wasn't your fault. You didn't do anything wrong.' And I know that's true. But some small part of me would always think, 'You weren't there.' The irony is, Dan was the only person who could wipe those doubts from my head."

MANY SURVIVORS VIEW A SINCERE apology as a valuable form of restitution. True apologies—those that aren't disingenuous or entirely self-serving—are rare. But the function of a genuine apology precisely corresponds with what most survivors seek in the wake of their violation. The philosopher Nick Smith describes what a proper apology can accomplish. The person apologizing accepts blame for the injury and explains why the conduct was wrong. Doing so "validates the victim's beliefs." An apology also expresses a commitment to the equality and humanity of the victim. Instead of viewing her as an "obstacle" to advancing his interests, he treats her as a "person with dignity." And if the apology includes a promise not to repeat the actions, the victim feels more secure in the knowledge that the abuser won't ever again hurt her or anyone else.

APOLOGIES ARE AN IMPORTANT COMPONENT of a model for resolving disputes that is known as restorative justice. Restorative justice offers a path to healing that, for many victims, is an appealing alternative to traditional legal accountability. I've heard this repeatedly from accusers with serious misgivings about more conventional processes, with all their well-known failings.

sujatha baliga is an attorney and the recipient of a MacArthur "Genius" award for her restorative justice work. As baliga describes it, restorative justice "brings those who have harmed, their victims, and affected families and communities into processes that repair the harm and rebuild relationships." The aim of restorative justice is to heal everyone involved, starting with the survivor, rather than to penalize the abuser. Because the process is not adversarial, the accuser and the accused are meant to join forces.

baliga says that in cases of sexual violence, most survivors want the person who hurt them to accept responsibility. Many survivors want their family and friends to be present for this admission. Many want the person who harmed them to understand that *what happened was wrong* and to sincerely commit to never repeating the offense. Some survivors want to avoid ever having to see the person who offended against them. Over time, both parties, and, ideally, those close to them, gather to discuss how to repair the damage caused by the violation. "At the end of the process," baliga explains, "a plan to meet the survivor's self-identified needs is made by consensus of everyone present. The responsible person is supported by family and community to do right by those they've harmed."

Restorative justice has an important virtue: the approach casts the survivor as a credible source of information about her experience and the depths of her pain. Her worth is never in doubt, which can provide survivors with needed validation.

LEGAL SCHOLARS LESLEY WEXLER, Jennifer K. Robbennolt, and Colleen Murphy have described several core commitments that are central to restorative justice. The first is acknowledgment. Participation in most restorative justice programs is conditioned on the offender admitting to the wrongful behavior. When a victim describes what happened and is believed, she receives important validation, not only from the offender and from close members of their community. Her reality is affirmed—she has interpreted events correctly, and she is not to blame.

Taking responsibility—as with a sincere apology—is a second key dimension of restorative justice. For many victims, this is the essence of holding an abuser to account. Excuses and justifications are not acceptable. For some victims, it's important that the offender accept responsibility not only for the original violation but also for a response that worsened the injury. This might include accountability for "denial, deception, or retaliation." Survivors may also seek acceptance of responsibility by those who were complicit in the abuse or its harmful aftermath.

Apart from acknowledgment and acceptance of responsibility, restorative justice is premised on the idea that the offender should seek to repair the harm caused by the abuse. Archbishop Desmond Tutu once said, "If you take my pen and say you are sorry, but don't give me the pen back, nothing has happened." A similar idea holds true for victims of abuse. Restorative justice models ask the survivor to identify ways for the offender to make amends. Financial compensation may be helpful, both as symbolic recognition of the wrong, and as a way to defray the real economic costs resulting from abuse. Victims might ask the person who harmed them to engage in community service, especially if it advances justice for others who have been similarly wronged. Since the process aims to return the survivor to the place she occupied before she was hurt, what it takes to repair the harm is customized to the individual.

A final facet of restorative justice is preventing repetition of the offense. "Part of affirming the dignity and status of the harmed individual is taking steps to avoid perpetuating similar wrongdoing in the future," write the legal scholars Wexler, Robbennolt, and Murphy. They note that many survivors are "motivated to take action against offenders in the hope that similar harm will not befall others in the future and to regain a sense that they themselves are safe from continuing harassment." An abuser who promises not to engage in further misconduct may well be moving in this direction, but what really matters is that he makes good on this promise. A real commitment to rehabilitation must unfold over time. For survivors, the thought that the abuser will never hurt again can be among the greatest sources of healing.

SOFIA WAS A FIFTEEN-YEAR-OLD GIRL who was sexually assaulted by Michael, an eighteen-year-old boy who attended her high school. After the assault, Michael's friends took to social media to accuse Sofia of lying about what happened. With no witnesses, many believed Michael's denials.

Michael was eventually arrested. Instead of prosecuting the case, the district attorney sent it to a nonprofit agency trained in restorative justice practices. Michael was assured that, if he cooperated, nothing he said could be used against him in school disciplinary proceedings or the juvenile justice system—an essential guarantee by prosecutors—and he readily agreed. Sofia and her family were then contacted, and they also agreed to participate in the process.

baliga and a colleague met separately with Sofia, Michael, and their supporters. After consultation with both teens, it was decided that each of their mothers and Michael's sister would join the final gathering. In preparation, the facilitators talked with Michael about the impact of his behavior and its possible origins. They spoke with Sofia about what she wanted to say to Michael about the assault and how it affected her. Anticipating that it would be too difficult to confront Michael directly, Sofia asked her mother to speak on her behalf. But once the big meeting arrived, her plan shifted. As baliga recalls, "Sofia's demeanor instantly changed from timid to emboldened, and a powerful dialogue ensued about the impact of the assault on Sofia's life and on her family."

Since the assault, Sofia had lost weight. She was having nightmares and sleeping in her mother's bed. She had stopped going to school because of rumors that she lied about the rape for attention. After listening to Sofia, Michael addressed the question she had posed: *What were you thinking when you did this?* "I know you're a good girl, and I thought all good girls have to fight a little the first time," Michael answered. Michael's sister "gasped," baliga recollects, "and the room went silent for a little while."

"Even as the words came out of his own mouth," baglia continues, "we could all see Michael realize how wrong this was. He bent over and put his face in hands, and when he looked up, Sofia's mother squinted at him in disbelief, shaking her head. After what felt like an eternity, Michael's mother finally broke the silence, saying to her own daughter, 'See? I brought you so you'd know even nice boys like your brother can think things like this, do things like this.' Upon hearing Michael's mother take Sofia's 'side,' both Sofia and her mother broke down in tears, and Michael's mother stood up and hugged them. Then she sat back down, placed her hand gently on her son's arm, and shared stories of sexual violence endured in the past by members of her own family."

As the conversation progressed, Michael expressed his own confusion about consent. He talked about ambiguous media depictions and the ways his friends related their own sexual experiences. He then suggested that he had believed what he did was "okay because he felt that Sofia had expressed interest in him." Sofia "looked him directly in the eyes and told him that this had no bearing on his choice to assault her when she said no." Michael appeared to absorb this. It seemed that he gained a new understanding of consent—one that would diminish the likelihood he would assault again. And Sofia reclaimed her power.

The meeting then turned to a plan to repair Sofia's harm. Michael volunteered to post an apology on social media, including the words "she didn't lie," in an effort to rehabilitate her damaged reputation among their peers. Sofia asked that Michael spend a month at home to give her "space" at school, and he agreed.

The restorative justice process helped Sofia move forward with her life. In the weeks after the meeting, her mother reported that Sofia had "even more self-confidence than she'd had before the assault." She returned to wearing clothes that fit her body; she moved back into her own bedroom; she was more willing to assert her opinions and feelings (including with the men in her family) than ever before. Much of what was broken by the assault had been mended. Sofia had been able to reckon with Michael and force him to grapple with the fullness of his violation. She received the support of both her family and his. She saw that he faced consequences for his actions. In the end, Michael was held to account. All this happened because Sofia was valued. Knowing she was considered worthy helped return her to solid, equal ground.

When restorative justice practices function as intended, the survivor is credited. Her story is believed. Her injury is placed front and center, with the ultimate aim of repair. She is regarded as entirely deserving of care.

SURVIVORS ARE MOST LIKELY TO encounter restorative justice approaches to sexual misconduct on college campuses, where education and community building are central to the institutional mission. This is unlike other settings—notably the criminal justice system—where other goals are paramount. Many survivors welcome the option of restorative justice on campus, since the close confines of a college community and the ripple effects of pursuing a traditional complaint can make adversarial approaches uniquely unappealing. A comprehensive study of sexual assault on one college campus found that, in the aftermath of abuse, survivors were concerned about "losing their friends," "imposing a polluted identity on a current or former loved one," and "being seen as 'that girl' or 'that guy.'" Alternative methods of resolving disputes—like negotiation, mediation, and restorative justice—can respond to these concerns.

But the turn to restorative justice in higher education is relatively new. For decades, when it came to sexual assault cases, federal guidance frowned on using alternative dispute resolution models rather than more formal disciplinary processes.*

One reason is that colleges have an interest in pushing accusers toward informal resolution of their complaints. As compared to a full-fledged Title IX proceeding, which involves an investigation and hearing, informal responses are generally less costly from both a public-relations and a litigation standpoint. Abusers and other students on campus have also been known to pressure accusers to resolve their complaints through informal channels, where the stakes for the accused are lower.

For survivors who feel compelled to participate in an alternative to the conventional campus dispute model—and even for those who choose it freely—the outcome may be disappointing. Because restorative justice "lends itself to much more warm and fuzzy and kind and gentle" consequences for the abuser, as one Title IX expert suggests, survivors can wind up perceiving that the severity of their complaint was minimized. This same Title IX expert often hears women say that, looking back, they regret not treating their sexual assault with more seriousness. A lawyer who represents survivors says, "It almost never works. The apology from the perpetrator is never sincere. The victim never feels safe, and the friends can never stop torturing the victim."

When survivors don't trust that their institutions are committed

---

* The Trump administration supported an increased role for informal resolution procedures while at the same time issuing guidelines that made traditional processes more burdensome for the accuser. In March 2021, President Biden ordered the Department of Education to conduct a comprehensive review of those guidelines, raising the prospect that some will be revised.

to meaningful change, nonpunitive approaches to sexual misconduct can seem suspect. For instance, Berkeley High School in Northern California has a troubled history of allegedly failing to address sexual harassment and assault. Over the past decade, the school district has been the target of multiple lawsuits and federal investigations. In February 2020, after a list of "boys to watch out 4" was written on a girls' bathroom stall, student activists organized to protest a school culture they described as enabling sexual misconduct and coercing victims into silence. Part of the problem, the students explained, was that school officials were unwilling to impose real consequences for abuse. "Since forever we've been listening to what they can't do," one junior fumed. When told that the administration was working on a plan to implement "restorative justice circles," the organizers were outraged by the perceived inadequacy of the response. "We don't think it's fair for them to say, 'Here's a little *feelings circle* after everything that's happened,'" said one student activist. "We want real punishments. We don't want a circle where we talk about how hurt we are."

Here's the larger worry: restorative justice practices risk aligning with a larger cultural tolerance for abuse. Because these practices depend heavily on the involvement of family members and friends, they are susceptible to the same biases that infect the larger community. Even with the best of intentions, participants can unwittingly reinforce widely shared views of whose suffering matters, and whose does not. So too can restorative justice leave intact prevailing conceptions of sexuality and gender roles, including the belief that "men seek sex and women grant access," which researchers Jennifer Hirsch and Shamus Khan observe in their multiyear study of sexual assault on campus. Without deliberately attacking the cultural norms that give rise to sexual abuse, restorative justice practices can replicate those norms and the inequalities that sustain them.

The legal scholar Sarah Deer has voiced similar concerns about peacekeeping, which is a traditional Native American approach to justice upon which many restorative justice practices are based. These models are appropriate for resolving many kinds of disputes, Deer says, but not necessarily those involving sexual assault. She writes that one of the potential weaknesses of restorative justice "is the assumption of some degree of preexisting equality between the parties—and clearly a rape survivor and her perpetrator are at unequal places." Inequalities that are overlooked are apt to be reproduced, to the detriment of the victim.

Despite these dangers, restorative justice can provide survivors with precisely the validation they seek. For example, at The College of New Jersey, which has made restorative justice a priority, about half the students who pursue sexual assault complaints elect a restorative justice process. The school was inspired to develop the alternative model after repeatedly hearing from students who didn't want to move forward formally, but nevertheless insisted, "I want this person to know that they did something wrong."

TRANSFERRING THE "BURDEN OF DISGRACE": THE POINT OF CONSEQUENCES

In 2015, a literary scout at the Weinstein Company named Lauren O'Connor filed a complaint against the media mogul with the human resources department. The complaint detailed O'Connor's own experiences of verbal harassment while describing what she called "a toxic environment for women at this company." Women who work for Weinstein "are essentially used to facilitate his sexual conquests of vulnerable women who hope he will get them work," O'Connor recounted in the internal complaint. Her efforts to complain to HR had been unsuccessful, she said. Short of physical assault, she had been advised that nothing could be done.

The O'Connor complaint would become a central piece of evidence in the *New York Times* investigation into Weinstein. At the time she wrote it, O'Connor was painfully aware of her vulnerability. "I am a 28 year old woman trying to make a living and a career," she noted. "Harvey Weinstein is a 64 year old, world famous man and this is his company. The balance of power is me: 0, Harvey Weinstein: 10." Yet despite the obvious risks in coming forward, O'Connor could no longer remain silent. She had tried to be a professional. "Instead," she wrote, "I am sexualized and diminished."

O'Connor's assessment of the power imbalance proved correct. Even after learning of the allegations against Weinstein in her complaint, the company's board members were persuaded that there was no need to investigate. She was disposable, and he was untouchable. O'Connor reached a settlement with Weinstein, which included a nondisclosure provision. She "withdrew her complaint and thanked him for the career opportunity he had given her."

"Power operates on multiple levels," O'Connor would later observe in January 2019, as Weinstein awaited his trial in New York. "It operates in professional hierarchy. Right? You have juniors and seniors and presidents and CEOs and COOs. Power operates across the media. Do you have platform? Do you have voice? Do you not have platform? Do you not have voice? Power operates across finances. Do you have money? Do you not have money? And it operates across gender. So when we talk about, you know, Harvey Weinstein being stacked at 10 and me stacked at zero, those are the measurements."

It was five years after O'Connor filed her internal complaint that Weinstein was convicted by the New York jury. The following day, O'Connor and several of his other accusers gathered to reflect on what it meant for him to be held criminally responsible. For all the women assembled, the conviction represented a long-overdue reversal of the power dynamic that Weinstein perpetually exploited. "Yesterday, the scales of justice restored the balance of power. They tipped in favor of survivors of assault and workplace inequity," O'Connor proclaimed. "The balance of power is now survivors and silence breakers, ten, abusers and predators, zero."

Other accusers articulated similar sentiments. The conviction was a "triumph for survivors everywhere." A "landmark moment." A "measure of vindication for all people who've been sexually abused." By reallocating blame, Weinstein's conviction had empowered his accusers. "I'm not shaming myself anymore because the shame belongs with him," remarked Larissa Gomes. The conviction—a collective judgment of fault—allows victims to "put the shame and the blame on their perpetrator and take it off themselves," said Jessica Barth, another accuser.

For Louise Godbold, yet another accuser, the conviction meant that survivors everywhere mattered. "This was never about Harvey," Godbold explained. "This was about what we as a society will tolerate . . . The message is clear: hurt other people and there will be consequences."

HOLDING THE ABUSER TO ACCOUNT is almost universally important to survivors. But the function of accountability is not what you might think. For many, *suffering* by the abuser isn't the point, nor is punishment for its own sake a high priority. Rather than see the abuser deprived of liberty, victims often want him stripped of what Judith Lewis Herman calls "undeserved honor or status." Herman's study of victims shows that most who turned to the legal system were motivated by a wish to publicly expose the offender—not to cause needless humiliation, but to divest him of "undeserved respect and privilege." Victims hoped their own "standing in their families and communities" would then be elevated relative to the abuser. As Herman writes, "The main purpose of exposure was not to get even by inflicting pain. Rather, they sought vindication from the community as a rebuke to the offenders' display of contempt for their rights and dignity."

Legal theorists call this the expressive function of punishment. Philosopher Jean Hampton, among other theorists, has suggested that punishing an offender can equalize the social standing of his victim. When a person is violated, her status is diminished. The abuser has treated her as less valuable than he, which is not what she deserves. Punishment of the abuser communicates that this is wrong and affirms the opposing message: the victim is no less important than he. On the contrary, she is valued, respected, and worthy of protection. "The crime represents the victim as demeaned relative to the wrongdoer; the punishment 'takes back' the demeaning message," Hampton writes.

A set of experiments designed by the legal scholar Kenworthey Bilz to test the effects of punishment on social standing supports the expressive theory of punishment. Study participants were shown edited clips of the movie *The Accused*, which is loosely based on a gang rape that took place in 1983 in New Bedford, Massachusetts. After viewing the film, participants were presented with one of two outcomes. In the punishment version, the offenders—characterized in the study as one "college boy" and two "townies"—were convicted of rape. The no-punishment version featured the men pleading guilty before trial to a lesser nonsexual offense. In order to measure the effects of these outcomes on social standing, participants were then asked to consider how members of the community would rate the victim and the offenders along various dimensions, including the extent to which each was "admired," "valuable," and "respected."

Bilz found that when the offenders were punished, they lost social standing and the victim gained social standing. At the same time, a failure to punish the offenders for rape had the opposite effect: the victim lost social standing and the offenders gained it. This increase in social standing was even greater for the unpunished "college boy" (as compared to the "townie" offender), whose perceived social status was higher from the outset. Bilz concluded that punishment is a communication device that "expresses, and perhaps even alters, the social standing of victims and offenders."

Brenda Adams is a lawyer who represents many victims of campus sexual assault. What she sees in her practice is wholly consistent with the expressive theory of punishment. Her clients often want meaningful consequences imposed on their abuser—not to exact revenge, but to reconfigure a balance of power that the violation destroyed. "This single event has completely changed the survivor's life forever. They will never ever be the same," Adams told me. "So the thought that the person who did that to them is not going to have his life changed in any way is a concept they cannot wrap their mind around." No sanction can undo the harm suffered. But a collective judgment that impacts the abuser's life may help return the survivor to her rightful place in the community.

For the participants in Bilz's study, the conviction of the rapists *itself* counted as punishment that restored a victim's social standing. (Participants never learned if the rapists received any jail time.) Punishment need not entail "hard treatment." Bilz writes, "Legislative bodies can 'reprimand' their errant members; nations may face censure for human rights violations; first-time or juvenile offenders may be issued 'warnings' in lieu of fines or incarceration; various employers, religions, and parents might choose to formally rebuke misbehavior rather than deliver actual, material hard treatment." To serve an expressive function, a consequence must be *perceived* by the relevant audiences as punishment, but that perception is invariably subjective.

ACCOUNTABILITY AS VINDICATION

Every accuser I've spoken with over the years has expressed the significance of holding her abuser to account in one way or another, and
each wanted her violation to trigger a consequence—again, a meaningful disruption of the status quo. What varied was the nature of the
desired consequence.

Rebecca Campbell, the psychologist who researches law enforcement's response to sexual assault, has observed a similar range of desired outcomes. In her work, Campbell is careful to note that not all
survivors look to police and prosecutors—many see the prison system
as inhumane, and a "racist, classist, and sexist system in its own right."
Some victims who do turn to the criminal justice system may not view
incarceration as the right metric for accountability, while others see
imprisonment as the only way to express the severity of their violation.
Campbell writes, "The choice whether to engage the criminal justice
system and the meaning of justice is different for each survivor."

A criminal conviction may itself count as a form of accountability.
Jennifer Gonzalez, the prosecutor handling the Chicago case against
R. Kelly, told me that sex crimes victims often see a criminal conviction as meaningful regardless of the jail sentence attached to it. For
many survivors, the conviction itself has the effect of "shouldering
the weight" of their violation. "If someone isn't held accountable, she
shoulders that weight alone for the rest of her life," says Gonzalez. In
a similar vein, Alaleh Kianerci, who prosecuted Brock Turner, told
me that a guilty verdict assures the victim she was believed, which
brings relief. The sentencing hearing provides another vehicle for
healing because it gives the victim an outlet to express the depths of
her suffering—and to do so with the full backing of the state behind
her. "You're finally going to take the power back," Kianerci informs
survivors.

What does it mean to be vindicated by the criminal justice system? One survivor told me she simply hoped her allegation would result in a formal indictment rather than be folded into other pending charges. Even if it meant that her abuser wouldn't serve any additional jail time, what mattered was that he would be charged with *her* assault. Another survivor insisted that her abuser should be sentenced to *some* jail time for what he did to her—the length of incarceration wasn't important at all. It could be one extra day, she said. But she opposed an outcome where the man would serve concurrent sentences for his assault on her and on another victim. And many survivors do attach significance to the amount of time in prison. The sentence itself can be seen as reflective of the victim's injury and whether it matters.

IN HER LETTER TO THE sentencing judge, Rachael Denhollander, the first woman to publicly accuse Larry Nassar of sexual assault, said the following: "I am writing to urge you today to impose the maximum available sentence." In her letter, Denhollander described her own experience of abuse and its enduring impact. She noted the shocking number of victims of Nassar's abuse. And she posed a question that she viewed as the most important: "How much is a little girl worth?"

For Denhollander, the term of incarceration was a tangible expression of the victims' value. "Does the destruction of these precious children matter enough to provide every measure of justice the law can offer?" she asked, adding, "The sentence you hand down will answer these questions." To Denhollander, anything less than the maximum prison sentence would tell the victims they were less than fully valued. By contrast, when Nassar was sentenced to the maximum time, it affirmed for her that the women's lives were worth "everything."

Prison time is clearly an imperfect measure of justice, but many

survivors view comparatively light sentences—or no jail time at all—
as proof of how little they matter compared to the abuser. For instance, a military woman whose confessed rapist served two months
in jail and retired with full benefits said this: "I was never one of
the Air Force's own. My rapist was." One accuser told me that she
"just wanted the sentence to show the weight of this crime, that it
shouldn't be less important than another because I knew my assailant." She explained this to the judge, who gave her rapist no jail time.

IN LATE 2018, A FORMER Baylor University student and ex-president
of his fraternity resolved a sexual assault case against him by pleading no contest to a lesser charge of unlawful restraint. The incident
took place at a fraternity party, where the victim felt immediately se-
dated after drinking from a cup that she'd left unattended while she
danced. She recalls the defendant raping her before she blacked out.

The negotiated plea allowed the man's record to be swept clean—
he would have no criminal history going forward. Provided he complete three years of probation, pay a $400 fine, and undergo drug,
alcohol, and psychological treatment, he could avoid any jail time.

The victim's lawyer said that, in forty years practicing law, he had
"never seen a sweetheart deal like this," adding that "it stinks to high
hell." The victim too was outraged. "I have been through hell and back
and my life has been forever turned upside down," she reflected.
"This guy violently raped me multiple times, choked me, and when
I blacked out, he dumped me face down on the ground and left me
to die."

In a letter to the victim and her lawyer, the prosecutor apologized
for not advising them about the plea before it was reported in the
press. The deal was "not the outcome we had hoped for or that I had
originally offered," the prosecutor acknowledged. But because she
had just tried and lost "a very similar case," she worried about taking

this one to trial. In the earlier case, wrote the prosecutor, the jury "was looking for any excuse not to find an innocent looking young defendant guilty," especially where there was one victim and not more.

In the Baylor fraternity case, the victim was unconvinced that this rationale justified settling for a non-jail sentence. "It sounds like [the prosecutor] is agreeing with the jurors that he's too good looking to be convicted, or he only raped one girl, so we will let him go," the victim remarked. She told the judge who accepted the plea deal that she was "devastated." Rapists "will be emboldened by their power over women," she warned, "and their ability to escape justice and punishment."

SURVIVORS MAY ALSO VIEW INCARCERATION as a way to keep an abuser from reoffending. In cases of multiple offenses or "gratuitous sadism," victims often mention this goal as vital to a just outcome. For many, if their allegation is to matter, it must prompt a response that protects themselves and future potential victims.

Let's return to Abby Honold, the University of Minnesota student who was violently raped during a football tailgate by a fellow student. After pleading guilty to sexually assaulting Honold and another woman, the man was sentenced to more than six years of prison. As Honold sees it, what happened to her amounted to something important because, in the end, it kept other women safe from a serial rapist. "I'm happy that for the last few years he hasn't been able to hurt people. That was really what I wanted as an outcome," she told me. "I know that there's nobody being hurt by him right now, and that I don't have to worry about it, even though it shouldn't be my responsibility. But I think a lot of victims end up feeling that responsibility very deeply—myself included."

Honold also says the resolution of the case helped her to heal. The conviction and sentence were not only an "acknowledgement from the community that this did happen," she explains, but also a way for the collective to say, "we're so sorry and you shouldn't have been treated this way." For Honold, whose experiences with police and prosecutors were mostly negative, this was a crucial expression from the state—an expression of solidarity.

———

Communal condemnation conveys that sexual misconduct will not be tolerated. This alters the conditions that facilitate abuse—and it vindicates survivors. When trusted institutions fail to condemn abusers, these same institutions can be held to account in the court of public opinion and in courts of law. For many survivors, this kind of accountability is essential.

Marissa Hoechstetter told me that the New York gynecologist who assaulted her while she was pregnant should never have been permitted to plead guilty to abusing only two patients and avoid any jail time. It compounded her violation, she says, when the prosecutor dismissed her complaint and the complaints of dozens of other women. Hoechstetter has become an advocate for better approaches to the prosecution of sexual assault. But she recognizes that accountability entails more than criminal justice.

Hoechstetter maintains that for many years, a callous disregard for victims protected her abuser from consequences and allowed him to continue hurting patients in his care. She and seventy-seven other women are suing NewYork-Presbyterian for allegedly enabling nearly two decades of abuse while having been on notice of the doctor's predations. The women's list of demands includes reforms that would protect other women from abusive doctors. "What are we doing to keep other patients safe?" Hoechstetter asks. "Because when we continue to call out these serial predators as anomalies or aberrations, it distracts us from the fact that this is way more common and pervasive than we want to admit." For it to matter, she insists that an allegation of sexual misconduct should prompt real institutional change that will prevent further abuse.

———

An internal workplace investigation can serve a similar function for victims of sexual harassment. A true finding of credibility forces members of the workplace community—including management and leadership—to respond, providing needed accountability for the abuser and others complicit in the abuse. Without a collective response of this sort, the victim is denied vindication.

In late 2017, more than a dozen women—former law clerks, law professors, a law student—came forward with sexual harassment allegations against Alex Kozinski, who sat for more than three decades as a federal judge on the Ninth Circuit Court of Appeals in California. After Kozinksi resigned from the bench while denying wrongdoing, the judicial panel investigating him closed its inquiry, claiming it no longer had the authority to proceed. For at least three of his accusers—Leah Litman, Emily Murphy, and Katherine Ku—this outcome was wholly unsatisfying. The women, all lawyers, note that their allegations were carefully corroborated. But in the end, they write, "We cannot now point to findings of an official investigation that establish validated, agreed-upon hard truths of what happened."

Kozinski returned to public life only months after his resignation. His accusers say his public appearances have been "disappointingly easy," unmarked by any mention of the women's claims. This silence reinforces a culture of complicity and further normalizes sexual abuse. "The lack of a formal process offers a simple, if hollow, way to discount the accusations against him—as mere allegations," write Litman, Murphy, and Ku. When powerful men are momentarily disgraced in the eyes of family, friends, or the general public, the stigma of sexual misconduct allegations—including those that are corroborated or admitted—is often fleeting.

Even without official findings, the three Kozinski accusers suggest that people in the accused's orbit could nevertheless acknowledge the allegations against him. This would provide at least *some* vindication of the women who came forward.

———

Many survivors find that a civil lawsuit offers the best prospect for vindication, especially when the criminal system has failed to deliver. John Clune, the former sex crimes prosecutor–turned–civil litigator in Boulder, says that often his clients first turn to law enforcement in the hope their abuser will be held criminally responsible. "It's only in the aftermath of the police not doing anything about what happened that they'll start looking for other options," Clune told me. "That's when they start seeking out attorneys for other remedies like civil lawsuits," he explains, in an effort to "take back at least a small piece of control."

A civil lawsuit offers a special kind of accountability. Victims who prevail can take satisfaction from the knowledge that their injury *cost* their abuser, or their employer, or both. Apart from compensating survivors for what they suffered, a damage award can be even "more important as a public symbol of the perpetrator's guilt." The status quo has been meaningfully disrupted.

Robert Vance, the Philadelphia lawyer who represents many low-wage workers, says that while his clients are grateful for economic relief, the feeling that they've been believed and supported is just as important. Most settlement agreements include a provision stating that a payment doesn't constitute an admission of liability. But Vance told me his clients see it differently. "When the case settles, that validates what they've been saying. Because quite naturally their view is,

'If nothing was wrong, if you didn't do anything, then you wouldn't pay me for what you did to me.'" A settlement is vindication. It's a token of all that has been endured. It's a reversal of long-standing disregard for victims who insist they deserve better. "At the end of the process," says Vance, they have become "more powerful people."

When we provide survivors with the validation and the vindication they seek and deserve, we weaken the forces that sink their allegations. The credibility complex has remarkable staying power, as we've seen. Still, bit by bit, it *can* be dismantled.

CONCLUSION

In May 2011, almost ten years before Harvey Weinstein was convicted of sexual assault, Nafissatou Diallo, a Black woman from Guinea, was working as a housekeeper at the Sofitel, an upscale hotel in Midtown Manhattan. She had arrived in New York with her young daughter eight years earlier, unable to read or write in any language, and she was granted asylum. To earn money, she braided hair and helped in a friend's store before landing work at the hotel in 2008. For cleaning fourteen rooms a day, she earned $25 an hour. According to her supervisors, Diallo was a model employee.

One Saturday around noon, she entered the hotel presidential suite, Room 2806, to clean, thinking it had been vacated. Diallo says that when she entered, she immediately encountered a naked man with white hair. The man was Dominique Strauss-Kahn, then managing director of the International Monetary Fund and a potential candidate for the French presidency. "You're beautiful," Diallo recalls him saying, as he wrestled her toward the bedroom of the suite, while she insisted, "Sir, stop this. I don't want to lose my job." She would later remember feeling "so afraid."

As Diallo has described it, the assault happened quickly. While he pulled her to the bed and tried to put his penis in her mouth, she tightened her lips and moved her face. She tried pushing him away and, in hopes of scaring him, mentioned that her supervisor was nearby. Strauss-Kahn moved her toward the bathroom, pulled her uniform up around her thighs, tore her stockings—she was wearing two pairs at the time—reached under her underwear, and forcefully grabbed the outside of her vaginal area. He roughly pushed her to her knees with her back against the wall, then held her head on both sides and forced her to perform oral sex on him. She remembers getting up, spitting, and running into the hallway. "I was so alone. I was so scared," she says.

The entire incident was over within minutes, as key card records confirm. She recounted that her supervisor soon found her in the hallway, visibly shaken, and asked what was wrong, to which Diallo replied, "If somebody try to rape you in this job, what do you do?" The supervisor's response would set in motion a chain of events that would, after a long ordeal, bring Diallo a measure of justice. The man she accused was a "VIP guest," said the supervisor, while adding, but "I don't give a damn." About an hour later, after another supervisor and two hotel security officers were looped in, the hotel called 911. In the meantime, Strauss-Kahn checked out of the hotel and left for the airport, forgetting his phone in the room.

The police escorted Diallo to the hospital, where a nurse performed a gynecological exam and observed redness.* The stains on Diallo's uniform were quickly established as semen, which would later be matched to Strauss-Kahn's DNA, as would the DNA found on Diallo's stockings. Within hours of the hotel's call to 911, Strauss-

---

* According to the medical records, Diallo also reported pain in her left shoulder, but—as often happens when women, especially Black women, describe their medical symptoms—her complaint went nowhere: no X-rays were ordered, and no pain medication was given or prescribed. About six weeks after the initial hospital visit, with the benefit of an MRI, an orthopedic surgeon would diagnose torn cartilage in her left shoulder.

Kahn was taken into custody at the airport. His lawyers first floated an alibi, suggesting he was not even in the room during the alleged encounter. But the defense soon shifted to a claim that the sex was consensual. Days after his arrest, the District Attorney's Office presented the case to a Manhattan grand jury, which charged Strauss-Kahn with multiple sex crimes, including forcible oral sex.

FROM THE TIME SHE CAME forward, Diallo and her credibility were under attack in the court of public opinion. Speculation by segments of the press and commentators ran the gamut. She was out for Strauss-Kahn's money. She was a pawn being manipulated in an effort to derail his presidential bid. She was a "professional con artist," a "scam artist," a "pathological liar," a "disgraced maid," a "prostitute," and the "infamous Sofitel maid/hooker."

Three months after Strauss-Kahn was arrested, the District Attorney's Office recommended that all charges be dismissed. "Undeniably," prosecutors wrote to the court, "for a trial jury to find the defendant guilty, it must be persuaded beyond a reasonable doubt that the complainant is credible. . . . If we do not believe her beyond a reasonable doubt, we cannot ask a jury to do so."

What happened to shake their confidence? Prosecutors said that over the course of their investigation, Diallo's story about what happened in the immediate wake of the incident had shifted—she apparently waffled on whether she had briefly begun cleaning a nearby room after fleeing Strauss-Kahn's suite. Prosecutors also pointed to Diallo's unrelated "falsehoods," including her submission of certifications needed for low-income housing and, recently, a description of having been gang raped by soldiers in Guinea—a claim she then retracted. Other than Diallo's account of the incident in question, prosecutors explained, "all of the evidence that might be relevant to the contested issues of force and lack of consent is simply inconclusive."

Rips in her pantyhose were consistent with a forced sexual encounter but also, prosecutors noted, consistent with consensual sex. Likewise, the available physical and forensic evidence couldn't prove that force was used.

Even the existence of another accuser didn't change the calculus. During the course of the investigation, a French journalist had also come forward with a sexual assault allegation against Strauss-Kahn—she said he tried to rape her in an empty apartment while she was conducting an interview with him. But based on case law limiting the admission of "uncharged crimes" evidence, prosecutors deemed it unlikely that they would be allowed to introduce the journalist's testimony at trial. All told, prosecutors were left with "grave concerns about the complainant's reliability" that they maintained made it "impossible to resolve the question of what exactly happened in the defendant's hotel suite."

Diallo's lawyers decried the dismissal as a denial of justice and a harmful abandonment—of Diallo, and of all future victims of sexual assault.

BUT THE STORY DOES NOT end there. In August 2011, days after the criminal case was dismissed, Diallo filed a civil suit against Strauss-Kahn, alleging that his sexual assault caused her physical and psychological harm, as well as permanent damage to her reputation. She was suing, she said, "to vindicate her rights, to assert her dignity as a woman, to hold Dominique Strauss-Kahn accountable for the violent and deplorable acts that he committed against her in Room 2806, to teach her young daughter that no man—regardless of how much money, power and influence he has—should ever be allowed to violate her body, and to stand up for all women who have been raped, sexually assaulted or abused throughout the world but who are too afraid to speak out."

With the credibility complex in mind, we can understand much of what happened to Diallo as quintessential credibility discounting, and we can see Strauss-Kahn's treatment as reflecting a hefty credibility boost. From the hospital to the criminal justice system to the court of public opinion, the fallout from Diallo's allegation mirrors the experiences of many of the women whose stories appear in these pages. Diallo was variously distrusted, blamed, and disregarded by commentators—and then dismissed by prosecutors who could point to their heavy burden of proving guilt beyond a reasonable doubt. Physical evidence corroborated Diallo's story, yet prosecutors worried about how jurors would respond to her, and they expressed misgivings of their own. The evidence fell short of the unequivocal proof we've long expected: serious physical injury, a recovered weapon, DNA match to an unknown stranger. Because Diallo's credibility was downgraded, Strauss-Kahn's consent defense, however far-fetched, would win the day—without a jury ever hearing the case. All who were watching saw yet another accuser dismissed. For the already skeptical, the notion that women falsely cry rape was again confirmed.

The case was shot through with power from beginning to end. In November 2020, I spoke with Diallo's lawyer, Douglas Wigdor, who told me, "There's no doubt in my mind that if she was not an immigrant from Africa, she would have been treated very differently." The fact that Strauss-Kahn was among the world's most powerful men, and white, further disadvantaged Diallo. The credibility complex worked, as it routinely does, to entrench the status quo.

There were also glimmers of hope: Along the way to dismissal of the criminal case, on several pivotal occasions, people *believed* Diallo—her allegation wasn't distrusted, she wasn't blamed, she wasn't disregarded. Diallo's supervisor made clear that Strauss-Kahn's VIP status should not immunize him from consequences for his actions. The police gathered enough evidence to make an arrest, for prosecutors to present the case to a grand jury, and for that grand jury to indict. Black civic leaders and some women's rights groups rallied in support of Diallo and demanded accountability for Strauss-Kahn. These moments confirmed that Diallo's allegation was important, and *she mattered*. Those who didn't discount her credibility empowered her, and she was able to move forward with her civil suit using evidence that police had gathered in the course of their criminal investigation.

In December 2012, the civil suit was resolved. Strauss-Kahn finally agreed to settle Diallo's claim for an undisclosed amount of money. Wigdor issued a statement: "While the agreement to resolve Ms. Diallo's claims with DSK is the final chapter in what has been a long and arduous year and a half, the agreement to settle this matter will provide her with a new beginning so that she and her daughter can move forward and begin the process of healing."

———

I thought about Nafissatou Diallo that morning in late February 2020 as I sat in the New York City courtroom awaiting the Harvey Weinstein verdict. I wondered if her story would have ended differently had it occurred in the present day. The parallels were striking: same prosecutor's office, similar allegations, a defense of consent, a powerful man accused. This time around, the powerful man was about to be held accountable—which was altogether new. But still the prospect of criminal justice for a woman, coming forward alone—like Diallo did—is far from certain, especially when she is a woman of color. The obstacles that Diallo encountered, within the legal system and outside of it, remain. Countless accusers confront them. As the Weinstein jurors announced their verdict, I reflected on what it would take to truly turn the tides.

If we want to see real change, we must dismantle the credibility complex. And that can only happen if we remake law and culture so that trust, blame, and care are no longer meted out along axes of power.

Our everyday interactions are a perfect starting point. We know that most survivors of sexual assault and harassment will initially report to someone within their orbit. Friends, family members, co-workers, and mentors become a certain type of "first responder." The psychologist Kimberly Lonsway calls the moment of first disclosure a "fork in the road," since members of a trusted inner circle will shape the aftermath of abuse for the survivor. We are these trusted people. And we can indeed do better.

Guideposts can help.

First, by better calibrating the level of certainty we choose for ourselves, we'll increase the odds of fairly responding to an allegation. When setting an appropriate confidence level for belief, we must be mindful of context. If the stakes are relatively low—if liberty, education, or employment aren't on the line for the accused—our individual standard of persuasion should be much less stringent than the standards imposed in courts of law. Outside a criminal process, there's simply no reason to demand evidence beyond a reasonable doubt. In other forums—for instance, where the accused's job is in jeopardy—we should demand a level of certitude that is lower than the most onerous standard of proof, but higher than the level needed to respond in our personal lives.

Next, we can improve our process of reasoning about allegations and denials. How? By discarding the stranger rape paradigm and the archetypes it generates—the perfect victim *and* the monster abuser. The myths that maintain their hold are powerful because we don't see their influence. Once we do, their influence dissipates, opening space for science, psychology, and accurate understandings of abuse along with the hierarchies that enable it.

Also, we can resist the lure of blame-shifting when women behave in ways we know are most likely to trigger our judgments: when women drink; when their dress and conduct is too "sexual"; when women don't scream loud enough, fight hard enough, flee fast enough; when women don't sever all ties with the abuser. And we can recognize our long-standing reluctance to hold men responsible for their misconduct.

Finally, we can shrink the care gap. The women I've spoken with did not ask much of the friends and family members to whom they disclosed. Yet their loved ones nevertheless managed to disappoint. One accuser told me that all she hoped for was an "I hear you, I believe you, and I'm here to support you . . ." Perhaps she would have wanted someone to share in the emotional burden. Maybe she would have appreciated some company if she chose to report to the police. She might have wanted her friends to cut ties with her abuser. And perhaps just knowing these measures were on offer would have helped. Whatever form it took, the support of her family and friends would have showed they understood that her abuse was wrong and it harmed her. It would have demonstrated she was important to them. This alone would have made all the difference in the world.

———

Our reckoning with sexual misconduct begins with the individual—and it must not end there. Cultural progress demands legal change. Among many crucial reforms, rules that bake in the credibility discount—all the places I describe in this book—require an overhaul. Reform is urgently needed wherever distrust, blame, and disregard find outlet in our legal doctrines.

To upend rules that embed distrust, we must extend the time horizons that allow complaints to proceed—time limits for reporting workplace harassment and overly strict statutes of limitation that apply to the filing of criminal and civil cases. These requirements should better comport with the realities of abuse and its aftermath. We must ensure that the discovery phase of litigation no longer allows overly searching inquiries into sexual harassment plaintiffs' pasts while shielding defendants' patterns of abuse.

To reverse rules that shift blame onto the victim, we must eliminate voluntary intoxication defenses in rape law and modernize the definition of consent to dissolve verbal resistance requirements. And on the civil side, we must remove the presumption that harassing conduct is welcome and formalize the exact opposite understanding— that harassing conduct is *un*welcome.

To jettison rules that disregard harm to survivors, we must abolish the force requirement and remaining vestiges of the marital rape exemption. In sexual harassment law, we must eliminate the "severe or pervasive" standard, raise damage caps, and expand protections for vulnerable workers, including domestic workers, farmworkers, independent contractors, interns, and volunteers.

In some states, many of the changes I outline are underway. But the legal system discounts credibility in ways that are difficult to fix by law reform alone. Cultural biases creep in whenever actors exercise discretion or judgment, which happens throughout both criminal and civil processes. Police officers choose how to investigate and whether to arrest. Prosecutors determine what charges, if any, to pursue and whether to offer a pretrial disposition. Judges hand down evidentiary rulings, sentencing decisions, and rulings on the law. Jurors assess credibility, weigh evidence, and, in civil cases, estimate damages.

From top to bottom, start to finish, the law is applied *by people*. This is what we're up against—which doesn't mean that legal reform is hopeless, but only that its reach is limited. If we are to meaningfully alter the ways our laws are enforced, our culture itself must evolve. We must put an end to the credibility discount and the credibility boost. This is a colossal challenge—and each one of us has the power to meet it. We begin the work of cultural transformation the moment we respond fairly to a single allegation of abuse.

ACKNOWLEDGMENTS

When I thought about writing a book about credibility, I knew it would have to be driven by the stories of survivors. Their willingness to trust me with their accounts was an inspiration and a constant reminder of all that is endured. I am grateful beyond words for their candor and equally inspired by their courage, and I have tried my best to honor their experiences. More women than I can count have shared their stories with me over several decades, before there was ever a book in my mind. They too are in these pages, even though they are not named.

I am also grateful for my conversations with lawyers, psychologists, sociologists, philosophers, activists, law enforcement officers, and journalists—some who also recounted their own experiences of abuse. The insights of these experts enriched the book immeasurably.

My deep appreciation extends to: Kate Abramson, Brenda Adams, Katie Baker, Kevin Becker, Scott Berkowitz, Rebecca Campbell, Eve Cervantez, John Clune, Jillian Corsie, Sarah Deer, Paula England, Deborah Epstein, Jennifer Freyd, Terry Fromson, Jennifer Gonzalez, Fatima Goss Graves, Chloe Grace Hart, Venkayla Haynes, Caroline Heldman, Marissa Hoechstetter, Nancy Hogshead-Makar, Abby Honold, Jim Hopper, Nicole Johnson, Debra Katz, Alaleh Kianerci, Jennifer Langhinrichsen-Rohling, Lauren Leydon-Hardy,

Jennifer Long, Kimberly Lonsway, Rachel Lovell, James Markey, Rose McGowan, Tom McDevitt, Aja Newman, Jennifer Reisch, Marissa Ross, Lynn Hecht Schafran, Joseph Sellers, Rachael Stirling, Sharyn Tejani, Lauren Teukolsky, Carol Tracy, Alison Turkos, Vanessa Tyson, Robert Vance, Amelia Wagoner, Carolyn West, Douglas Wigdor, Ari Wilkenfeld, Janey Williams.

Many survivors conveyed their belief in the importance of the book. Their optimism about what it could accomplish was a powerful motivator. One encounter in particular stands out. I had the pleasure of meeting Tarana Burke when this book was at an early stage of inception, and our exchange continued to resonate as I wrote.

From the beginning, my agent, Jennifer Gates, saw an urgent need for *Credible*. Without her, this book would not exist. Jen's remarkable vision, creativity, and smarts propelled the project forward, as did her steadfast faith in the power of these ideas and their potential to upend the way we respond to abuse.

The indomitable Karen Rinaldi, my publisher and editor, is a force of nature who immediately understood why this book mattered and knew exactly what it would take to get here. Karen is the person you most want in your corner. Her wisdom is unparalleled. My gratitude extends to the phenomenal team at Harper Wave, including Sophia Lauriello, Penny Makras, Yelena Nesbit, Brian Perrin, and Rebecca Raskin.

Amanda Moon saw with perfect clarity what this book could be. Her brilliant editorial instincts sharpened my argument, strengthened my voice, and tamed an unwieldy set of ideas. Working together was always a joy.

Natalie Meade checked every fact with precision and offered suggestions that went well above and beyond.

In 2019, it was my privilege to receive Northwestern University's Dorothy Ann and Clarence L. Ver Steeg Distinguished Research

Fellowship Award. My thanks to John and Jane Ver Steeg for their generosity and genuine excitement about the book.

Many people at Northwestern's Pritzker School of Law provided extraordinary support. Tom Gaylord made it his mission to ensure that my research was, without fail, current and comprehensive. Molly Heiler and Sarah Shoemaker offered the very best administrative assistance. A mighty team of students attended to early chapters with enthusiasm and intelligence: Riley Clafton, Emily Jones, Anastasiya Lobacheva, and Isabel Matson. James Speta, Daniel Rodriguez, and Kimberly Yuracko, my current and former deans, gave unwavering encouragement. My fabulous colleagues also helped in ways that truly mattered. For conversations along the way, special thanks to Shannon Bartlett, David Dana, Erin Delaney, Jocelyn Francoeur, Paul Gowder, Tonja Jacobi, Emily Kadens, Heidi Kitrosser, Jay Koehler, Jennifer Lackey, Candy Lee, Bruce Markell, Jide Nzelibe, James Pfander, David Schwartz, and Juliet Sorensen. Peter DiCola, Sarah Lawsky, and Janice Nadler also read drafts, shared incisive feedback, and imparted excellent advice throughout the process.

I am exceedingly fortunate to be surrounded by the best of friends. For years, they have never stopped showing interest in the book—both its progress and its contents. And they provided the kind of cheerleading (and, in several instances, draft-reading) that no one has a right to expect. My heartfelt thanks to Jeff Berman, Julie Bornstein, Susan Gallun, Andrew Gold, Kate Masur, Molly Mercer, Jenn Nicholson Paskus, Kaari Reierson, Maura Shea, Sarah Silins, Peter Slevin, Marc Spindelman, J. D. Trout, Kimberly Wasserman, Lisa Weiss, Nichole Williams, and Daria Witt. Extra thanks to Bobbi Kwall, who wanted to hear all the details.

Alan, my brother, is possessed of endless optimism and good humor, which appreciably eased the burden of writing a book during a pandemic.

My parents, Barbara and Frank, are my role models in all realms, to whom of course I owe everything.

Dylan would not want to be thanked, and certainly not at length. My gratitude knows no bounds.

Max and Leo, my teenagers, are a source of infinite pride and happiness. They watched, sacrificed, and rallied from exceptionally close quarters as this book came into being, transforming what might have been an impossible situation. For this, Max and Leo each have my greatest appreciation. They also have my everlasting respect, love, and adoration, along with an abiding promise to work as ever toward a more just world.

NOTES

AUTHOR'S NOTE

ix "I am both a survivor *and* still a victim, and somehow I will always and forever be both": Donna Freitas, *Consent: A Memoir of Unwanted Attention* (New York: Little, Brown and Company, 2019), 289.

ix abuse that is typical . . . female victim: Michele C. Black et al., "The National Intimate Partner and Sexual Violence Survey: 2010 Summary Report," National Center for Injury Prevention and Control, Centers for Disease Control and Prevention (2011): 18–19, 24, https://www.cdc.gov/violenceprevention/pdf/NISVS_Report2010-a.pdf.

INTRODUCTION

1 The vast majority . . . a prosecution, or a conviction: Kimberly A. Lonsway and Joanne Archambault, "The 'Justice Gap' for Sexual Assault Cases: Future Directions for Research and Reform," *Violence Against Women* 18, no. 2 (2012): 149–50.

1 Around the country . . . lead to an arrest: "The Criminal Justice System: Statistics," RAINN, accessed January 2, 2021, https://www.rainn.org/statistics/criminal-justice-system.

1 In some jurisdictions, the arrest rate is even lower: Anna Madigan, "Rape Cases in Virginia Often Go Unsolved," NBC 12, December 9, 2019, https://www.nbc12.com/2019/12/10/rape-cases-virginia-often -go-unsolved/; Jim Mustian and Michael R. Sisak, "Despite #MeToo,

'Clearance Rate' for Rape Cases at Lowest Point Since the 1960s," *USA Today*, December 27, 2018, https://www.usatoday.com/story /news/nation/2018/12/27/rape-cases-clearance-rate-hits-low-despite -metoo/2421259002.

2 This was over a decade after Tarana Burke . . . women and girls of color: Abby Ohlheiser, "The Woman Behind 'Me Too' Knew the Power of the Phrase When She Created It—Ten Years Ago," *Washington Post*, October 19, 2017, https://www.washingtonpost.com /news/the-intersect/wp/2017/10/19/the-woman-behind-me-too -knew-the-power-of-the-phrase-when-she-created-it-10-years-ago.

2 And several states extended . . . filing a sexual harassment claim: Andrea Johnson et al., "Progress in Advancing Me Too Workplace Reforms in #20StatesBy2020," National Women's Law Center (July 2019): https://nwlc-ciw49tixgw5lbab.stackpathdns.com/wp-content /uploads/2019/07/final_2020States_Report-9.4.19-v.pdf.

3 The social anthropologist Adam Kuper . . . "matter of ideas and values, a collective cast of mind": Adam Kuper, *Culture: The Anthropologists' Account* (Cambridge, MA: Harvard University Press, 1999), 227.

3 What's key here . . . power imbalances: Richard Johnson, "What Is Cultural Studies Anyway?" *Social Text*, no. 16 (1986): 39.

4 As cultural psychologists recognize . . . allegations of abuse: Kimin Eom and Heejung S. Kim, "Cultural Psychology Theory," in *Theory and Explanation in Social Psychology*, eds. Bertram Gawronski and Galen V. Bodenhausen (New York: Guilford Publications, 2014), 328; Alan Page Fiske et al., "The Cultural Matrix of Social Psychology," in *The Handbook of Social Psychology*, 4th ed., eds. Daniel T. Gilbert, Susan T. Fiske, and Gardner Lindzey (New York: McGraw-Hill, 1998), 915.

4 "Law operates even when it appears not to" . . . "form our identities": Naomi Mezey, "Law as Culture," *Yale Journal of Law & the Humanities* 13, no. 1 (2001): 48.

5 "law does more than reflect or encode . . . composition of social relations": Susan S. Silbey, "Making a Place for a Cultural Analysis of Law," *Law and Social Inquiry* 17, no. 1 (1992): 41; Austin Sarat and

Thomas R. Kearns, "The Cultural Lives of Law," in *Law in the Domains of Culture* (Ann Arbor: University of Michigan Press, 2000).

CHAPTER 1: ALONG AXES OF POWER: WORKINGS OF THE CREDIBILITY COMPLEX

13 McGowan tweeted . . . had raped her: Liz Calvario, "Rose Mc-Gowan Reveals She Was Raped by a Hollywood Executive," Indie-Wire, October 14, 2016, https://www.indiewire.com/2016/10/rose-mcgowan-tweets-raped-by-hollywood-executive-1201736965.

13 blockbuster exposés: Jodi Kantor and Megan Twohey, "Harvey Weinstein Paid Off Sexual Harassment Accusers for Decades," *New York Times*, October 5, 2017, https://www.nytimes.com/2017/10/05/us/harvey-weinstein-harassment-allegations.html; Ronan Farrow, "From Aggressive Overtures to Sexual Assault: Harvey Weinstein's Accusers Tell Their Stories," *New Yorker*, October 10, 2017, https://www.newyorker.com/news/news-desk/from-aggressive-overtures-to-sexual-assault-harvey-weinsteins-accusers-tell-their-stories.

13 In her memoir *Brave* . . . "be the same": Rose McGowan, *Brave* (New York: HarperCollins Publishers, 2018), 122.

14 "I kept thinking . . . just. a. girl": McGowan, *Brave*, 126–27.

14 As Kantor and Twohey would ultimately report . . . "she is discredited": Jodi Kantor and Megan Twohey, *She Said: Breaking the Sexual Harassment Story That Helped Ignite A Movement* (New York: Penguin Press, 2019), 101.

14 As McGowan puts it . . . "not the case": Rose McGowan, "Rose McGowan On Lisa Bloom Memo In New Book, 'She Said,'" interview by Michael Martin, *All Things Considered*, NPR, September 14, 2019, https://www.npr.org/2019/09/14/760876409/rose-mcgowan-on-lisa-bloom-memo-in-new-book-she-said.

14 McGowan says that just after the assault . . . "feel better," she says: McGowan, *Brave*, 128–29.

15 "inextricable from gender": Trina Grillo, "Anti-Essentialism and Intersectionality: Tools to Dismantle the Master's House," *Berkeley Women's Law Journal* 10, no. 1 (1995): 19.

15 As the historian Estelle Freedman wrote . . . "white female virtue": Estelle B. Freedman, *Redefining Rape: Sexual Violence in the Era of Suffrage and Segregation* (Cambridge, MA: Harvard University Press, 2013), 27.

16 The same is *not* true . . . "rather than as white": Grillo, "Anti-Essentialism and Intersectionality," 19.

17 "Black women who are raped don't matter": Venkayla Haynes, "Black Women Who Are Raped Don't Matter," Medium, June 13, 2019, https://medium.com/@VenkaylaHaynes/black-women-who-are-raped-dont-matter-b5fc0791a642.

18 Black women are not . . . "only more so": Angela P. Harris, "Race and Essentialism in Feminist Legal Theory," *Stanford Law Review* 42, no. 3 (1990): 595.

18 long-standing myths . . . confront Black accusers: Shaquita Tillman et al., "Shattering Silence: Exploring Barriers to Disclosure for African American Sexual Assault Survivors," *Trauma, Violence, & Abuse* 11, no. 2 (2010): 65.

18 "The hearings devolved . . . erotomaniac": Jane Mayer, "What Joe Biden Hasn't Owned Up To About Anita Hill," *New Yorker*, April 27, 2019, https://www.newyorker.com/news/news-desk/what-joe-biden-hasnt-owned-up-to-about-anita-hill.

18 In fact, around that time . . . almost a decade: Jane Mayer and Jill Abramson, *Strange Justice: The Selling of Clarence Thomas* (New York: Houghton Mifflin Harcourt, 1994), 114–15.

19 Reflecting on her experience . . . "black women's sexuality": Anita Hill, *Speaking Truth to Power* (New York: Anchor Books, 1997), 281.

19 Anita Hill identifies . . . "hurts everyone": Hill, *Speaking Truth to Power*, 279, 277.

19 One study found . . . altogether: LaDonna Long and Sarah E. Ullman, "The Impact of Multiple Traumatic Victimization on Disclosure and Coping Mechanisms for Black Women," *Feminist Criminology* 8, no. 4 (2013): 301–4.

20 "cultural mandate . . . unfair treatment in the criminal justice system": Tillman et al., "Shattering Silence," 64–65.

20 Other than sexual assaults against Native women . . . share the same

race: André B. Rosay, "Violence Against American Indian and Alaska Native Women and Men," *National Institute of Justice Journal* 277 (2016): 4; Rachel E. Morgan, "Race and Hispanic Origin of Victims and Offenders, 2012–2015," Bureau of Justice Statistics (2017): 15, https://www.bjs.gov/content/pub/pdf/rhovo1215.pdf.

20   "the stereotype . . . incarcerated black men": Salamishah Tillet, "Why Harvey Weinstein's Guilt Matters to Black Women," *New York Times*, February 26, 2020, https://www.nytimes.com/2020/02 /26/opinion/harvey-weinstein-black-women.html?action=click &module=Opinion&pgtype=Homepage.

20   "a form of self-denial . . . degradation": Hill, *Speaking Truth to Power*, 277.

20   Tarana Burke . . . less visible than celebrities: Sandra E. Garcia, "The Woman Who Created #MeToo Long Before Hashtags," *New York Times*, October 20, 2017, https://www.nytimes.com/2017/10/20 /us/me-too-movement-tarana-burke.html.

20   "This is a way of shutting down black women . . . all other harm": Ben Sisario and Nicole Sperling, "Pressured by Simmons over Exposé, Oprah Winfrey Faced a Big Decision," *New York Times*, January 17, 2020, https://www.nytimes.com/2020/01/17/movies/oprah-winfrey -russell-simmons-movie.html.

20   "Though the female members . . . about a Black rapist": Jamil Smith, "She Can't Breathe," in *Believe Me: How Trusting Women Can Change the World*, eds. Jessica Valenti and Jaclyn Friedman (New York: Seal Press, 2020), 216.

21   "Women of color" . . . overlapping layers of identity: Kimberlé Crenshaw, "Mapping the Margins: Intersectionality, Identity Politics, and Violence Against Women of Color," *Stanford Law Review* 43, no. 6 (1991): 1250.

21   more than half are victimized in their lifetime: Rosay, "Violence Against American Indian and Alaska Native Women and Men," 40.

21   "It's more expected than unexpected": Timothy Williams, "For Native American Women, Scourge of Rape, Rare Justice," *New York Times*, May 22, 2012, https://www.nytimes.com/2012/05/23/us/native -americans-struggle-with-high-rate-of-rape.html.

22 In the lower forty-eight states . . . against Native victims: Rosay, "Violence Against American Indian and Alaska Native Women and Men," 41.

23 Gretchen Small served . . . "don't count": Victoria McKenzie and Wong Maye-E, "In Nome, Alaska, Review of Rape 'Cold Cases' Hits a Wall," Associated Press, December 20, 2019, https://apnews.com/b6d9f5f6fd71d2b75e3b77ad9a5c0e76.

23 this feels bad to admit . . . no one helps: Williams, "For Native American Women, Scourge of Rape, Rare Justice."

23 "I stayed silent . . . to be assaulted": Sarah McBride, "Why I'm Not Staying Silent About Being A Trans Woman Who Was Sexually Assaulted," BuzzFeed, October 20, 2017, https://www.buzzfeed.com/sarahemcbride/why-its-so-hard-for-trans-women-to-talk-about-sexual-assault?utm_term=.yqEVXwqo6#.wcORNxZj3.

27 That night, on the phone . . . "these days": Barbara Bradley Hagerty, "The Campus Rapist Hiding in Plain Sight," *Atlantic*, July 15, 2019, https://www.theatlantic.com/education/archive/2019/07/why-dont-more-college-rape-victims-come-forward/593875.

27 when two more women . . . he was charged with Honold's assault: Hagerty, "The Campus Rapist Hiding in Plain Sight."

28 Among the population most vulnerable . . . complain to police: Sofi Sinozich and Lynn Langton, "Special Report: Rape and Sexual Assault Among College-Age Females, 1995–2013," Bureau of Justice Statistics (December 2014): 1, https://www.bjs.gov/content/pub/pdf/rsavcaf9513.pdf.

28 Women in college report at lower rates—20 percent, according to one estimate: Sinozich and Langton, "Special Report," 1.

28 less than 5 percent, according to another: Bonnie S. Fisher, Francis T. Cullen, and Michael G. Turner, "The Sexual Victimization of College Women," Bureau of Justice Statistics (December 2000): 23, https://www.ncjrs.gov/pdffiles1/nij/182369.pdf.

28 Reporting rates for women of color . . . even lower: Colleen Murphy, "Another Challenge on Campus Sexual Assault: Getting Minority Students to Report It," *Chronicle of Higher Education*, June 18, 2015, https://www.chronicle.com/article/Another-Challenge-on

-Campus/230977; Jennifer C. Nash, "Black Women and Rape: A Review of the Literature," Brandeis University Feminist Sexual Ethics Project, (June 12, 2009): 4–5, https://www.brandeis.edu/projects/fse /slavery/united-states/slav-us-articles/nash2009.pdf.

28   for every Black woman who reports . . . do not report theirs: "Black Women and Sexual Assault," The National Center on Violence Against Women in the Black Community (October 2018): 1, https:// ujimacommunity.org/wp-content/uploads/2018/12/Ujima-Womens -Violence-Stats-v7.4-1.pdf.

28   they are more likely . . . by a stranger: Bonnie S. Fisher et al., "Reporting Sexual Victimization to the Police and Others: Results from a National-Level Study of College Women," *Criminal Justice and Behavior* 30, no. 1 (2003): 30–31.

28   more than three-quarters of victims know their perpetrator: Michael Planty et al., "Female Victims of Sexual Violence, 1994–2010," Bureau of Justice Statistics (May 2016): 4, https://www.bjs.gov/content/pub /pdf/fvsv9410.pdf.

28   nine of ten victims say that no weapon was used: Planty et al., "Female Victims of Sexual Violence," 5.

29   Black girls are especially vulnerable . . . before age fourteen: Thema Bryant-Davis et al., "Struggling to Survive: Sexual Assault, Poverty, and Mental Health Outcomes of African American Women," *American Journal of Orthopsychiatry* 80, no. 1 (2010): 64.

29   sexual abuse during childhood . . . in adulthood: Kevin Lalor and Rosaleen McElvaney, "Child Sexual Abuse, Links to Later Sexual Exploitation/High-Risk Sexual Behavior, and Prevention/Treatment Programs," *Trauma, Violence, & Abuse* 11, no. 4 (2010): 159–77.

29   "negative social reactions" . . . about the misconduct: Courtney E. Ahrens, "Being Silenced: The Impact of Negative Social Reactions on the Disclosure of Rape," *American Journal of Community Psychology* 28 (2006): 270–73; Debra Patterson, Megan Greeson, and Rebecca Campbell, "Understanding Rape Survivors' Decisions Not to Seek Help from Formal Social Systems," *Health & Social Work* 34, no. 2 (2009): 130–33.

30   This awareness . . . stranger rape paradigm: Manon Ceelen et al.,

"Characteristics and Post-Decision Attitudes of Non-Reporting Sexual Violence Victims," *Journal of Interpersonal Violence* 34, no. 9 (2019): 1969; Marjorie R. Sable and Denise L. Mauzy, "Barriers to Reporting Sexual Assault for Women and Men: Perspectives of College Students," *Journal of American College Health* 55, no. 3 (2006): 159; Kaitlin Walsh Carson et al., "Why Women Are Not Talking About It: Reasons for Nondisclosure of Sexual Victimization and Associated Symptoms of Posttraumatic Stress Disorder and Depression," *Violence Against Women* 26, no. 3–4 (2019): 273, 275; Amy Grubb and Emily Turner, "Attribution of Blame in Rape Cases: A Review of the Impact of Rape Myth Acceptance, Gender Role Conformity and Substance Use on Victim Blaming," *Aggression and Violent Behavior* 17, no. 5 (2012): 444.

31 We see this across industries . . . "for causing the offending actions": Chai R. Feldblum and Victoria A. Lipnic, "Select Task Force on the Study of Harassment in the Workplace: Report of Co-Chairs Chai R. Feldblum & Victoria A. Lipnic," U.S. Equal Employment Opportunity Commission (June 2016): 16, https://www.eeoc.gov/sites/default/files/migrated_files/eeoc/task_force/harassment/report.pdf.

31 In 1975, Lin Farley . . . "behavior of men": Lin Farley, *Sexual Shakedown: The Sexual Harassment of Women on the Job* (New York: Warner Books, 1980), 11–12.

31 "something to just live through": Catharine A. MacKinnon, "Where #MeToo Came From, and Where It's Going," *Atlantic*, March 24, 2019, https://www.theatlantic.com/ideas/archive/2019/03/catharine-mackinnon-what-metoo-has-changed/585313.

31 Only once sexual harassment was named . . . and illegal: Reva B. Siegel, "Introduction: A Short History of Sexual Harassment," in *Directions in Sexual Harassment Law*, eds. Catharine A. MacKinnon and Reva B. Siegel (New Haven: Yale University Press, 2004), 2.

32 Alejandra began working . . . to her employer: Complaint at 9, 10–11, *Sanchez v. ABM Industries*, Case No. 19CECG00566 (Superior Court, Fresno County, California February 13, 2019).

32 "I spent many years suffering": Yesenia Amaro, "'I Spent Many Years Suffering.' Women in Fresno Allege Sexual Harassment at Janitorial

Company," *Fresno Bee*, February 13, 2019, https://www.fresnobee.com/news/local/article226219730.html.

33 Maria de Jesus Ramos Hernandez . . . unlikely to complain: Diana Vellos, "Immigrant Latina Domestic Workers and Sexual Harassment," *American University Journal of Gender and the Law* 5, no. 2 (1997): 425–26 (citing Carla Marinucci, "Despair Drove Her to Come Forward," *San Francisco Examiner*, January 10, 1993, at A11).

33 She was a perfect target for her harasser: Maria Ontiveros, "Three Perspectives on Workplace Harassment of Women of Color," *Golden Gate University Law Review* 23, no. 3 (1993): 818.

34 Rowena Chiu began working . . . to share or not: Kantor and Twohey, *She Said*, 63–68.

35 There were many reasons why . . . burying her own assault: Rowena Chiu, "Harvey Weinstein Told Me He Liked Chinese Girls," *New York Times*, October 5, 2019, https://www.nytimes.com/2019/10/05/opinion/sunday/harvey-weinstein-rowena-chiu.html. The remainder of this section is drawn from Chiu's essay and from Kantor and Twohey, *She Said*, 247–61.

CHAPTER 2: OF PERFECT VICTIMS AND MONSTER ABUSERS: HOW MYTHS DISTORT OUR CREDIBILITY JUDGMENTS

38 According to one estimate . . . raped by an acquaintance: Black et al., "The National Intimate Partner and Sexual Violence Survey: 2010 Summary Report," 21, https://www.cdc.gov/violenceprevention/pdf/nisvs_report2010-a.pdf.

38 Most of us are familiar . . . "sexual assault victims": Kimberly A. Lonsway and Joanne Archambault, "Dynamics of Sexual Assault: What Does Sexual Assault Really Look Like?" (2019): 7–8, 13, https://pdfs.semanticscholar.org/cd1c/ccb807f8e341ae164610125007d4dd27742e.pdf.

38 "prejudicial, stereotyped, or false beliefs about rape, rape victims, and rapists": Martha R. Burt, "Cultural Myths and Supports for Rape," *Journal of Personality and Social Psychology* 38, no. 2 (1980): 217.

38 "to deny and justify male sexual aggression against women": Kimberly

A. Lonsway and Louise F. Fitzgerald, "Rape Myths: In Review," *Psychology of Women Quarterly* 18, no. 2 (1994): 133.

39   As the writer Rebecca Solnit writes . . . "being owed sex is everywhere": Rebecca Solnit, *Men Explain Things to Me* (Chicago: Haymarket Books, 2014), 131.

39   "His rights trump hers": Solnit, *Men Explain Things to Me*, 131.

39   Researchers have found . . . cluster of misconceptions: Kimberly A. Lonsway, Lilia M. Cortina, and Vicki J. Magley, "Sexual Harassment Mythology: Definition, Conceptualization, and Measurement," *Sex Roles* 58, no. 9 (2008): 604; Jin X. Goh et al., "Narrow Prototypes and Neglected Victims: Understanding Perceptions of Sexual Harassment," *Journal of Personality and Social Psychology* (forthcoming, January 2022), https://doi.org/10.1037/pspi0000260.

43   In 2019 . . . "act enough 'like a rape victim'": Ryan Leigh Dostie, "She Didn't Act Like a Rape Victim," *New York Times*, July 22, 2019, https://www.nytimes.com/2019/07/22/opinion/armed-forces -rape.html.

43   Other victims have developed . . . during abuse: Jennifer M. Heidt, Brian P. Marx, and John P. Forsyth, "Tonic Immobility and Childhood Sexual Abuse: A Preliminary Report Evaluating the Sequela of Rape-Induced Paralysis," *Behavior Research and Therapy* 43, no. 9 (September 2005): 1167.

43   As neurobiologists discover . . . under attack: Jim Hopper, "Freezing During Sexual Assault and Harassment," *Psychology Today*, April 3, 2018, https://www.psychologytoday.com/us/blog/sexual-assault-and -the-brain/201804/freezing-during-sexual-assault-and-harassment.

44   The law's resistance requirement . . . over the past century: Michelle J. Anderson, "Reviving Resistance in Rape Law," *University of Illinois Law Review* 1998, no. 4 (1998): 957.

45   In 1906 . . . Brown walked free: *Brown v. State*, 106 N.W. 536, 536–38 (Wis. 1906).

46   In 1983 . . . were not enough: *State v. Powell*, 438 So.2d 1306, 1307, 1308 (La. Ct. App. 1983).

46   it remains "a model standard of behavior" . . . judge rape accusers: Anderson, "Reviving Resistance," 962.

46 Some like Alabama retain a formal requirement . . . on resistance: Model Penal Code § 213.1 Reporters' Note (American Law Institute, Tentative Draft No. 3, 2017).

46 Still today . . . "a rape has occurred.": Joshua Dressler, *Understanding Criminal Law*, 8th ed. (Durham, NC: Carolina Academic Press, 2018), 555.

46 With rare exception . . . as a victim of assault: Deborah Tuerkheimer, "Affirmative Consent," *Ohio State Journal of Criminal Law* 13, no. 2 (2016): 448.

47 For instance, in New York . . . "expression of lack of consent": N.Y. Penal Law § 130.05(2)(d) (McKinney, 2013).

47 Both "suppressed" and "intensified" . . . sexual assault survivors: Kimberly A. Lonsway and Joanne Archambault, "Victim Impact: How Victims Are Affected by Sexual Assault and How Law Enforcement Can Respond," End Violence Against Women International (2019): 19, https://www.evawintl.org/Library/DocumentLibraryHandler.ashx ?id=656.

47 For example . . . and civilians alike: Faye T. Nitschke, Blake M. McKimmie, and Eric J. Vanman, "A Meta-Analysis of the Emotional Victim Effect for Female Adult Rape Complainants: Does Complainant Distress Influence Credibility?," *Psychological Bulletin* 145, no. 10 (2019): 953.

48 Skepticism of Marie's account . . . investigation into her rapist: T. Christian Miller and Ken Armstrong, *A False Report: A True Story of Rape in America* (New York: Crown, 2018), 105–7, 111. (The miniseries is based on reporting originally published by ProPublica and The Marshall Project, which later became this book.)

48 A meta-analysis finds . . . for no good reason: Nitschke, McKimmie, and Vanman, "A Meta-Analysis of the Emotional Victim Effect," 953, 955, 973.

49 It was once believed that the uterus . . . resulting in "hysterical" symptoms: Lisa Appignanesi, *Mad, Bad and Sad: Women and the Mind Doctors* (New York: W.W. Norton & Company, 2008), 142.

50 As one forensic psychiatrist testified . . . told the jury: Patrick Ryan and Maria Puente, "Rosie Perez Testifies at Harvey Weinstein

Trial: Annabella Sciorra Said 'I Think It Was Rape.'" *USA Today*, January 24, 2020, https://www.usatoday.com/story/entertainment /celebrities/2020/01/24/weinstein-trial-prosecution-calls-rape-trauma -expert-testify/4556867002.

50 This vilification . . . real consequences: Jennifer S. Hirsch and Shamus Khan, *Sexual Citizens: A Landmark Study of Sex, Power, and Assault on Campus* (New York: W. W. Norton & Company, 2020), 157.

52 Barbara Bowman . . . fall of 2014: Barbara Bowman, "Bill Cosby Raped Me. Why Did It Take 30 Years for People to Believe My Story?," *Washington Post*, November 13, 2014, https://www.washington post.com/posteverything/wp/2014/11/13/bill-cosby-raped-me-why -did-it-take-30-years-for-people-to-believe-my-story.

52 In the end . . . on his couch: Graham Bowley and Sydney Ember, "Andrea Constand was the 'Linchpin' of the Bill Cosby Case," *New York Times*, May 17, 2017, https://www.nytimes.com/2017/05/17/arts /television/bill-cosby-andrea-constand.html.

52 In late 2019 . . . "hardcore pedophile": Matthias Gafni, "After a Rape Mistrial in the #MeToo Era, Accusations Fly. What Happened in the Jury Room?," *San Francisco Chronicle*, November 10, 2019, https://www.sfchronicle.com/bayarea/article/After-a-rape-mistrial -in-the-MeToo-era-14823146.php.

54 In the wake of misconduct allegations . . . "containing of multitudes": Megan Garber, "Les Moonves and the Familiarity Fallacy," *Atlantic*, July 30, 2018, https://www.theatlantic.com/entertainment /archive/2018/07/les-moonves-and-the-familiarity-fallacy/566315.

CHAPTER 3: WHOSE TRUTH?: HOW VICTIMS ARE DISTRUSTED

56 In January 2016 . . . "Bitch": Lisa Miller, "One Night at Mount Sinai," The Cut, October 15, 2019, https://www.thecut.com/2019/10 /mount-sinai-david-newman.html.

57 Soon after . . . "'she's crazy'": Miller, "One Night at Mount Sinai."

58 When the police spoke . . . "she was on morphine": Miller, "One Night at Mount Sinai."

58 One physician said . . . "dragged through the mud on this": Yanan

Wang, "Prominent Manhattan E.R. Doctor, Author, TED-talker Charged with Sexually Abusing Patients," *Washington Post*, January 20, 2016, https://www.washingtonpost.com/news/morning-mix/wp/2016/01/20/prominent-manhattan-e-r-doctor-author-ted-talker-charged-with-sexually-abusing-patients.

58 Friends and colleagues . . . "someone's career": Anna Merlan, "Doctor Accused of Ejaculating on Unconscious Patient Will Reportedly Be Charged With Sexual Abuse," *Jezebel*, January 19, 2016, https://jezebel.com/doctor-accused-of-ejaculating-on-unconscious-patient-wi-1753772879.

58 Even people . . . "earns him the benefit of the doubt from me": Miller, "One Night at Mount Sinai."

59 Within a week . . . investigated the allegation: Miller, "One Night at Mount Sinai."

60 the believability of that claim . . . "how the world works": Karen Jones, "The Politics of Credibility," in *A Mind of One's Own: Feminist Essays on Reason and Objectivity*, 2nd ed., eds. Louise M. Antony and Charlotte E. Witt (New York: Routledge, 2018), 155.

61 Philosophers refer to this spectrum . . . "the truth of other propositions": Franz Huber, "Belief and Degrees of Belief," in *Degrees of Belief*, eds. Franz Huber and Christoph Schmidt-Peri (Dordrecht: Springer Netherlands, 2009), 1.

64 In one survey . . . 51 to 100 percent: Amy Dellinger Page, "Gateway to Reform? Policy Implications of Police Officers' Attitudes Toward Rape," *American Journal of Criminal Justice* 33, no. 1 (2008): 54, 55.

64 A study of a different set . . . complaints are false: Martin D. Schwartz, "National Institute of Justice Visiting Fellowship: Police Investigation Of Rape—Roadblocks And Solutions," National Institute of Justice (2010): 28, https://www.ncjrs.gov/pdffiles1/nij/grants/232667.pdf.

64 one Midwestern police officer . . . "questions of the veracity": Rachel M. Venema, "Police Officer Schema of Sexual Assault Reports: Real Rape, Ambiguous Cases, and False Reports," *Journal of Interpersonal Violence* 31, no. 5 (2016): 879.

64 an Idaho sheriff . . . "actually consensual sex": Danielle Paquette, "The Rape Myth That Lives on in Idaho," *Washington Post*, March 18,

2016, https://www.washingtonpost.com/news/wonk/wp/2016/03/18
/idaho-sheriff-said-most-rape-victims-hes-worked-with-are-lying
-the-numbers-disagree.

64 The confirmation bias . . . "hard to dislodge": Jennifer L. Eberhardt,
*Biased: Uncovering the Hidden Prejudice That Shapes What We See,
Think, and Do* (New York: Penguin Publishing Group, 2019), 33.

64 Studies using the most reliable . . . between 2 and 8 percent:
Kimberly A. Lonsway, Joanne Archambault, and David Lisak, "False
Reports: Moving Beyond the Issue to Successfully Investigate and
Prosecute Non-Stranger Sexual Assault," End Violence Against
Women International (2009): 2, https://www.nsvrc.org/publications
/articles/false-reports-moving-beyond-issue-successfully-investigate
-and-prosecute-non-s.

64 A recent meta-analysis . . . about 5 percent: Claire E. Ferguson and
John M. Malouff, "Assessing Police Classifications of Sexual Assault
Reports: A Meta-Analysis of False Reporting Rates," *Archives of Sex-
ual Behavior* 45, no. 5 (2016): 1185.

65 Research suggests . . . most likely to be true: Kimberly Lonsway,
"Trying to Move the Elephant in the Living Room: Responding to
the Challenge of False Rape Reports," *Violence Against Women* 16, no.
12 (2010): 1361; Dara Lind, "What We Know About False Rape Allegations," Vox, June 1, 2015, https://www.vox.com/2015/6/1/8687479
/lie-rape-statistics.

65 "Someone filing a false report . . . most people": Lonsway, "Trying
to Move the Elephant in the Living Room," 1361.

65 Based on academic research . . . is incorrect: Sandra Newman, "What
Kind of Person Makes False Rape Accusations?," Quartz, May 11,
2017, https://qz.com/980766/the-truth-about-false-rape-accusations.

66 He later apologized . . . women's claims: Alex Marshall, "Plácido
Domingo Walks Back Apology on Harassment Claims," *New York
Times*, February 27, 2020, https://www.nytimes.com/2020/02/27/arts
/music/placido-domingo-apology.html.

66 The story detailed . . . "made them uncomfortable": Jocelyn
Gecker, "Women Accuse Opera Legend Domingo of Sexual Harass-

ment," Associated Press, August 13, 2019, https://apnews.com/c2d51
d690d004992b8cfba3bad827ae9.

66 In the weeks following . . . "get any worse": Jocelyn Gecker and
Jocelyn Noveck, "11 More Women Accuse Opera Singer Placido Domingo of Sexual Harassment, Inappropriate Behavior," *USA Today*,
September 5, 2019, https://www.usatoday.com/story/entertainment
/celebrities/2019/09/05/placido-domingo-accused-sexual-harassment
-11-more-women/2218067001.

67 Weeks after . . . "against Mr. Domingo": Anastasia Tsioulcas,
"Met Opera Chief: 20 Women's Accusations Against Plácido Domingo 'Not Corroborated,'" NPR, September 23, 2019, https://www
.npr.org/2019/09/23/763542627/met-opera-chief-20-womens
-accusations-against-pl-cido-domingo-not-corroborated.

67 Soon after . . . future performances: Michael Cooper, "Plácido
Domingo Leaves Met Opera Amid Sexual Harassment Inquiry," *New
York Times*, September 24, 2019, https://www.nytimes.com/2019/09
/24/arts/music/placido-domingo-met-opera-harassment.html.

67 Brock Turner . . . in 2015: Maya Salam, "Brock Turner Is Appealing
His Sexual Assault Conviction," *New York Times*, December 2, 2017,
https://www.nytimes.com/2017/12/02/us/brock-turner-appeal
.html.

70 In 2016 . . . "just look at what they can do to you": Barry Levine
and Monique El-Faizy, *All the President's Women: Donald Trump and
the Making of a Predator* (New York: Hachette Books, 2019), 213.

70 In 2018 . . . "accuse you of something": Jennifer Williams and Alexia
Underwood, "Read: Trump's Bizarre, Rambling Solo Press Con-
ference on Kavanaugh, Rosenstein, and More," Vox, September 26,
2018, https://www.vox.com/2018/9/26/17907608/trump-kavanaugh
-rosenstein-press-conference-un-nafta-full-text-transcript; Jeremy Dia-
mond, "Trump Says It's 'a Very Scary Time for Young Men in America,'" CNN, October 2, 2018, https://www.cnn.com/2018/10/02
/politics/trump-scary-time-for-young-men-metoo/index.html.

70 The Kavanaugh allegations . . . "axe to grind": Sandra E. Garcia, "A
Mom's #HimToo Tweet Ignites a Viral Meme, and Her Embarrassed

Son Clarifies," *New York Times*, October 9, 2018, https://www.nytimes
.com/2018/10/09/us/him-too-tweet-hashtag.html.

71 Cosby's lawyer said . . . "and lots more money": Natalie Hope Mc-
Donald, "Opening Statements in Cosby Trial Focus on Andrea Constand's Seven-Figure Settlement," Vulture, April 10, 2018, https://
www.vulture.com/2018/04/cosby-trial-defense-tries-paint-constand
-as-gold-digger.html.

71 One study . . . to digest their reactions: Francine Banner, "Honest
Victim Scripting in the Twitterverse," *William & Mary Journal of
Women and the Law* 22, no. 3 (2016): 510.

71 Women whose sexual identity . . . attention-seeking liars: Nicole L.
Johnson and MaryBeth Grove, "Why Us? Toward an Understanding
of Bisexual Women's Vulnerability for and Negative Consequences of
Sexual Violence," *Journal of Bisexuality* 17, no. 4 (2017): 443.

72 This effect . . . well publicized: Lonsway and Fitzgerald, "Rape
Myths: In Review," 135.

72 Duke lacrosse: Duff Wilson, "Former Duke Players Cleared of
All Charges," *New York Times*, April 11, 2007, https://www.nytimes
.com/2007/04/11/us/12dukecnd.html.

72 *Rolling Stone*: Sydney Ember, "Rolling Stone to Pay $1.65 Million
to Fraternity Over Discredited Rape Story," *New York Times*, June 13,
2017, https://www.nytimes.com/2017/06/13/business/media/rape-uva
-rolling-stone-frat.html.

72 "The truth about rape . . . satisfying story": Jia Tolentino, *Trick Mirror:
Reflections on Self-Delusion* (New York: Random House, 2019), 250.

73 Emily Martin . . . tell their story: Alana Semuels, "Low-Wage
Workers Aren't Getting Justice for Sexual Harassment," *Atlantic*,
December 27, 2017, https://www.theatlantic.com/business/archive
/2017/12/low-wage-workers-sexual-harassment/549158.

73 Sandra Pezqueda's story . . . was fired: Semuels, "Low-Wage
Workers Aren't Getting Justice for Sexual Harassment."

74 Whether she is . . . "the injustice of appearance": Deborah L. Rhode,
The Beauty Bias: The Injustice of Appearance in Life and Law (New York:
Oxford University Press, 2010).

76 Bessel van der Kolk . . . "(to the hospital)": Bessel A. van der Kolk,

The Body Keeps the Score: Brain, Mind, and Body in the Healing of Trauma (New York: Penguin Books, 2014), 195.

77 In addition . . . our hippocampus: Jim Hopper, "Why Can't Christine Blasey Ford Remember How She Got Home?," *Scientific American*, October 5, 2018, https://blogs.scientificamerican.com/observations /why-cant-christine-blasey-ford-remember-how-she-got-home.

78 In her testimony . . . "with one another": "Kavanaugh hearing: Transcript," *Washington Post*, September 27, 2018, https://www .washingtonpost.com/news/national/wp/2018/09/27/kavanaugh -hearing-transcript.

78 Dahlia Lithwick . . . "Everyone": Dahlia Lithwick, "The Room Where It Happened," in *Believe Me: How Trusting Women Can Change the World*, eds. Jessica Valenti and Jaclyn Friedman (New York: Seal Press, 2020), 27–28.

78 Less than a week . . . felt "unsure": "NPR/PBS NewsHour/Marist Poll Results October 2018," NPR/PBS NewsHour/Marist (2018): 19, http://maristpoll.marist.edu/wp-content/uploads/2018/10/NPR _PBS-NewsHour_Marist-Poll_USA-NOS-and-Tables_1810021305 .pdf#page=3.

79 Rachel Mitchell . . . "raises significant questions": Rachel Mitchell to All Republican Senators, "Analysis of Dr. Christine Blasey Ford's Allegations," Memorandum, Nominations Investigative Counsel United States Senate Committee for the Judiciary, September 30, 2018, 2–3, https://apps.washingtonpost.com/g/documents/politics/rachel -mitchells-analysis/3221.

79 In an essay . . . against her: Hopper, "Why Can't Christine Blasey Ford Remember How She Got Home?"

79 "Ignorance of how memory works . . . get away with": Jim Hopper, "How Reliable Are the Memories of Sexual Assault Victims?," *Scientific American*, September 27, 2018, https://blogs.scientificamerican.com /observations/how-reliable-are-the-memories-of-sexual-assault- victims.

80 In a study . . . that were not pursued: Misty Luminais, Rachel Lovell, and Daniel Flannery, "Perceptions of Why the Sexual Assault Kit Backlog Exists in Cuyahoga County, Ohio and Recommendations

for Improving Practice," Begun Center for Violence Prevention Research and Education (2017): 1, https://digital.case.edu/islandora /object/ksl:2006061457.

80 Campbell was the lead researcher . . . preset notions: Rebecca Campbell et al., "The Detroit Sexual Assault Kit Action Research Project Final Report," Michigan State University (2015): 109, https:// www.ncjrs.gov/pdffiles1/nij/grants/248680.pdf.

81 perceived overemotionality . . . underemotionality: Emma Sleath and Ray Bull, "Police Perceptions of Rape Victims and the Impact on Case Decision Making: A Systematic Review," *Aggression and Violent Behavior* 34 (2017): 108.

81 Across police departments big and small . . . high rates: Police have systematically mishandled rape cases in jurisdictions including Los Angeles; Washington, D.C.; Baltimore; St. Louis; Philadelphia; New Orleans; New York; and Missoula, Montana. Corey Rayburn Yung, "How to Lie with Rape Statistics: America's Hidden Rape Crisis," *Iowa Law Review* 99, no. 3 (2014): 1218–19; Joseph Goldstein, "New York Examines Over 800 Rape Cases for Possible Mishandling of Evidence," *New York Times*, January 10, 2013, https://www.nytimes .com/2013/01/11/nyregion/new-york-reviewing-over-800-rape -cases-for-possible-mishandling-of-dna-evidence.html; Jon Krakauer, *Missoula: Rape and the Justice System in a College Town* (New York: Anchor Books, 2016), 367–70.

81 High "clearance" numbers . . . low arrest rates: Yung, "How to Lie with Rape Statistics: America's Hidden Rape Crisis."

81 In Pittsburgh . . . unfounded in 2017: Lucy Perkins, "Pittsburgh Police Dismiss Nearly One-Third Of Rape Cases As 'Unfounded,'" WESA, May 15, 2019, https://www.wesa.fm/post/pittsburgh-police -dismiss-nearly-one-third-rape-cases-unfounded#stream/0.

81 In Prince William County, Virginia . . . nearly 40 percent in 2016: Bernice Yeung et al., "When It Comes to Rape, Just Because a Case Is Cleared Doesn't Mean It's Solved," ProPublica, November 15, 2018, https://www.propublica.org/article/when-it-comes-to-rape-just -because-a-case-is-cleared-does-not-mean-solved.

82 an earlier analysis found similarly high rates . . . Oxnard, Califor-

nia: Alex Campbell and Katie J. M. Baker, "This Police Department Tosses Aside Rape Reports When a Victim Doesn't Resist 'To the Best of Her Ability,'" BuzzFeed News, September 8, 2016, https://www .buzzfeednews.com/article/alexcampbell/unfounded.

82 researchers estimate . . . about 5 percent: Ferguson and Malouff, "Assessing Police Classifications of Sexual Assault Reports: A Meta-Analysis of False Reporting Rates," 1185.

82 A ProPublica investigation . . . only 3 percent of its cases: Lena V. Groeger et al., "Could Your Police Department Be Inflating Rape Clearance Rates?," ProPublica, November 15, 2018, https://projects .propublica.org/graphics/rape_clearance.

82 "No matter the jurisdiction . . . sexual violence seldom results in an arrest": Melissa S. Morabito et al., U.S. Department of Justice, "Decision Making in Sexual Assault Cases: Replication Research on Sexual Violence Case Attrition in the U.S." (February 2019): VI, https://www .ncjrs.gov/pdffiles1/nij/grants/252689.pdf.

83 In 2011, Lara McLeod . . . never even arrested: Katie J. M. Baker, "The Police Told Her to Report Her Rape, Then Arrested Her for Lying," BuzzFeed News, September 27, 2015, https://www .buzzfeednews.com/article/katiejmbaker/the-police-told-her-to -report-her-rape-then-arrested-her-for.

84 More than one hundred thousand . . . around the country: "Where the Backlog Exists and What's Happening to End It," End The Backlog, accessed April 19, 2019, http://www.endthebacklog.org/backlog /where-backlog-exists-and-whats-happening-end-it.

84 In her study . . . "shelved, literally": Campbell et al., "The Detroit Sexual Assault Kit Action Research Project Final Report," 105.

85 the first time . . . up her skirt: Irin Carmon, "The Woman Who Taped Harvey Weinstein," The Cut, February 18, 2020, https://www .thecut.com/2020/02/ambra-battilana-gutierrez-on-the-harvey -weinstein-trial.html.

85 "Being from another country . . . believed in the system": Carmon, "The Woman Who Taped Harvey Weinstein."

85 The following day . . . "I won't do it again": Ronan Farrow, *Catch and Kill* (New York: Little, Brown and Company, 2019), 68.

85   "After analyzing" . . . Manhattan District Attorney's Office: James
     C. McKinley Jr., "Harvey Weinstein Won't Face Charges After Grop-
     ing Report," *New York Times*, April 10, 2015, https://www.nytimes
     .com/2015/04/11/nyregion/harvey-weinstein-wont-face-charges
     -after-groping-report-manhattan-prosecutor-says.html.

85   According to Gutierrez . . . "the front page": Carmon, "The Woman
     Who Taped Harvey Weinstein."

86   The defense team claimed . . . events prevailed: Megan Twohey et
     al., "For Weinstein, a Brush With the Police, Then No Charges," *New
     York Times*, October 15, 2017, https://www.nytimes.com/2017/10/15
     /nyregion/harvey-weinstein-new-york-sex-assault-investigation.html.

86   Fourteen years later . . . criminal court: Rajini Vaidyanathan,
     "Larry Nassar Case: The 156 Women Who Confronted a Predator,"
     BBC News, January 25, 2018, https://www.bbc.com/news/world-us
     -canada-42725339.

88   Back in 2004 . . . "not a crime": Kenneth Ouellette, "Independent
     Investigation for Brianne Randall and Meridian Township, Mich-
     igan," Meridian Township, Michigan (2019): http://www.meridian
     .mi.us/home/showdocument?id=17575.

88   The detective chose . . . to prosecutors: Richard Gonzales, "Mich-
     igan Officer Says He Botched Investigation, Believed Larry Nassar's
     'Lies,'" NPR, March 26, 2019, https://www.npr.org/2019/03/26/7070
     48511/michigan-officer-says-he-botched-investigation-believed
     -larry-nassars-lies.

88   Girls and women came forward . . . USA Gymnastics: Kerry
     Howley, "Everyone Believed Larry Nassar," The Cut, November 19,
     2018, https://www.thecut.com/2018/11/how-did-larry-nassar-deceive
     -so-many-for-so-long.html.

88   This was how . . . "medically appropriate": Jean Casarez et al., "She
     Filed a Complaint Against Larry Nassar in 2014. Nothing Hap-
     pened," CNN, February 1, 2018, http://www.cnn.com/2018/02/01
     /us/msu-amanda-thomashow-complaint-larry-nassar/index.html.

90   a gaslighter . . . "without grounds": Kate Abramson, "Turning Up
     the Lights on Gaslighting," *Philosophical Perspectives* 28 (2014): 2.

92   More women would later come forward . . . Andrew Yang: Gra-

ham Kates, "Dozens of Women Have Accused Doctor of Sexual Assault Following Evelyn Yang Interview, Lawyer Says," CBS News, February 17, 2020, https://www.cbsnews.com/news/dr-robert-hadden -dozens-more-women-accuse-doctor-sexual-assault-since-evelyn-yang -interview-lawyer-says.

92 Many of these women have sued . . . pattern of abuse: Complaint, *Jane Doe 16 v. Columbia Univ.*, Case No. 1:20-cv-01791 (S.D.N.Y. February 28, 2020).

93 "untruthful, dishonest, or vicious" accusers: *People v. Yannucci*, 15 N.Y.S.2d 865, 866 (App. Div.2d Dep't 1939), *rev'd on other grounds*, 238 N.Y. 546 (1940).

93 without a corroboration requirement . . . "there is no truth": *Davis v. State*, 48 S.E. 180, 181–82 (Ga. 1904).

93 "The natural instinct . . . as a witness": *State v. Neel*, 60 P. 510, 511 (Utah 1900).

94 a rape charge "is one which is easily made . . . with caution": *People v. Rincon-Pineda*, 538 P.2d 247, 252 (Cal. 1975).

94 To support the exceptional requirement . . . "the defendant": Model Penal Code § 213.6 cmt. at 428 (American Law Institute, Official Draft and Revised Comments 1980).

94 To justify a hard "prompt outcry" rule . . . "psychopathy of the complainant": Model Penal Code § 207.4 cmt. at 265 (American Law Institute, Tentative Draft No. 4 1955). The 1962 Proposed Official Draft directs the reader to Tentative Draft No. 4 for commentary related to the "prompt outcry" rule. Model Penal Code § 213.6 at 151 (American Law Institute, Proposed Official Draft 1962).

94 The new explanation rests . . . "sexual aggression": Model Penal Code § 213.6 cmt. at 421 (American Law Institute, Official Draft and Revised Comments 1980).

94 to rationalize the instruction . . . "in private": Model Penal Code § 213.6(5) (American Law Institute, Official Draft and Revised Comments 1980).

95 More than a dozen states . . . in rape cases: Early drafts of the proposed Model Penal Code revision provide a useful overview of the prompt complaint rule, corroboration, and cautionary jury instructions

in state law. American Law Institute, Model Penal Code: Sexual Assault and Related Offense, Preliminary Draft No. 5 184–89 (September 8, 2015).

95 Under Title VII . . . time-barred: 42 U.S.C. § 2000e-5(e)1 (2000).

96 In two cases . . . against her: *Faragher v. City of Boca Raton*, 524 U.S. 775 (1998); *Burlington Indus. v. Ellerth*, 524 U.S. 742 (1998).

96 the defense "indirectly imposes" . . . "is always 'unreasonable'": Deborah L. Brake and Joanna L. Grossman, "The Failure of Title VII as a Rights-Claiming System," *North Carolina Law Review* 86, no. 4 (2008): 879, 881.

96 Lower courts . . . seventeen days: *Conatzer v. Med. Prof'l Building Servs.*, 255 F.Supp.2d 1259, 1270 (N.D. Okla. 2003); *Marsicano v. Am. Soc'y of Safety Eng'rs*, No. 97 C 7819, 1998 WL 603128, at *7 (N.D. Ill. 1998).

97 "nuts and sluts" defense: Legal scholar Susan Estrich coined this term in 1991 to describe how Clarence Thomas supporters discredited Anita Hill during his confirmation hearings. Alessandra Stanley, "The Curious Case of Susan Estrich," *New York Times*, September 9, 2016, https://www.nytimes.com/2016/09/11/style/susan-estrich-feminist -roger-ailes-fox-news.html.

CHAPTER 4: BLAME-SHIFTING: HOW VICTIMS ARE FAULTED

102 In 2016 . . . she told a reporter: Alanna Vagianos, "10 Years Later, She Confronted the Cop Who Said Her Rape Was 'Consensual,'" *Huffington Post*, October 25, 2017, https://www.huffpost.com/entry /second-assault-jillian-corsie-rape-amy-rosner_n_5d31d6d7e4b020c d9942b934.

103 When we attribute . . . off the hook: Gloria J. Fischer, "Effects of Drinking by the Victim or Offender in a Simulated Trial of an Acquaintance Rape," *Psychological Reports* 77 (1995): 579–86.

103 This penchant for . . . "responsible for the assault": Grubb and Turner, "Attribution of Blame in Rape Cases," 444.

104 researchers have consistently found . . . victim blaming: Grubb and Turner, "Attribution of Blame in Rape Cases," 445; Antonia Abbey,

Pam McCauslan, and Lisa Thomson Ross, "Sexual Assault Perpetration by College Men: The Role of Alcohol, Misperception of Sexual Intent, and Sexual Beliefs and Experiences," *Journal of Social & Clinical Psychology* 17, no. 2 (1998): 169–70, 184; Alan J. Lambert and Katherine Raichle, "The Role of Political Ideology in Mediating Judgments of Blame in Rape Victims and Their Assailants: A Test of the Just World, Personal Responsibility and Legitimization Hypothesis," *Personality and Social Psychology Bulletin* 26, no. 7 (2000): 854, 858, 860–61; Clifford R. Mynatt and Elizabeth Rice Allgeier, "Risk Factors, Self-Attributions, and Adjustments Problems Among Victims of Sexual Coercion," *Journal of Applied Social Psychology* 20, no. 2 (1990): 142, 146–53.

104 According to this theory . . . "careless or foolish": Melvin J. Lerner and Dale T. Miller, "Just World Research and the Attribution Process: Looking Back and Ahead," *Psychological Bulletin* 85, no. 5 (1978): 1031.

104 When one of Harvey Weinstein's lawyers . . . "any vulnerable circumstance ever": Michael Barbaro, host, "The Woman Defending Harvey Weinstein," *The Daily* (podcast), February 7, 2020, transcript, https://www.nytimes.com/2020/02/07/podcasts/the-daily/weinstein-trial.html.

104 After the interview aired . . . using the hashtag #WhereIPutMyself: Megan Twohey, "A Question That Almost Went Unasked," *New York Times*, February 14, 2020, https://www.nytimes.com/2020/02/14/podcasts/daily-newsletter-weinstein-trial-coronavirus.html/.

105 Research suggests . . . "victim of rape": Grubb and Turner, "Attribution of Blame in Rape Cases," 446.

106 "If I was truly honest" . . . "poor judgment": Chessy Prout with Jenny Abelson, *I Have the Right To: A High School Survivor's Story of Sexual Assault, Justice, and Hope* (New York: Margaret K. McElderry Books, 2018), 139, 157.

107 Research confirms . . . sexual victimization: Karen G. Weiss, "Too Ashamed to Report: Deconstructing the Shame of Sexual Victimization," *Feminist Criminology* 5, no. 3 (2010): 294.

107 In her exposé . . . "do something like this to us": Katie J. M. Baker,

"My Weekend in America's So-Called 'Rape Capital,'" Jezebel, May 10, 2012, https://jezebel.com/my-weekend-in-americas-so-called-rape-capital-5908472.

107 Research shows that self-blaming . . . healing: Sarah E. Ullman, *Talking About Sexual Assault: Society's Response to Survivors* (Washington, D.C.: American Psychological Association, 2010), 79.

108 Donna Freitas, the author . . . "so long?": Freitas, *Consent*, 288.

108 this ideal stems . . . the "good girl": Grubb and Turner, "Attribution of Blame in Rape Cases," 447.

109 While intoxicated rapists . . . when they are intoxicated: Grubb and Turner, "Attribution of Blame in Rape Cases," 449; Deborah Richardson and Jennifer L. Campbell, "Alcohol and Rape: The Effect of Alcohol on Attributions of Blame for Rape," *Personality and Social Psychology Bulletin* 8, no. 3 (1982): 472; Calvin M. Simms, Nora E. Noel, and Stephen A. Maisto, "Rape Blame as a Function of Alcohol Presence and Resistant Type," *Addictive Behaviors* 32, no. 12 (2007): 2773–74; T. Cameron Wild, Kathryn Graham, and Jürgen Rehm, "Blame and Punishment for Intoxicated Aggression: When Is the Perpetrator Culpable?" *Addiction* 93, no. 5 (1998): 681–82; "The bottle may grant a pardon to the perpetrator" from Karla J. Stormo et al., "Attributions About Acquaintance Rape: The Role of Alcohol and Individual Differences," *Journal of Applied Social Psychology* 27, no. 4 (1997): 299.

109 women who are assaulted . . . internalize this message: Heather D. Flowe and John Maltby, "An Experimental Examination of Alcohol Consumption, Alcohol Expectancy, and Self-Blame on Willingness to Report a Hypothetical Rape," *Aggressive Behavior* 44, no. 3 (2018): 230.

109 In her book, *Blurred Lines* . . . "fifth vodka shot": Vanessa Grigoriadis, *Blurred Lines: Rethinking Sex, Power, and Consent on Campus* (New York: Houghton Mifflin Harcourt, 2017), 93.

109 This belief is critical . . . came her way: Duncan Kennedy, *Sexy Dressing Etc.: Essays on the Power and Politics of Cultural Identity* (Cambridge, MA: Harvard University Press, 1995), 171–72.

110 In her memoir . . . with her beauty: McGowan, *Brave*, 235–36.

110 On college campuses . . . "What were you wearing?": Isabella Gomez, Mercedes Leguizamon, and Christina Zdanowicz, "Sexual As-

sault Survivors Are Reclaiming the Words Used to Discredit Them: 'What Were You Wearing?'" CNN, April 16, 2018, https://www.cnn.com/2018/04/16/health/what-were-you-wearing-exhibit-trnd/index.html.

110 As Peggy Orenstein explains . . . "young men's": Peggy Orenstein, *Girls & Sex: Navigating the Complicated New Landscape* (New York: HarperCollins Publishers, 2016), 7–9.

111 In *Pushout* . . . blamed for their violation: Monique W. Morris, *Pushout: The Criminalization of Black Girls in Schools* (New York: The New Press, 2015), 125, 127–28, 129–30.

111 Research shows . . . "held to a higher standard": Nicole Therese Buchanan, "Examining the Impact of Racial Harassment on Sexually Harassed African-American Women," (PhD diss., University of Illinois, Urbana-Champaign, 2002), 23–24, https://www.ideals.illinois.edu/handle/2142/82025.

111 Among the cluster of stereotypes . . . "Black slave women": Patricia Hill Collins, *Black Feminist Thought: Knowledge, Consciousness, and the Politics of Empowerment*, 2nd ed. (New York: Routledge, 2000), 81.

111 "If Black women . . . when they are raped": Roxanne Donovan and Michelle Williams, "Living at the Intersection: The Effects of Racism and Sexism on Black Rape Survivors," in *Violence in the Lives of Black Women: Battered, Black, and Blue*, ed. Carolyn M. West (New York: Routledge, 2013), 98.

112 Psychologists have found . . . disclosing their abuse: Donovan and Williams, "Living at the Intersection," 98.

112 Vanessa Grigoriadis . . . "'just how it is'": Grigoriadis, *Blurred Lines*, 98.

112 Karmenife later created . . . "have it rest on my shoulders": Marie Solis, "Meet the Sexual Assault Survivor Who Rewrote Her Experience in a Powerful Photo Series," Mic, February 29, 2016, https://www.mic.com/articles/136394/meet-the-sexual-assault-survivor-who-rewrote-her-experience-in-a-powerful-photo-series.

112 "a thing to be stolen, sold, bought, bartered, or exchanged by others": Catharine A. MacKinnon, *Toward a Feminist Theory of the State* (Cambridge: Harvard University Press, 1989), 172.

113 England and a colleague . . . "for casual sex": Paula England and Jonathan Bearak, "The Sexual Double Standard and Gender Differences in Attitudes Toward Casual Sex Among U.S. University Students," *Demographic Research* 30 (2014): 1336.

114 One team of sociologists . . . labeled "sluts": Elizabeth A. Armstrong et al., "'Good Girls': Gender, Social Class, and Slut Discourse on Campus," *Social Psychology Quarterly* 77, no. 2 (2014): 100, 102, 111, 112.

114 Winston said . . . pursue charges: Walt Bogdanich, "A Star Player Accused, and a Flawed Rape Investigation," *New York Times*, April 16, 2014, https://www.nytimes.com/interactive/2014/04/16/sports/errors-in-inquiry-on-rape-allegations-against-fsu-jameis-winston.html.

114 The film depicts . . . "a whore": *The Hunting Ground*, directed by Kirby Dick, Los Angeles: Chain Camera Pictures, 2015.

116 Charlotte can recall only . . . her assault: *State v. Finley*, No. A13–0803 (Minn. Ct. App. April 28, 2014).

116 the drafters specifically rejected . . . "end result": Model Penal Code § 213.1 cmt. 5 at 315 (American Law Institute, Official Draft and Revised Comments 1980).

116 More than half the states . . . victim's responsibility: Allison C. Nichols, "Out of the Haze: A Clearer Path for Prosecution of Alcohol-Facilitated Sexual Assault," *New York University Annual Survey of American Law* 71, no. 2 (2016): 222.

117 This is what happened to Audrey . . . the victim of rape: *State v. Haddock*, 664 S.E.2d 339, 475–76, 483 (N.C. Ct. App. 2008).

117 Researchers have consistently demonstrated . . . sober women: Georgina S. Hammock and Deborah R. Richardson, "Perceptions of Rape: The Influence of Closeness of Relationship, Intoxication and Sex of Participant," *Violence and Victims* 12, no. 3 (1997): 238; Kellie Rose Lynch et al., "Who Bought the Drinks? Juror Perceptions of Intoxication in a Rape Trial," *Journal of Interpersonal Violence* 28, no. 16 (2013): 3207; Richardson and Campbell, "Alcohol and Rape," 469; Regina A. Schuller and Anne-Marie Wall, "The Effects of Defendant

and Complainant Intoxication on Mock Jurors' Judgments of Sexual Assault," *Psychology of Women Quarterly* 22, no. 4 (1998): 557, 565.

118 In one study . . . perceived as victims: Lynch et al., "Who Bought the Drinks?," 3207–8, 3217.

120 Melissa Nelson . . . sided with Knight: *Nelson v. Knight*, 834 N.W. 2d 64, 65–67, 70, 72, 73 (Iowa 2013).

121 has called this . . . temptation enough: Lynne Henderson, "Rape and Responsibility," *Law and Philosophy* 11, no. 1 (1992): 130–31.

121 The leading case on "unwelcomeness" . . . decided in 1986: *Meritor Sav. Bank v. Vinson*, 477 U.S. 57 (1986).

121 The story begins more than a decade earlier . . . sex with him: Tanya Katerí Hernández, "'What Not to Wear'—Race and Unwelcomeness in Sexual Harassment Law: The Story of *Meritor Savings Bank v. Vinson*," in *Women and the Law: Stories*, eds. Elizabeth M. Schneider and Stephanie M. Wildman (New York: Foundation Press, 2011), 281–83.

121 She later recounted . . . "how it started": DeNeen L. Brown, "She said her boss raped her in a bank vault. Her sexual harassment case would make legal history," *Washington Post*, October 13, 2017, https://www .washingtonpost.com/news/retropolis/wp/2017/10/13/she-said-her -boss-raped-her-in-a-bank-vault-her-sexual-harassment-case-would -make-legal-history.

121 Over the next two and a half years . . . forced intercourse: Brief of Respondent Mechelle Vinson at 4, *Meritor*, 477 U.S. 57 (No. 84–1979).

121 She chose . . . "I need my job": Hernández, "'What Not to Wear,'" 283, 284.

122 When the stress . . . denied the accusations: Hernández, "'What Not to Wear,'" 284–85.

122 The case was tried . . . "about sex": Hernández, "'What Not to Wear,'" 286.

122 Any "intimate or sexual relationship" . . . "victim of sexual discrimination": *Vinson v. Taylor*, Civ. Action No. 78–1793 (D.D.C. February 26, 1980).

122 "All too often . . . would-be perpetrators": Brief of Respondent Mechelle Vinson at 45, *Meritor*, 477 U.S. 57 (no. 84–1979).

122 Vinson was cast . . . "contributed to the outcome": Hernández, "'What not to Wear,'" 301.

123 Vinson's case eventually . . . in place today: *Meritor*, 477 U.S. at 68, 69 (emphasis added).

123 Regardless of what they are wearing . . . loose-fitting shirt: Buchanan, "Examining the Impact of Racial Harassment on Sexually Harassed African-American Women."

123 "The mere fact" . . . "'asked for it'": Hernández, "'What Not to Wear,'" 303–6.

126 In one typical case . . . "name(s) of the disease(s)": *Kroontje v. CKE Rests.*, No. Civ. 13–4066-KES, 2014 WL 1513895, at *5–6 (D.S.D. April 16, 2014).

126 Even with the rape shield rule in place . . . woman-initiated sex: Deborah Tuerkheimer, "Judging Sex," *Cornell Law Review* 97, no. 6 (2012): 1490.

127 The admission of sexual history evidence . . . protection of our laws: Michelle J. Anderson, "From Chastity Requirement to Sexuality License: Sexual Consent and a New Rape Shield Law," *George Washington Law Review* 70, no. 1 (2002): 107.

129 The story of a woman named Crystal . . . "brought trouble onto herself": Margaret Moore Jackson, "Confronting 'Unwelcomeness' From the Outside: Using Case Theory to Tell the Story of Sexually-Harassed Women," *Cardozo Journal of Law and Gender* 14, no. 1 (2007): 75–76.

129 One analysis of the case law . . . "or force": Janine Benedet, "Hostile Environment Sexual Harassment Claims and the Unwelcome Influence of Rape Law," *Michigan Journal of Gender and Law* 3, no 1 (1996): 139, 136, 142, 143, 150.

CHAPTER 5: THE CARE GAP: HOW VICTIMS ARE DISREGARDED

132 When the two arrived . . . "sex on him": "Vanessa Tyson's Full Statement on Justin Fairfax," *New York Times*, February 6, 2019, https://www.nytimes.com/2019/02/06/us/politics/vanessa-tyson -statement.html.

133 Fairfax denied . . . Fairfax maintained: Tara Law, "Professor Comes Forward With Graphic Details of Alleged Sexual Assault by Virginia Lt. Governor," *Time*, February 6, 2019, https://time.com/5523274 /vanessa-tyson-virginia-sexual-assault.

133 He also compared . . . "protect black men": "Justin Fairfax Accuser Vanessa Tyson Describes Alleged Sexual Assault: 'I Couldn't Feel My Neck,'" CBS News, April 1, 2019, https://www.cbsnews.com/news /justin-fairfax-accuser-vanessa-tyson-speaks-out-sexual-assault.

133 Fairfax later sued . . . has appealed: Laura Vozzella, "Judge Dismisses Lt. Gov. Fairfax's Defamation Suit over CBS Interviews on Sexual Assault Claims," *Washington Post*, February 11, 2020, https:// www.washingtonpost.com/local/virginia-politics/judge-dismisses-lt -gov-fairfaxs-defamation-suit-over-cbs-interviews-on-sexual-assault -claims/2020/02/11/d76e6a42-4d15-11ea-9b5c-eac5b16dafaa_story .html; *Fairfax v. CBS Broadcasting, Inc.*, No. 1:19-cv-01176-AJT-MSN, at *29–30 (E.D. Va. February 11, 2020); Dan Packel, "Justin Fairfax Swaps Lawyers as Appeal in CBS Defamation Case Moves Forward," *National Law Journal*, May 27, 2020, https://www.law.com/national lawjournal/2020/05/27/justin-fairfax-swaps-lawyers-as-appeal-in -cbs-defamation-case-moves-forward/?slreturn=20200526163659.

134 "One thing . . . glance away from this": Associated Press, "Vanessa Tyson, Who Accused Virginia Lt. Gov. Justin Fairfax of Sexual Assault, Talks Women Reporting Abuse," *USA Today*, February 13, 2019, https://www.usatoday.com/story/news/nation/2019/02/13 /justin-fairfax-accuser-vanessa-tyson-talks-women-reporting-abuse /2857038002.

134 She understands . . . often it doesn't: Vanessa Tyson, "Understanding the Personal Impact of Sexual Violence and Assault," *Journal of Women, Politics & Policy* 40, no. 1 (2019): 176.

135 "This is the *truly* grotesque factor . . . sympathy and empathy": Rebecca Traister, "Why Donald Trump—and Other Powerful Men— Love to Cast Themselves as Victims," Intelligencer, *New York Magazine*, October 24, 2019, https://nymag.com/intelligencer/2019/10 /why-donald-trump-loves-to-cast-himself-as-a-victim.html.

136 "Women's careers . . . what they've done": Jia Tolentino, "Jian

Ghomeshi, John Hockenberry, and the Laws of Patriarchal Physics," *New Yorker*, September 17, 2018, https://www.newyorker.com/culture/cultural-comment/jian-ghomeshi-john-hockenberry-and-the-laws-of-patriarchal-physics.

136 this allocation of credibility . . . "making these accusations": Kate Manne, *Down Girl: The Logic of Misogyny* (New York: Oxford University Press, 2018), 194, 218–19.

136 This general preference . . . settle rather than destabilize: Daniel Kahneman, *Thinking, Fast and Slow* (New York: Farrar, Straus and Giroux, 2011), 304–9.

137 "All the perpetrator asks . . . burden of pain": Judith Herman, *Trauma and Recovery: The Aftermath of Violence—From Domestic Abuse to Political Terror* (New York: Basic Books, 1992), 7.

137 by coming forward, "the victim demands . . . remembering": Herman, *Trauma and Recovery*, 7–8.

137 "Empathy is biased" . . . "prejudice does": Paul Bloom, *Against Empathy: The Case for Rational Compassion* (New York: Ecco, 2016), 31.

138 for nearly two decades . . . "listen to us": Rebecca Greenfield, "Marriot Sued by Housekeeper Over Guest Sexual Misconduct," Bloomberg, January 28, 2019, https://www.bloomberg.com/news/articles/2019-01-28/marriott-sued-over-guest-sexual-misconduct-as-metoo-expands; Complaint, *Vallejo v. Marriott Hotel Services, Inc.*, Case No. 30–2019–01046612-CU-OE-CJC (Superior Court, Orange County, California January 28, 2019).

139 Like many of the thirty women . . . *be flattered*: Susan Chira and Catrin Einhorn, "How Tough Is It to Change a Culture of Harassment? Ask Women at Ford," *New York Times*, December 19, 2017, https://www.nytimes.com/interactive/2017/12/19/us/ford-chicago-sexual-harassment.html.

140 Jenna Ries . . . "reviewing the tape": Complaint at 8, 9, 13, 15, *Ries v. McDonald's USA*, Case No. 19–829-CD (Mich. Ingham Cty. Circuit Ct. November 12, 2019), https://www.aclu.org/sites/default/files/field_document/1_complaint_filed.pdf.

140 In *Boys & Sex* . . . "ignore pain": Peggy Orenstein, *Boys & Sex: Young*

Men on Hookups, Love, Porn, Consent, and Navigating the New Masculinity (New York: HarperCollins Publishers, 2020), 176.

141 Girls are "trained" . . . "more seriously than their own": Orenstein, *Boys & Sex*, 176.

141 This training cultivates . . . provides to others: Robin West, *Caring for Justice* (New York: New York University Press, 1997), 114.

141 Girls grow up . . . "work wives": Laura A. Rosenbury, "Work Wives," *Harvard Journal of Law & Gender* 36, no. 2 (2013): 346.

141 For many women and girls . . . central feature of subordination: West, *Caring for Justice*, 79, 82.

141 "Patriarchal ideology" . . . "essence of misogyny": Manne, *Down Girl*, 46–47.

141 Research shows . . . paramount: Cordelia Fine, *Delusions of Gender: How Our Minds, Society, and Neurosexism Create Difference* (New York: W. W. Norton & Company, 2010), 24–26.

142 Laurie Penny . . . "male suffering simply matters more": Laurie Penny, "Gaming's #MeToo Moment and the Tyranny of Male Fragility," *Wired*, September 6, 2019, https://www.wired.com/story/video games-industry-metoo-moment-male-fragility.

144 Decades ago . . . "I could not stop laughing.": E. Jean Carroll, *What Do We Need Men For? A Modest Proposal* (New York: St. Martin's Press, 2019), 242.

144 As one participant . . . began to cry: Beth A. Quinn, "The Paradox of Complaining: Law, Humor, and Harassment in the Everyday Work World," *Law and Social Inquiry* 25, no. 4 (2000): 1167.

144 Research shows that even when unwanted . . . workplace free of abuse: Vicki Magley et al., "Outcomes of Self-Labeling Sexual Harassment," *Journal of Applied Psychology* 84, no. 3 (1999): 390.

145 Stereotypes of Latinx . . . what seems inevitable: Waleska Suero, "'We Don't Think of It as Sexual Harassment': The Intersection of Gender & Ethnicity on Latinas' Workplace Sexual Harassment Claims," *Chicanx Latinx Law Review* 33, no. 1 (2015): 146.

145 Comedian Anna Akana . . . "violating thing": Susan Cheng,

"Asian-American Women in Hollywood Say It's Twice as Hard for Them to Say #MeToo," BuzzFeed News, February 24, 2018, https://www.buzzfeednews.com/article/susancheng/what-metoo-means-for-asian-american-women-in-hollywood.

145 Across a range of workplaces . . . downplaying it: Feldblum and Lipnic, "Select Task Force on the Study of Harassment in the Workplace," v.

146 A good illustration . . . "I don't know if I'm wrong": Susan W. Hinze, "'Am I Being Over-Sensitive?' Women's Experience of Sexual Harassment During Medical Training," *health* 8, no. 1 (2004): 103, 109–10.

146 Donna Freitas describes . . . "never left me again": Freitas, *Consent*, 76–77.

146 the law of private harms . . . sexual harassment: Catharine A. MacKinnon, *Sexual Harassment of Working Women* (New Haven and London: Yale University Press: 1979), 164–74.

147 Along with other activists . . . in 1979: MacKinnon, *Sexual Harassment of Working Women*, 174.

147 In *Meritor Savings* . . . "severe or pervasive": *Meritor Sav. Bank, FSB v. Vinson*, 477 U.S. 57, 67 (1986).

147 It does not suffice . . . perceive it this way: *Harris v. Forklift Sys., Inc.*, 510 U.S. 17, 21 (1993).

148 Three decades after . . . "comments and gestures": Sandra F. Sperino and Suja A. Thomas, *Unequal: How America's Courts Undermine Discrimination Law* (New York: Oxford University Press, 2017), 31.

148 Unless it makes work "hellish for women" . . . the law's concern: *Anderson v. G.D.C., Inc.*, 281 F.3d 452, 459 (4th Cir. 2002); *Hathaway v. Runyon*, 132 F.3d 1214, 1223 (8th Cir. 1997); *Baskerville v. Culligan Int'l Co.*, 50 F.3d 428, 430 (7th Cir. 1995).

148 One woman said she endured . . . "sexually hostile work environment claim": *Cockrell v. Greene Cty. Hosp. Bd.*, No. 7:17-cv-00333-LSC, 2018 WL 1627811, at *4–5 (N.D. Ala. April 4, 2018).

148 To support this conclusion, the court cited an earlier case . . . "eleven months": *Cockrell*, 2018 WL 1627811, at *5 (citing *Mendoza v. Borden, Inc.*, 195 F.3d 1238, 1247–48 [11th Cir. 1999]).

149 The dismissal of allegations . . . "less evidence of harassment": Sperino and Thomas, *Unequal*, 37.

149 Employers are not liable . . . "not uncommon in the workplace": *Swyear v. Fare Foods Corp.*, 911 F.3d 874, 881 (7th Cir. 2018) (citing *Passananti v. Cook Cty.*, 689 F.3d 655, 667 [7th Cir. 2012]).

149 A supervisor who . . . inquired about her menstrual cycle.: *Little v. CRSA*, 744 F. App'x 679, 680–81 (11th Cir. 2018).

149 A boss who . . . "wear low-cut blouses and short skirts": *Berger v. Rollins, Inc.*, No. CV 15–4102, 2017 WL 1361789, at *3 (E.D. La. April 12, 2017).

149 A supervisor who . . . propositioned her for sex: *Ogletree v. Necco*, No. 1:16-cv-1858-WSD, 2016 WL 7010869, at *1 (N.D. Ga. November 30, 2016).

150 when the harassing conduct . . . "isolated incidents of harassment": *Saidu-Kamara v. Parkway Corp.*, 155 F. Supp. 2d 436, 439–40 (E.D. Pa. 2001).

150 The court pointed to a string of cases . . . would amount to sexual harassment under the law: *Saidu-Kamara*, 155 F. Supp. 2d at 440.

150 Nor would it be actionable harassment . . . go to bed with him: *Anderson v. Family Dollar Stores of Ark., Inc.*, 579 F.3d 858, 862 (8th Cir. 2009).

150 For a manager to bombard . . . touch her breast: *Stacy v. Shoney's, Inc.*, 142 F.3d 436, 436 (6th Cir. 1998).

150 For a supervisor . . . "as if to grab her": *Saxton v. American Tel. & Tel., Co.*, 10 F.3d 526, 528 (7th Cir. 1993).

150 One woman said . . . unwanted touching of her shoulders, arms, and buttocks by male employees: *Landers v. CHLN, Inc.*, No. CIV.A. 07–75-EBA, 2009 WL 803777, at *1 (E.D. Ky. March 25, 2009).

151 Another woman recounted . . . "slut," and "tramp": *Baldwin v. Blue Cross/Blue Shield of Alabama*, 480 F.3d 1287, 1294–95 (11th Cir. 2007).

151 One woman described . . . attempting to kiss her: *Weiss v. Coca-Cola Bottling Co.*, 990 F.2d 333, 337 (7th Cir. 1993).

151 tort claim . . . distinct set of obstacles: Martha Chamallas, "Will Tort Law Have Its #MeToo Moment?," *Journal of Tort Law* 11, no. 1 (2018): 57–58.

151 In order to prove . . . "extreme and outrageous": Martha Chamallas, "Discrimination and Outrage: The Migration from Civil Rights to Tort Law," *William & Mary Law Review* 48, no. 6 (2007): 2124–31.

152 When courts dismiss a claim . . . too trivial to matter: Kalley R. Aman, "No Remedy for Hostile Environment Sexual Harassment? Balancing a Plaintiff's Right to Relief Against Protection of Small Business Employers," *Journal of Small and Emerging Business Law* 4, no. 2 (2000). The cases examined in this section are discussed in this piece.

152 One supermarket employee . . . "requisite outrageousness": *Hoy v. Angelone*, 691 A.2d 476, 479, 483 (Pa. Super. Ct. 1997).

152 In another case dismissed . . . "suggestive comments": *Blount v. Sterling Healthcare Grp., Inc.*, 934 F. Supp. 1365, 1368 (S.D. Fla. 1996).

152 On a separate occasion . . . "outrageousness required": *Pucci v. US-Air*, 940 F. Supp. 305, 307, 309 (M.D. Fla. 1996).

153 one defendant sought to question . . . "allegedly attacked": *Jacquez v. Duran*, No. CV 00–1185 JP/JHG, 2001 WL 37124997, at *1 (D.N.M. July 26, 2001).

153 Some courts maintain . . . less offensive: Patrick J. Hines, "Bracing the Armor: Extending Rape Shield Protections to Civil Proceedings," *Notre Dame Law Review* 86, no. 2 (2011): 899.

153 On this theory, courts have admitted . . . and the like: *Ten Broeck DuPont, Inc. v. Brooks*, 283 S.W.3d 705, 712 (Ky. 2009).

154 Women who worked in a Minnesota coal mine . . . "raped on the stand": Clara Bingham and Laura Leedy Gansler, *Class Action: The Landmark Case that Changed Sexual Harassment Law* (New York: Doubleday, 2002), 321–23.

154 "The measure of injury . . . deeply held values": Martha Chamallas and Jennifer B. Wriggins, *The Measure of Injury: Race, Gender, and Tort Law* (New York: New York University Press, 2010), 190.

155 workplace abuse can cause productivity . . . readily measured in dollars: Chamallas, "Discrimination and Outrage," 2147–50.

155 Under federal law . . . $50,000 to $300,000: 42 U.S.C. § 1981a(b)(3) (2012).

155 Many states also cap damages . . . pain and suffering: "Caps on Com-

pensatory Damages: A State Law Summary," Center for Justice & Democracy at New York Law School, June 2019, https://centerjd.org /content/fact-sheet-caps-compensatory-damages-state-law-summary.

155 In this "hierarchy of value" . . . conducive to compensation: Chamallas and Wriggins, *The Measure of Injury*, 171.

155 Caps also serve . . . "willing to accept.": Chamallas and Wriggins, *The Measure of Injury*, 175.

156 In 2011, a New York court reduced the damages . . . damages to $50,000: *New York State Div. of Human Rights v. Young Legends, LLC*, 934 N.Y.S.2d 628, 630, 632–33 (N.Y. App. Div. 2011).

157 When Black women . . . Black women and their claims: Jennifer Wriggins, "Rape, Racism and the Law," *Harvard Journal of Law and Gender* 6, no. 1 (1983): 106, 188 & n.93.

157 In a sentiment . . . "You never know about them": Carol Bohmer, "Judicial Attitudes Toward Rape Victims," *Judicature* 57, no. 7 (1974): 303.

157 "It is extremely damaging . . . in the face of their occurrence": West, *Caring for Justice*, 146.

158 Jenny Teeson . . . do whatever he wished: Karen Zraick, "Inside One Woman's Fight to Rewrite the Law on Marital Rape," *New York Times*, April 13, 2019, https://www.nytimes.com/2019/04/13/us/marital -rape-law-minnesota.html.

159 Writing in 1765 . . . "suspended during the marriage": William Blackstone, *Commentaries on the Laws of England*, vol. 1 (Oxford: Clarendon Press, 1765), 442.

159 from our country's origins . . . her very person: Freedman, *Redefining Rape*, 7.

159 Because the husband subsumed . . . known as the marital rape exemption: Jill Elaine Hasday, "Contest and Consent: A Legal History of Marital Rape," *California Law Review* 88, no. 5 (2000): 1389–92, 1397.

159 the 1962 Model Penal Code . . . "permitted him sexual liberties.": Model Penal Code § 213.1 (American Law Institute, Official Draft and Revised Comments 1980).

160 The "improper inference . . . marital status of the parties": Michelle

J. Anderson, "Diminishing the Legal Impact of Negative Social Attitudes Toward Acquaintance Rape Victims," *New Criminal Law Review* 13, no. 4 (2010): 663.

160 Although it's now illegal . . . she is unconscious: "Marital Rape and Sexual Assault," AEquitas (April 2020): 1–6, available by request at https://aequitasresource.org/resources.

160 "The state did not . . . must be inconsequential": West, *Caring for Justice*, 146.

160 after decades of reform . . . imminent threat of it: Stephen J. Schulhofer, "Reforming the Law of Rape," *Law & Inequality* 35, no. 2 (2017): 342–43.

161 "Typically an excessive and unrealistic amount . . . forced sexual interaction": Catharine A. MacKinnon, "Rape Redefined," *Harvard Law & Policy Review* 10, no. 2 (2016): 465.

161 cases involving weapons . . . rare exception: Black et al., "National Intimate Partner and Sexual Violence Survey: 2010 Summary Report," 44–45, 54–55; Michael Planty et al., "Female Victims of Sexual Violence, 1994–2010," U.S. Department of Justice (2016): 5, https://www.bjs.gov/content/pub/pdf/fvsv9410.pdf; Patricia Tjaden and Nancy Thoennes, "Full Report of the Prevalence, Incidence, and Consequences of Violence Against Women," U.S. Department of Justice (2000): 49–50, https://www.ncjrs.gov/pdffiles1/nij/183781.pdf.

161 Lisak has found . . . "into submission": David Lisak, "Understanding the Predatory Nature of Sexual Violence," *Sexual Assault Report* 14, no. 4 (2011): 56, https://web.archive.org/web/20180918030047/http://www.davidlisak.com/wp-content/uploads/pdf/SARUnderstandingPredatoryNatureSexualViolence.pdf.

161 In the typical . . . legally sufficient force.: Anderson, "Diminishing the Legal Impact of Negative Social Attitudes," 646.

162 The victim, unnamed . . . not guilty of rape: *Commonwealth v. Berkowitz*, 609 A.2d 1338, 1340, 1344–47 (Pa. Super. Ct. 1992), *order aff'd in part, vacated in part on other grounds*, 641 A.2d 1161 (Pa. 1994).

162 In one such case . . . for lack of force.: *State v. Mirabal*, 278 A.D.2d 526, 527 (N.Y. App. Div. 2000).

162 In another case . . . also for lack of force.: *State v. Elias*, 337 P.3d 670, 672, 676 (Idaho 2014).

162 The same result . . . surprised: Deborah Tuerkheimer, "Rape On and Off Campus," *Emory Law Journal* 65, no. 1 (2015): 24–38.

163 "Because the law" . . . "ignored or devalued": Lynn Hecht Schafran, "Barriers to Credibility: Understanding and Countering Rape Myths," Legal Momentum (n.d.): 9, https://www.webpages.uidaho.edu/gbabcock/PDFs/Rape%20Barriers_to_Credibility%20myths.pdf.

163 "The willingness to abuse power" . . . "pervasive and effective": Traister, "Why Donald Trump—and Other Powerful Men—Love to Cast Themselves as Victims."

164 The strategic use of the history . . . metaphorical lynching: Traister, "Why Donald Trump—and Other Powerful Men—Love to Cast Themselves as Victims."

164 Throughout the sixteenth and seventeenth centuries . . . vulnerable women: Michelle D. Brock, "No, There Is No Witch Hunt Against Powerful Men," *Washington Post*, October 18, 2017, https://www.washingtonpost.com/news/made-by-history/wp/2017/10/18/no-there-is-no-witch-hunt-against-powerful-men.

165 In 1920 . . . "surprisingly large": Edward L. Thorndike, "A Constant Error in Psychological Ratings," *Journal of Applied Psychology* 4, no. 1 (1920): 25, 29. For subsequent research on the halo effect, see Kahneman, *Thinking, Fast and Slow*, 4, 82–85, 114, 199–200.

165 Dahlia Lithwick . . . "most reliable" witness: Lithwick, "The Room Where It Happened," 30.

166 But two Swedish graduate students . . . upstanders: Claudia Koerner, "Brock Turner Has Lost His Appeal and Remains Guilty of Sexual Assault," BuzzFeed News, August 8, 2018, https://www.buzzfeednews.com/article/claudiakoerner/brock-turner-has-lost-his-appeal-and-remains-guilty-of.

166 Their testimony . . . Turner's guilt: Elena Kadvany, "Brock Turner Juror to Judge: 'Shame on You,'" *Palo Alto Weekly*, June 13, 2016, https://www.paloaltoonline.com/news/2016/06/13/brock-turner-juror-to-judge-shame-on-you.

166 he faced . . . fourteen years: Liam Stack, "Light Sentence for Brock Turner in Stanford Rape Case Draws Outrage," *New York Times*, June 6, 2016, https://www.nytimes.com/2016/06/07/us /outrage-in-stanford-rape-case-over-dueling-statements-of-victim -and-attackers-father.html.

166 His sister wrote . . . "life as he knew it": Lindsey Bever, "What the Stanford Sex Offender's Loved Ones Said to Keep Him out of Prison," *Washington Post*, June 8, 2016, https://www.washingtonpost .com/news/grade-point/wp/2016/06/08/what-the-stanford-sex -offenders-loved-ones-said-to-keep-him-out-of-prison.

166 His father wrote . . . "20 plus years of life": Tyler Kingkade, "Brock Turner's Dad Gave Tone-Deaf Plea for Lenient Sentence in Son's Sexual Assault Case," *Huffington Post*, June 5, 2016, https://www.huff post.com/entry/brock-turner-dad-action-stanford-sexual-assault_n _57548e2fe4b0c3752dcdf574?ir=College&section=us_college&utm _hp_ref=college#document/p3/a300156.

166 In her letter . . . "before that night . . .": Katie J. M. Baker, "Here's the Powerful Letter the Stanford Victim Read to Her Attacker," Buzz-Feed News, June 3, 2016, https://www.buzzfeednews.com/article /katiejmbaker/heres-the-powerful-letter-the-stanford-victim-read -to-her-ra#.xf2YDd8Xv.

167 In 2019, Miller came forward . . . "than his potential": Chanel Miller, *Know My Name: A Memoir* (New York: Viking Press, 2019), 233–41.

167 When an election . . . "by the justice system": Maggie Astor, "California Voters Remove Judge Aaron Persky, Who Gave a 6-Month Sentence for Sexual Assault," *New York Times*, June 6, 2018, https:// www.nytimes.com/2018/06/06/us/politics/judge-persky-brock -turner-recall.html.

167 Dozens of women . . . repeated sex acts: Julie K. Brown, "How a Future Trump Cabinet Member Gave a Serial Sex Abuser the Deal of a Lifetime," *Miami Herald*, November 28, 2018, https://www.miami herald.com/news/local/article220097825.html.

167 After the investigation . . . explicit images of girls: Matt Stieb, "Everything We Know About Jeffrey Epstein's Upper East Side Mansion," Intelligencer, *New York Magazine*, July 9, 2019, https://nymag.com

/intelligencer/2019/07/everything-we-know-about-jeffrey-epsteins
-new-york-mansion.html?utm_source=nym&utm_medium=f1&utm
_campaign=feed-part.

168 Instead of pursuing charges . . . "victims to object": Mimi Rocah
and Berit Berger, "Jeffrey Epstein's Deal with Federal Prosecutors
Wasn't Normal. The Men Who Arranged It Need to Face the Music," NBC News, February 23, 2019, https://www.nbcnews.com/think
/opinion/jeffrey-epstein-s-deal-federal-prosectors-wasn-t-normal
-men-ncna974911.

168 Epstein was permitted . . . released in 2009: Moira Donegan, "Too
Many Men Think Teenage Girls Are Fair Game. That Gave Jeffrey
Epstein Cover," *Guardian*, July 10, 2019, https://www.theguardian
.com/commentisfree/2019/jul/10/teenage-girls-jeffrey-epstein-fair
-game.

168 the media . . . expose his crimes: Ed Pilkington, "Jeffrey Epstein:
How US Media—with One Star Exception—Whitewashed the
Story," *Guardian*, July 13, 2019, https://www.theguardian.com/us
-news/2019/jul/13/jeffrey-epstein-alex-acosta-miami-herald-media.

168 the jailers who allowed . . . one young woman: David Ovalle, "Jeffrey
Epstein Lawsuits Offer Sordid Details, Including Sex While on Work
Release," *Miami Herald*, August 20, 2019, https://www.miamiherald
.com/news/state/florida/article234189557.html; Lori Rozsa, "For 'Client' Jeffrey Epstein, an Unlocked Cell in a Florida Jail," *Washington
Post*, July 19, 2019, https://www.washingtonpost.com/investigations
/captain-at-jail-where-epstein-served-time-in-2008-ordered-that
-his-cell-door-be-left-unlocked/2019/07/19/93e38934-a972-11e9-8
6dd-d7f0e60391e9_story.html.

168 the New York prosecutors who recommended . . . classification
guidelines: Jan Ransom, "Cyrus Vance's Office Sought Reduced Sex-
Offender Status for Epstein," *New York Times*, July 9, 2019, https://
www.nytimes.com/2019/07/09/nyregion/cyrus-vance-epstein.html.

168 the power brokers who . . . legitimized his conduct: Tiffany Hsu
et al., "Jeffrey Epstein Gave $850,000 to M.I.T., and Administra-
tors Knew," *New York Times*, January 15, 2020, https://www.nytimes
.com/2020/01/10/business/mit-jeffrey-epstein-joi-ito.html.

168 "the broad cultural antipathy . . . real harm,": Donegan, "Too Many Men Think Teenage Girls Are Fair Game."

169 "No one particularly cares" . . . directed at Black women and girls: Moya Bailey, "'Surviving R. Kelly' Serves Up a Toxic Cocktail of Misogynoir and Masculinity," *bitchmedia*, January 22, 2019, https://www.bitchmedia.org/article/surviving-rkelly-moya-bailey-misogynoir.

169 Black girls are often treated . . . matter least: Rebecca Epstein et al., "Girlhood Interrupted: The Erasure of Black Girls' Childhood," Center on Poverty and Inequality, Georgetown Law (2017): 2, 8, https://www.law.georgetown.edu/poverty-inequality-center/wp-content/uploads/sites/14/2017/08/girlhood-interrupted.pdf.

169 In 1994 . . . Aaliyah was eighteen: Nicole Hong, "R. Kelly Used Bribe to Marry Aaliyah When She Was 15, Charges Say," *New York Times*, December 5, 2019, https://www.nytimes.com/2019/12/05/nyregion/rkelly-aaliyah.html.

169 accounts of Kelly preying . . . Chicago newspaper: Ida Harris, "R. Kelly's Victims Were Ignored for 30 Years. It Has 'Everything to Do With the Fact That They Are Black Women,'" *Elle*, January 5, 2019, https://www.elle.com/culture/movies-tv/a25756816/r-kelly-lifetime-documentary-dream-hampton-interview.

169 Kelly's trial . . . "Daddy": Jim DeRogatis and Abdon M. Pallasch, "City Police Investigate R&B Singer R. Kelly in Sex Tape," *Chicago Sun-Times*, February 8, 2002, http://web.archive.org/web/20020212051418/http://www.suntimes.com/output/news/cst-nws-kelly08.html.

170 Still, despite the best . . . the show's executive producers: Harris, "R. Kelly's Victims Were Ignored for 30 Years."

170 Jim DeRogatis broke the story . . . "stop him": Jim DeRogatis, *Soulless: The Case Against R. Kelly* (New York: Abrams Press, 2019), 237, 263–64.

CHAPTER 6: "EVEN WORSE": WHY THE CREDIBILITY COMPLEX HARMS VICTIMS

175 One friend would later tell Williams . . . "you don't matter": Janey Williams, host, "You Don't Matter," *This Happened* (podcast), October 3, 2013.

175 the aftermath of abuse . . . "second rape" or "secondary victimization": Rebecca Campbell, "Rape Survivors' Experiences with the Legal and Medical Systems: Do Rape Victim Advocates Make a Difference?," *Violence Against Women* 12, no. 1 (2006): 1–2.

176 Research consistently shows . . . as a result: Heather L. Littleton, "The Impact of Social Support and Negative Disclosure Reactions on Sexual Assault Victims: A Cross-Sectional and Longitudinal Investigation," *Journal of Trauma & Dissociation* 11, no. 2 (2010): 212.

176 "Betrayal" . . . their loved ones: Jennifer J. Freyd and Pamela J. Birrell, *Blind to Betrayal: Why We Fool Ourselves We Aren't Being Fooled* (Hoboken, NJ: John Wiley & Sons, Inc., 2013), 23; Rachel E. Goldsmith et al., "Betrayal Trauma: Associations with Psychological and Physical Symptoms in Young Adults," *Journal of Interpersonal Violence* 27, no. 3 (2012): 557.

176 when we dismiss . . . moment of great vulnerability: Ullman, *Talking About Sexual Assault*, 59–82.

176 This is consistent . . . negative reactions to their disclosure: Littleton, "The Impact of Social Support and Negative Disclosure Reactions on Sexual Assault Victims," 223.

177 Researchers have found . . . without a personal connection: Ahrens, "Being Silenced," 266–71; Kimberly A. Lonsway, "Improving Responses to Sexual Assault Disclosures: Both Informal and Formal Support Providers," End Violence Against Women International (March 2020): 7, 9, https://evawintl.org/wp-content/uploads/2019-6_TB_Improving-Responses-to-SA-Disclosures.pdf.

177 In late 2019 . . . prominent sommelier: Julia Moskin, "A Celebrity Sommelier Is Accused of Sexual Assault," *New York Times*, November 1, 2019, https://www.nytimes.com/2019/11/01/dining/drinks/anthony-cailan-sexual-assault.html.

180 Over the course of more than two decades . . . victims whose institutions respond well: Carly Parnitzke Smith and Jennifer J. Freyd, "Dangerous Safe Havens: Institutional Betrayal Exacerbates Sexual Trauma," *Journal of Traumatic Stress* 26, no. 1 (2013): 120.

180 Study after study . . . initial violation: Lindsey L. Monteith et al., "Perceptions of Institutional Betrayal Predict Suicidal Self-Directed

Violence Among Veterans Exposed to Military Sexual Trauma," *Journal of Clinical Psychology* 72, no. 7 (2016): 751; Carly P. Smith and Jennifer J. Freyd, "Insult, Then Injury: Interpersonal and Institutional Betrayal Linked to Health and Dissociation," *Journal of Aggression, Maltreatment & Trauma* 26, no. 10 (2017).

181 "Traumatized people feel" . . . emotions in trauma victims: Herman, *Trauma and Recovery*, 52–53, 61.

182 compound harm to accusers: Carly Parnitzke Smith and Jennifer J. Freyd, "Institutional Betrayal," *American Psychologist* 69, no. 6 (2014): 585.

184 In her memoir . . . "all that she lived never occurred": Freitas, *Consent*, 314.

184 One study found . . . "demoralized, mistreated, and alone": Chris Linder and Jess S. Myers, "Institutional Betrayal as a Motivator for Campus Sexual Assault Activism," *NASPA Journal About Women in Higher Education* 11, no. 1 (2018): 6.

184 Lynn, a first-generation . . . "fell apart after that": Linder and Myers, "Institutional Betrayal," 6.

184 Victims who identified as lesbian, gay, or bisexual . . . worse psychological outcomes as a result: Carly P. Smith et al., "Sexual Violence, Institutional Betrayal, and Psychological Outcomes for LGB College Students," *Translational Issues in Psychological Science* 2, no. 4 (2016): 355–56.

184 Other research supports the finding . . . most harmful effects: Alec M. Smidt et al., "Out and in Harm's Way: Sexual Minority Students' Psychological and Physical Health after Institutional Betrayal and Sexual Assault," *Journal of Child Sexual Abuse* 1 (2019): 41–55.

186 Anna is one of many accusers . . . "find myself again": Walt Bogdanich, "Reporting Rape, and Wishing She Hadn't," *New York Times*, July 12, 2014, https://www.nytimes.com/2014/07/13/us/how-one -college-handled-a-sexual-assault-complaint.html.

187 While accused men . . . women who report an assault: Kiera Feldman, "Sexual Assault at God's Harvard," *New Republic*, February 17, 2014, https://newrepublic.com/article/116623/sexual-assault-patrick-henry -college-gods-harvard; Smith and Freyd, "Institutional Betrayal," 575.

187 It's not unheard-of . . . alcohol, drugs, and premarital sex: Emma Sarran Webster, "Baylor University Punished Sexual Assault Victims for Drinking," *Teen Vogue*, August 1, 2016, https://www.teenvogue.com/story/baylor-university-silenced-rape-sexual-assault-victims.

187 Campus officials can penalize . . . denied wrongdoing: Tatiana Schlossberg, "UConn to Pay $1.3 Million to End Suit on Rape Cases," *New York Times*, July 18, 2014, https://www.nytimes.com/2014/07/19/nyregion/uconn-to-pay-1-3-million-to-end-suit-on-rape-cases.html.

187 Annie E. Clark . . . "in that situation?": Caitlin McCabe, "5 Submit Complaint Against UNC over Sexual Assault," *Daily Tar Heel*, January 16, 2013, https://www.dailytarheel.com/article/2013/01/5-submit-complaint-against-unc-over-sexual-assault.

187 Clark and four other women . . . "especially at school": Jane Stancill, "UNC Found in Violation of Federal Law in Its Handling of Sex Assault and Discrimination," *News and Observer*, June 26, 2018, https://www.newsobserver.com/news/local/article213838729.html.

187 Another plaintiff in the case . . . "time and time again": Caitlin McCabe, "Group Files Sexual Assault Complaint Against UNC," *Daily Tar Heel*, January 16, 2013, https://www.dailytarheel.com/article/2013/01/group-files-sexual-assault-complaint-against-unc_0116.

187 "It's like the Wild West" . . . address sexual violence: Erica L. Green, "'It's Like the Wild West': Sexual Assault Victims Struggle in K-12 Schools," *New York Times*, May 11, 2019, https://www.nytimes.com/2019/05/11/us/politics/sexual-assault-school.html.

188 The girl sued . . . she was suspended: Complaint at 2, 3, 9, *Doe v. Gwinnett Cty. Pub. Sch.*, No. 1:18-cv-05278-CAP (N.D. Ga. November 16, 2018), https://www.publicjustice.net/wp-content/uploads/2019/04/2018.11.16-Doc.-1-Complaint.pdf.

188 Suspension may be the ultimate . . . report abuse: Aviva Stahl, "'This Is an Epidemic': How NYC Public Schools Punish Girls for Being Raped," *Vice*, June 8, 2016, https://www.vice.com/en_us/article/59mz3x/this-is-an-epidemic-how-nyc-public-schools-punish-girls-for-being-raped.

188 Virginia, a high school student . . . she was raped: Diana Lambert, "Former McClatchy High Student Says She Was Gang Raped

by Classmates. She Plans to Sue District," *Sacramento Bee*, March 18, 2018, https://www.sacbee.com/news/local/education/article204442509 .html.

189 After she was questioned . . . "harass and bully" her: Complaint at 6, 9, *Virginia M. v. Sacramento City Unified Sch. Dist.*, Case No. 34–2018–00226922 (Cal. Super. Ct. Sacramento County December 21, 2018).

189 When her lawsuit against the district settled . . . "like the whole world is against you": Equal Rights Advocates, "ERA Client Wins in Settlement with Sacramento School District; Spurs New Policies for 49,000 Students," press release, September 24, 2019, https://www .equalrights.org/news/era-client-wins-in-settlement-with-sacramento -school-district-spurs-new-policies-for-49000-students.

190 In her memoir, Miller writes . . . "*It mattered, what happened to you*": Miller, *Know My Name*, 3, 296–97.

190 Psychologists have identified . . . institutional betrayal: Kristen M. Reinhardt et al., "Came to Serve, Left Betrayed: Military Sexual Trauma and the Trauma of Betrayal," in *Treating Military Sexual Trauma*, ed. Lori S. Katz (New York: Springer Publishing Company, 2016), 61–78.

190 When "maintaining the cohesion of a military unit" . . . injury: Smith and Freyd, "Institutional Betrayal," 581 (citing Rebecca Campbell and Sheela Raja, "The Sexual Assault and Secondary Victimization of Female Veterans: Help-Seeking Experiences with Military and Civilian Social Systems," *Psychology of Women Quarterly* 29, no. 1 [2005]: 97–106).

190 Because the military . . . particularly damaging: Felicia J. Andresen et al., "Institutional Betrayal Following Military Sexual Trauma Is Associated with More Severe Depression and Specific Posttraumatic Stress Disorder Symptom Clusters," *Journal of Clinical Psychology* 75, no. 7 (2019): 1306.

190 Researchers have found . . . PTSD symptoms: Andresen et al., "Institutional Betrayal Following Military Sexual Trauma."

191 Military women are harassed . . . their male counterparts: "Department of Defense Annual Report on Sexual Assault in the Mil-

itary," Department of Defense (2018): 9, https://int.nyt.com/data /documenthelper/800-dod-annual-report-on-sexual-as/d659d6d0 126ad2b19c18/optimized/full.pdf#page=1; Lindsay Rosenthal and Lawrence Korb, "Twice Betrayed: Bringing Justice to the U.S. Military's Sexual Assault Problem," Center for American Progress (November 2013): 2, https://www.americanprogress.org/wp-content/uploads /2013/11/MilitarySexualAssaultsReport.pdf.

191 betrayed by their superiors: Ibid.

191 the case of Justin Rose . . . "worse than the first": Justin Rose, "I Was Sexually Assaulted by Another Marine. The Corps Didn't Believe Me," *New York Times Magazine*, September 7, 2018, https://www .nytimes.com/2018/09/07/magazine/sexual-assault-marine-corps .html.

192 A 2015 Human Rights Watch report . . . "Discharged for misconduct": "Embattled: Retaliation Against Sexual Assault Survivors in the US Military," Human Rights Watch (May 2015): 3, https://www .hrw.org/report/2015/05/18/embattled/retaliation-against-sexual -assault-survivors-us-military.

192 "These people were supposed to be my family" . . . "I was betrayed": Amy Herdy and Miles Moffeit, "For Crime Victims, Punishment," *Denver Post*, May 13, 2005, https://extras.denverpost.com/justice/tdp _betrayal.pdf.

192 she suffers a singular violation: Debra Patterson, "The Linkage Between Secondary Victimization by Law Enforcement and Rape Case Outcomes," *Journal of Interpersonal Violence* 26, no. 2 (2011): 329.

193 A 2019 study by the criminologist . . . dismissed rather than resolved: Morabito et al., "Decision Making in Sexual Assault Cases," VI.

193 women are suing . . . sexual assault cases: Valeriya Safronova and Rebecca Halleck, "These Rape Victims Had to Sue to Get the Police to Investigate," *New York Times*, May 23, 2019, https://www.nytimes .com/2019/05/23/us/rape-victims-kits-police-departments.html.

194 In May 2010, Marlowe . . . remained unprocessed: Complaint at 3–7, *Marlowe v. City & Cty. of San Francisco*, No. 3:16-cv-00076-MMC (N.D. Cal. October 21, 2016).

194 Marlowe sued the City of San Francisco . . . unconstitutional discrimination: *Marlowe v. City and Cty. of San Francisco*, Case No. 16-cv-00076-MMC (N.D. Cal. September 27, 2016), *aff'd* 753 F. App'x 479, *cert denied* 140 S. Ct. 244.

194 But similar complaints . . . some are now proceeding: *Smith v. City of Austin*, No. 1:18-cv-00505-LY (W.D. Tex. February 10, 2020); *Borkowski v. Baltimore Cty.*, No. 1:18-cv-2809-DKC (D. Md. September 10, 2018); *Doe v. Town of Greenwich*, 3:18-cv-01322-KAD (D. Conn. August 9, 2018); *Doe v. City of Memphis*, No. 2:13-cv-03002-JTF-cgc (W.D. Tenn. December 20, 2013); Safronova and Halleck, "These Rape Victims Had to Sue to Get the Police to Investigate" (describing undisclosed settlement paid by Village of Robins, IL, to victim).

195 Ybos had waited nine years . . . twelve-year-old girl: Barbara Bradley Hagerty, "An Epidemic of Disbelief," *Atlantic*, July 22, 2019, https://www.theatlantic.com/magazine/archive/2019/08/an-epidemic-of-disbelief/592807.

195 "Investigating and solving a rape case" . . . "'disappear' rape cases": Meaghan Ybos and Heather Marlowe, "Five Ways the Media-Driven Rape Kit 'Backlog' Narrative Gets It Wrong," The Appeal, March 5, 2018, https://theappeal.org/five-ways-the-media-driven-rape-kit-backlog-narrative-gets-it-wrong-99a02956df06.

195 "If I had a righteous victim" . . . the comment typical: Hagerty, "An Epidemic of Disbelief."

196 Lucia Evans had just finished her junior year . . . "disgusted with myself": Ronan Farrow, "From Aggressive Overtures to Sexual Assault: Harvey Weinstein's Accusers Tell Their Stories," *New Yorker*, October 10, 2017, https://www.newyorker.com/news/news-desk/from-aggressive-overtures-to-sexual-assault-harvey-weinsteins-accusers-tell-their-stories.

196 In October 2017 . . . complaint against Weinstein: Ronan Farrow, "Behind the Scenes of Harvey Weinstein's Arrest," *New Yorker*, May 25, 2018, https://www.newyorker.com/news/news-desk/behind-the-scenes-of-harvey-weinsteins-impending-arrest.

197 Evans says this meeting . . . "family through that?": Michael Bar-

baro, host, "The Harvey Weinstein Case, Part 1," *The Daily* (podcast), January 9, 2020, transcript, https://www.nytimes.com/2020/01/09 /podcasts/the-daily/harvey-weinstein-trial.html.

197 Detectives feared . . . near New York City: Farrow, "Behind the Scenes of Harvey Weinstein's Arrest."

197 While she considered whether to cooperate . . . "it feels right": Barbaro, "The Harvey Weinstein Case, Part 1."

197 Four months later . . . "I felt betrayed": Mackenzie Nichols, "Harvey Weinstein Accuser Lucia Evans Breaks Silence After D.A. Dropped Charge," *Variety*, September 18, 2019, https://variety.com/2019/film /news/harvey-weinstein-lucia-evans-breaks-silence-1203340104.

197 Prosecutors announced that they had learned . . . oral sex as consensual: Michael R. Sisak and Tom Hays, "Manhattan DA Drops Part of Harvey Weinstein Case," Associated Press, October 12, 2018, https:// apnews.com/472366b4c7c74178bde962f85416fac6.

197 Evans disputes . . . events: Barbaro, "The Harvey Weinstein Case, Part 1."

198 According to Farrow . . . "other women in the case": David Remnick, "Ronan Farrow on What the Harvey Weinstein Trial Could Mean for the #MeToo Movement," *New Yorker*, January 13, 2020, https://www.newyorker.com/news/q-and-a/ronan-farrow-on-what -the-harvey-weinstein-trial-could-mean-for-the-metoo-movement.

198 Evans remembers thinking . . . "obviously it was not": Riley Board, "Lucia Evans '05 on Midd, #MeToo," *Middlebury Campus*, February 13, 2020, https://middleburycampus.com/48206/news/48206.

198 Evans describes feeling . . . "still really a struggle": Lucia Evans, "Own Your Truth," video, September 24, 2019, https://www.youtube .com/watch?v=vQZgZWE5urI&feature=youtu.be.

CHAPTER 7: BEYOND BELIEF: WHEN SURVIVORS MATTER

199 In the fall of 2017 . . . without the detour: Alison Turkos, "Why I'm Suing Lyft," Medium, September 17, 2019, https://medium.com /@alturkos/why-im-suing-lyft-6a409e316d1f.

201 Turkos received . . . severely weakened the case: Complaint at 26–29, *Welch Demski v. City of New York*, No. 150089/2019 (N.Y. Sup. Ct. January 31, 2019).

201 Turkos also learned . . . "ignored, belittled, dismissed me": Turkos, "Why I'm Suing Lyft."

201 Nearly two years after . . . other potential victims: Complaint at 14, *Turkos v. Lyft, Inc.*, No. CGC-19–579280 (Cal. Super. Ct. September 17, 2019).

201 Several other women . . . complaints with indifference: Maria Cramer, "19 Women Sue Lyft as Sexual Assault Allegations Mount," *New York Times*, December 5, 2019, https://www.nytimes.com/2019/12/05/business/lyft-sexual-assault-lawsuit.html.

201 "Lyft is systematically" . . . "abhorrent to victims": Lauren Kaori Gurley, "Lyft Allegedly Kept a Driver on the Platform Who Held a Passenger at Gunpoint While Two Other Men Raped Her," *Vice*, September 17, 2019, https://www.vice.com/en_us/article/vb57w8/lyft-allegedly-kept-a-driver-on-the-platform-who-held-a-passenger-at-gunpoint-while-two-other-men-raped-her.

201 "I have put my face . . . to be heard and believed": Turkos, "Why I'm Suing Lyft."

201 Turkos has also sued . . . protect sexual assault victims: Complaint at 1, *Welch Demski v. City of New York*.

204 "spectrum of gender-based violence" . . . just beginning to tell their stories: Tarana Burke, "#MeToo Was Started for Black and Brown Women and Girls. They're Still Being Ignored," *Washington Post*, November 9, 2017, https://www.washingtonpost.com/news/post-nation/wp/2017/11/09/the-waitress-who-works-in-the-diner-needs-to-know-that-the-issue-of-sexual-harassment-is-about-her-too.

205 Psychologist Judith Lewis Herman likewise stresses . . . "repair the injury": Herman, *Trauma and Recovery*, 70.

205 In her study . . . "from victim to offender": Judith Lewis Herman, "Justice from the Victim's Perspective," *Violence Against Women* 11, no. 5 (2005): 579, 585.

206 Megan Ganz . . . "respect for women": Dan Harmon, host, "Don't Let Him Wipe or Flush," *Harmontown* (podcast), January 1, 2018,

https://www.harmontown.com/2018/01/episode-dont-let-him-wipe
-or-flush.

206 After the podcast aired, Ganz tweeted . . . "It's about vindication":
Michael Nordine, "Dan Harmon Delivers a 'Masterclass in How to
Apologize,' and the Woman He Wronged Wants You to Listen,"
IndieWire, January 11, 2018, https://www.indiewire.com/2018/01
/dan-harmon-megan-ganz-apology-1201916560.

207 For Ganz, the audience for this vindication . . . "doubts from my
head": Jonah Engel Bromwich, "Megan Ganz on Dan Harmon's Apology: 'I Felt Vindicated,'" *New York Times*, January 13, 2018, https://
www.nytimes.com/2018/01/13/arts/dan-harmon-megan-ganz
.html.

207 Many survivors . . . valuable form of restitution: Herman, "Justice
from the Victim's Perspective," 586.

207 The philosopher Nick Smith . . . her or anyone else: Nick Smith, *I
Was Wrong: The Meanings of Apologies* (New York: Cambridge University Press, 2008), 10.

207 sujatha baliga . . . restorative justice work: Jennifer Schuessler,
"MacArthur 'Genius' Grant Winners for 2019: The Full List," *New York
Times*, September 25, 2019, https://www.nytimes.com/2019/09/25
/arts/macarthur-genius-grant-winners-list.html.

209 Legal scholars . . . harmful aftermath: Lesley Wexler et al., "#Me-
Too, Time's Up, and Theories of Justice," *University of Illinois Law
Review* 2019, no. 1 (2019): 69–91.

209 Archbishop Desmond Tutu . . . "nothing has happened.": Lesley
Wexler et al., "#MeToo, Time's Up, and Theories of Justice," 78 (citing
Nancy Berlinger, *After Harm: Medical Error and the Ethics of Forgive-
ness* [Baltimore: Johns Hopkins University Press, 2005], 61).

210 A similar idea holds true for victims . . . sources of healing: Lesley
Wexler et al., "#MeToo, Time's Up, and Theories of Justice," 77–82.

212 Sofia was a fifteen-year-old girl . . . equal ground: sujatha baliga,
"A Different Path for Confronting Sexual Assault," Vox, October
10, 2018, https://www.vox.com/first-person/2018/10/10/17953016
/what-is-restorative-justice-definition-questions-circle.

212 Survivors are most likely . . . mission: Katherine Mangan, "Why More

Colleges Are Trying Restorative Justice in Sex-Assault Cases," *Chronicle of Higher Education*, September 17, 2018, https://www.chronicle.com/article/Why-More-Colleges-Are-Trying/244542?cid=at&utm_source=naicu.

212 the criminal justice system . . . paramount: Margo Kaplan, "Restorative Justice and Campus Sexual Misconduct," *Temple Law Review* 89 (2017): 717–18.

212 A comprehensive study . . . "'that guy'": Hirsch and Khan, *Sexual Citizens*, 211.

213 rather than more formal disciplinary processes . . . some will be revised: Katie Rogers and Erica L. Green, "Biden Will Revisit Trump Rules on Sexual Assault," *New York Times*, March 8, 2021, https://www.nytimes.com/2021/03/08/us/politics/joe-biden-title-ix.html.

213 Because restorative justice "lends itself" . . . "torturing the victim": Mangan, "Why More Colleges Are Trying Restorative Justice."

214 Berkeley High School . . . "how hurt we are": Tracy Clark-Flory, "How Berkeley High's Whisper Network Sparked a Movement," Jezebel, March 17, 2020, https://jezebel.com/how-berkeley-highs-whisper-network-sparked-a-movement-1841601179.

214 So too . . . sexual assault on campus: Hirsch and Khan, *Sexual Citizens*, 127.

215 The legal scholar Sarah Deer . . . "are at unequal places": Sarah Deer, *The Beginning and End of Rape: Confronting Sexual Violence in Native America* (Minneapolis: University of Minnesota Press, 2015), 124–25.

216 In 2015, a literary scout at the Weinstein Company . . . "sexualized and diminished": Kantor and Twohey, *She Said*, 135.

216 O'Connor's assessment of the power imbalance . . . "opportunity he had given her": Kantor and Twohey, "Harvey Weinstein Paid Off Sexual Harassment Accusers for Decades."

216 "Power operates on multiple levels" . . . "those are the measurements": Lauren O'Connor, "Ex-Harvey Weinstein Employee Breaks Silence on Her Memo That Helped Take Down Movie Mogul," video, 55:02, January 29, 2019, https://www.democracynow.org/2019/1/29/exclusive_ex_harvey_weinstein_employee_breaks.

217 "Yesterday, the scales of justice restored" . . . "there will be consequences": "'Silence Breakers' Speak Out on Weinstein Verdict," NowThis News, video, February 25, 2020, https://www.youtube.com /watch?v=7Xlj2mcK3x4.

218 Rather than see . . . "rights and dignity": Herman, "Justice from the Victim's Perspective," 589–90, 593–94, 597.

218 Philosopher Jean Hampton . . . "'takes back' the demeaning message": Jean Hampton, "An Expressive Theory of Retribution," in *Retributivism and Its Critics*, ed. Wesley Cragg (Stuttgart: Franz Steiner Verlag, 1992), 13.

219 A set of experiments . . . invariably subjective: Kenworthey Bilz, "Testing the Expressive Theory of Punishment," *Journal of Empirical Legal Studies* 13, no. 2 (2016): 364–90.

220 Campbell is careful to note . . . "for each survivor": Rebecca Campbell and Giannina Fehler-Cabral, "Why Police 'Couldn't or Wouldn't' Submit Sexual Assault Kits for Forensic DNA Testing: A Focal Concerns Theory Analysis of Untested Rape Kits," *Law & Society Review* 52, no.1 (2018): 99.

221 In her letter . . . "everything": Rachael Denhollander, *What Is a Girl Worth? My Story of Breaking the Silence and Exposing the Truth about Larry Nassar and USA Gymnastics* (Carol Stream, IL: Tyndale Momentum, 2019), 291–92, 313.

222 a military woman . . . "My rapist was": Debra Dickerson, "Rallying Around the Rapist," *New York Times*, March 18, 2003, https://www .nytimes.com/2003/03/18/opinion/rallying-around-the-rapist.html.

222 in forty years . . . "stinks to high hell": Eli Rosenberg and Kristine Phillips, "Accused of Rape, Former Baylor Fraternity President Gets No Jail Time After Plea Deal," *Washington Post*, December 11, 2018, https://www.washingtonpost.com/education/2018/12/11/accused -rape-former-frat-president-gets-no-jail-time-after-plea-deal-da.

223 In late 2018 . . . "escape justice and punishment": Holly Yan and Tina Burnside, "Ex-Baylor Frat President Indicted on 4 Counts of Sex Assault Won't Go to Prison," CNN, December 11, 2018, https://www .cnn.com/2018/12/11/us/baylor-ex-frat-president-rape-allegation /index.html.

223 In cases . . . a just outcome: Herman, "Justice from the Victim's Perspective," 595.

223 After pleading guilty . . . six years of prison: Brandon Stahl, "6 Years in Prison for Ex-U Student Who Raped Two Women," *Star Tribune*, August 30, 2016, http://www.startribune.com/6-year-term -for-ex-u-student-who-raped-one-woman-at-frat-party-another-at -his-apartment/391781041.

224 plead guilty . . . avoid any jail time: Jan Ransom, "19 Women Accused a Gynecologist of Abuse. Why Didn't He Go to Prison?," *New York Times*, October 22, 2019, https://www.nytimes.com/2019/10/22 /nyregion/robert-hadden-gynecologist-sexual-abuse.html.

224 Hoechstetter has become an advocate . . . prosecution of sexual assault: Marissa Hoechstetter, "Can a Prosecutor Be Progressive and Take Sex Crimes Seriously?," The Appeal, January 8, 2020, https://the appeal.org/progressive-prosecutors-metoo.

224 She and seventy-seven other women . . . the doctor's predations: Nelli Black, et al., "New Evidence Shows a Patient Warned Columbia University About OB-GYN's Alleged Sexual Assault Decades Ago," CNN, February 28, 2020, https://www.cnn.com/2020/02/28/politics /columbia-sexual-assault-letter-warning-invs/index.html.

226 When powerful men are momentarily disgraced . . . is often fleeting: Stassa Edwards, "Redemption Is Inevitable for Powerful Men," Jezebel, April 20, 2018, https://jezebel.com/redemption-is-inevitable -for-powerful-men-1825364533.

226 In late 2017, more than a dozen women . . . the allegations against him: Leah Litman et al., "A Comeback but No Reckoning," *New York Times*, August 2, 2018, https://www.nytimes.com/2018/08/02/opinion /sunday/alex-kozinski-harassment-allegations-comeback.html.

226 a damage award . . . "symbol of the perpetrator's guilt:" Herman, "Justice from the Victim's Perspective," 590.

CONCLUSION

229 Discussion of the Diallo/Strauss-Kahn story is drawn from the following sources: Christopher Dickey, "'DSK Maid' Tells of Her Al-

leged Rape by Strauss-Kahn: Exclusive," *Newsweek*, July 25, 2011, https://www.newsweek.com/dsk-maid-tells-her-alleged-rape-strauss -kahn-exclusive-68379; Recommendation for Dismissal at 8, *People v. Strauss-Kahn*, No. 02526/2011 (N.Y. Sup. Ct. August 22, 2011); Adam Martin, "Strauss-Kahn Held Without Bail: Graphic Details Released," *Atlantic*, May 16, 2011, https://www.theatlantic.com /international/archive/2011/05/strauss-kahn-held-without-bail -graphic-details-released/350724/; Adam Martin, "Strauss-Kahn Pins Defense on Datebook, Claim of Consent," *Atlantic*, May 17, 2011, https://www.theatlantic.com/international/archive/2011/05/strauss -kahn-pins-defense-datebook/350755/; John Eligon, "Strauss-Kahn Drama Ends with Short Final Scene," *New York Times*, August 23, 2011, https://www.nytimes.com/2011/08/24/nyregion/charges-against -strauss-kahn-dismissed.html; Vivienne Foley and Michael Pearson, "Strauss-Kahn, Accuser Settle Civil Lawsuit," CNN, December 10, 2012, https://www.cnn.com/2012/12/10/us/dsk-lawsuit/index.html; Complaint, *Nafissatou Diallo v. Dominique Strauss-Kahn*, Case No. 307065–2011 (New York Supreme Ct., Bronx County, August 8, 2011).

230 According to the medical records . . . torn cartilage in her left shoulder: Erika Stallings, "This Is How the American Healthcare System Is Failing Black Women," *O, The Oprah Magazine*, August 1, 2018, https://www.oprahmag.com/life/health/a23100351/racial-bias -in-healthcare-black-women/; Consumer Reports, "Is Bias Keeping Female, Minority Patients from Getting Proper Care for Their Pain?," *Washington Post*, July 29, 2019, https://www.washingtonpost .com/health/is-bias-keeping-female-minority-patients-from-getting -proper-care-for-their-pain/2019/07/26/9d1b3a78-a810-11e9-9214 -246e594de5d5_story.htmlavailable.

235 members of a trusted inner circle . . . aftermath of abuse for the survivor: Ahrens, "Being Silenced," 270–73.

237 In some states . . . are underway: Andrea Johnson et al., "Progress in Advancing Me Too Workplace Reforms in #20StatesBy2020," National Women's Law Center (2019), https://nwlc.org/wp-content /uploads/2019/07/final_2020States_Report-12.20.19-v2.pdf.

INDEX

ABOUT THE AUTHOR

DEBORAH TUERKHEIMER is a professor at the Northwestern Pritzker School of Law. She earned her undergraduate degree from Harvard College and her law degree from Yale Law School. She served for five years as an assistant district attorney in the New York County District Attorney's Office, where she specialized in domestic violence and child abuse prosecution.